987654321

# The Definitive Guide to Spring Web Flow

Erwin Vervaet

**Apress**®

**The Definitive Guide to Spring Web Flow**

**Copyright © 2008 by Erwin Vervaet**

ISBN-13 (pbk): 978-1-4302-1624-7

ISBN-13 (electronic): 978-1-4302-1625-4

9 8 7 6 5 4 3 2 1

Trademarked names may appear in this book. Rather than use a trademark symbol with every occurrence of a trademarked name, we use the names only in an editorial fashion and to the benefit of the trademark owner, with no intention of infringement of the trademark.

*Java™ and all Java-based marks are trademarks or registered trademarks of Sun Microsystems, Inc., in the US and other countries. Apress, Inc., is not affiliated with Sun Microsystems, Inc., and this book was written without endorsement from Sun Microsystems, Inc.*

SpringSource is the company behind Spring, the de facto standard in enterprise Java. SpringSource is a leading provider of enterprise Java infrastructure software, and delivers enterprise class software, support, and services to help organizations utilize Spring. The open source-based Spring Portfolio is a comprehensive enterprise application framework designed on long-standing themes of simplicity and power. With more than five million downloads to date, Spring has become an integral part of the enterprise application infrastructure at organizations worldwide. For more information visit: www.springsource.com.

Lead Editor: Steve Anglin
Technical Reviewers: Keith Donald, Karl David Moore
Editorial Board: Clay Andres, Steve Anglin, Ewan Buckingham, Tony Campbell, Gary Cornell, Jonathan Gennick, Matthew Moodie, Joseph Ottinger, Jeffrey Pepper, Frank Pohlmann, Ben Renow-Clarke, Dominic Shakeshaft, Matt Wade, Tom Welsh
Senior Project Manager: Kylie Johnston
Copy Editor: Heather Lang
Associate Production Director: Kari Brooks-Copony
Senior Production Editor: Laura Cheu
Compositor: Pat Christenson
Proofreader: Lisa Hamilton
Indexer: Becky Hornyak
Cover Designer: Kurt Krames
Manufacturing Director: Tom Debolski

Distributed to the book trade worldwide by Springer-Verlag New York, Inc., 233 Spring Street, 6th Floor, New York, NY 10013. Phone 1-800-SPRINGER, fax 201-348-4505, e-mail orders-ny@springer-sbm.com, or visit http://www.springeronline.com.

For information on translations, please contact Apress directly at 2855 Telegraph Avenue, Suite 600, Berkeley, CA 94705. Phone 510-549-5930, fax 510-549-5939, e-mail info@apress.com, or visit http://www.apress.com.

Apress and friends of ED books may be purchased in bulk for academic, corporate, or promotional use. eBook versions and licenses are also available for most titles. For more information, reference our Special Bulk Sales—eBook Licensing web page at http://www.apress.com/info/bulksales.

The information in this book is distributed on an "as is" basis, without warranty. Although every precaution has been taken in the preparation of this work, neither the author(s) nor Apress shall have any liability to any person or entity with respect to any loss or damage caused or alleged to be caused directly or indirectly by the information contained in this work.

The source code for this book is available to readers at http://www.apress.com.

# Contents at a Glance

# Contents

# About the Author

**ERWIN VERVAET** is an independent consultant based in Leuven, Belgium. Erwin has been using Java since its inception and has extensive experience applying it in a wide range of application domains. He also runs his own software and consultancy company, Ervacon (http://www.ervacon.com).

Erwin enjoys writing, teaching, and speaking about Java- and Spring-related subjects. As the originator of the Spring Web Flow project, he currently co-leads its development together with Keith Donald.

# About the Technical Reviewers

**KEITH DONALD** is a principal and founding partner of SpringSource (formerly Interface21), the company behind Spring. He is best known in the Spring community for creating Spring Web Flow with Erwin Vervaet. At SpringSource, Keith is the lead of the web application development products team. His team, based in Melbourne, Florida, helps sustain the development of Spring Web MVC and Web Flow and their associated integrations and is also responsible for future innovations in the domain of web application development frameworks.

Keith, together with Jay Zimmerman of NoFluffJustStuff Software Symposiums, is also the director of the Spring Experience conference series. He is responsible for the technical content of the conference, which takes place in Florida each December.

In addition, Keith is the principal architect behind SpringSource's state-of-the-art Spring training curriculum. This curriculum has provided practical training on Spring to over 3,000 students worldwide.

Keith, an experienced enterprise software developer and mentor, has built business applications for customers spanning a diverse set of industries including banking, network management, information assurance, education, and retail. He is particularly adept at translating business requirements into technical solutions.

Keith's blog can be found at `http://blog.springsource.com/main/author/keithd`.

**KARL DAVID MOORE** is a software engineer with over six years' commercial development experience. He holds a first class honors degree in software engineering from Sheffield Hallam University.

Karl has been a Spring Framework user since early 2004 and is an active contributor to the Spring forums, with over 8,000 posts. During his career, Karl has been extensively involved in all aspects of software development and has a particular passion for refactoring legacy systems. This has helped him foster a very strong interest in test-driven development, code quality, and attention to detail.

Karl enjoys researching and developing approaches to aid and simplify development, and evangelizing about techniques and tools to improve the skills of other developers.

You can find Karl's LinkedIn profile at `http://www.linkedin.com/in/karldmoore`.

# Acknowledgments

This book, and Spring Web Flow itself, only exist thanks to the input and help of many different people.

Spring Web Flow was lucky and gained an active community right from the start. A special thanks goes out to the early adopters and forum members, whose invaluable feedback has helped mold Spring Web Flow into what it is today. Several people deserve special credits for their active involvement in the project: Juergen Hoeller, Colin Sampaleanu, Rod Johnson, Ben Hale, Christian Dupuis, J. Enrique Ruiz, C_sar Ordiñana, Rossen Stoyanchev, Jeremy Grelle, Rob Harrop, Seth Ladd, Colin Yates, Steven Devijver, Greame Rocher, Sam Brannen, Maxim Petrashev, Marten Deinum, and Dave Syer. It goes without saying that countless others also deserve credit.

Writing a book is a big undertaking that could not be done without the support and feedback of several people. I would like to thank Keith Donald for his invaluable input into Spring Web Flow, as well as for his review efforts. Karl David Moore also went above and beyond the call of duty, doing extraordinarily thorough chapter reviews and helping me polish my quirky English. The fine people at Apress that molded this book into its current form also deserve accolades: Heather Lang, Laura Cheu, and Kylie Johnston. Several other people also directly or indirectly contributed to this book: Philip Van Bogaert, Henri Shih, Kris Meukens, and Mike Seghers. Thank you all.

A very special thanks goes out to my wife Bieke. She tirelessly kept the kids busy and did more than her fair share while I slaved away at this book. I can honestly say that without Bieke's support, this book would not have been possible.

# Introduction

When I started working on Spring Web Flow at the end of 2004, web applications already accounted for a large part of the Java enterprise development space. I had used Struts on several projects at that point but always felt something was missing. Working with a proprietary framework on a few projects in the financial industry sparked my interest. The framework I was using included a work flow engine, a fairly typical feature for frameworks targeted at high-end enterprise applications. What was novel about it, however, was that the work flow engine could also be used to define *page flows* in web applications. This brought a refreshingly intuitive approach to Java web application development.

Using a state diagram as the basis for page flows in web applications seemed much more natural than the request-centric solutions offered by the mainstream frameworks of the time. This was especially true for the more complex use cases that required the user to pass through a number of different steps in the completion of a business process. Over the course of 2004, I had been learning about the Spring Framework, which was gaining momentum at the time, and had been impressed by its design and implementation quality. I set out to add a page flow controller to the Spring Web MVC framework and created what would later become Spring Web Flow.

Initially, Spring Web Flow focused on using a state-diagram–based approach to make defining page navigation in web applications easy and intuitive. This gave web application developers a powerful way to express page navigation rules. Expressive page flow definitions also highlighted the need for better *navigational control*. The infamous Back button problem caused all sorts of difficulties in web applications that tried to control page navigation. Spring Web Flow clearly needed to address this issue.

Around that time, I read an article discussing the use of continuations to solve navigational problems in web applications. This struck me as fitting very well with Spring Web Flow's flow execution model and provided the missing link. Spring Web Flow now combined two very attractive and complementary features:

- An intuitive and easy to use method of *expressing page navigation rules* in web applications.

- A powerful and robust *navigational control* system.

Bringing a third attractive feature to the table required only a small step:

- Encapsulate page flows as black-box *application modules* with a well-defined input-output contract.

Spring Web Flow has come a long way in the last two years. It has grown from a simple "flow controller" for the Spring Web MVC framework into "a next generation Java web application controller framework that allows developers to model user actions as high-level modules called flows. The framework delivers improved productivity and testability while providing a strong solution to enforcing navigation rules and managing application state" (Johnson et al 2003). The next generation of the framework, Spring Web Flow 2, introduces exciting new features to help you build and run rich web applications. Clearly, Spring Web Flow is now a mature project that is used in many production deployments and has an active user community.

I wrote this book not only to teach you how to work with Spring Web Flow but also to help you understand the rationale and motivation behind the framework. I hope you enjoy reading this book and have fun working with Spring Web Flow!

# About the Spring Web Flow Project

The original incarnation of the Spring Web Flow project was a small open source project started by Erwin Vervaet in October 2004 called Ervacon Spring Web Flow (http://www.ervacon.com/products/springwebflow). The project caught the attention of Keith Donald, one of the developers on the Spring Framework team, and became an official Spring Framework subproject in February of 2005. After almost two years of active development and a number of preview releases and release candidates, the project released its first production ready 1.0 version in October of 2006. This version is the subject of this book.

Building on the solid foundation set by Spring Web Flow 1, development continued on the next generation of the product. Spring Web Flow 2, released in June of 2008, underwent a few architectural changes allowing it to more seamlessly integrate into a rich web environment. It has impressive support for JSF and AJAX techniques and further simplifies the flow definition syntax.

Spring Web Flow uses the well-known Apache 2 license, a free/open source software license (Apache Software Foundation 2004). The Apache 2 license is used by many other open source projects, such as the Spring Framework itself and the Apache HTTP Server. It allows use of Spring Web Flow for any purpose, whether commercial or noncommercial, and even allows for modification and redistribution.

Spring Web Flow is sometimes mistakenly written as "Spring WebFlow." This confusion has its origin in the Spring Web Flow package name, org.springframework.webflow, which writes webflow in one word. "Spring Web Flow" is also often abbreviated as "SWF."

The official Spring Web Flow home page is located at http://www.springframework.org/webflow. It is an essential resource for Spring Web Flow users wanting to keep an eye on the evolution of the project. If you're still left with questions after reading this book, you'll have a good chance of getting an answer on the very active Spring user forums: http://forum.springframework.org. The Ervacon Spring Web Flow Portal (http://www.ervacon.com/products/swf) also offers useful information such as Spring Web Flow tips and tricks and a practical introduction.

# About This Book

This book aims to teach you how to work with Spring Web Flow. It covers both basic and advanced use cases and provides an in-depth reference to all features Spring Web Flow currently offers. You'll also learn to extend the framework to take it beyond its out-of-the-box feature set. Once you've finished this book, you'll be able to call yourself a Spring Web Flow expert!

## Spring Web Flow 1 and Spring Web Flow 2

Before we continue, one important point needs to be clarified. This book deals with Spring Web Flow 1. The next generation of the framework, Spring Web Flow 2, is subject matter for another book.

Versions 1 and 2 are essentially two separate products. The core concepts are the same, but the two versions are quite different technically. As a result, Spring Web Flow 2 is not backward compatible with Spring Web Flow 1. Moving from version 1 to version 2 would be a migration rather than a simple upgrade. This book's Epilogue discusses the differences between the two versions in more detail and will help you decide which version is best for you.

Spring Web Flow 1 will be referred to as just "Spring Web Flow" in this book, omitting the version number. When talking about Spring Web Flow 2, the version number will be explicitly mentioned.

## Target Audience

This book is intended to be a reference for both new and advanced Spring Web Flow users. If you're a new user, you'll learn how to get started using Spring Web Flow and leverage all of its powerful features. As an advanced user, you'll learn about extending the framework and many of its best practices, and you'll find this book provides very interesting insights into the design of Spring Web Flow.

Before reading this book, you should have a solid understanding of Java and Java web application development including topics such as servlets and JavaServer Pages (JSP). Many of the samples in this book use the Spring Web MVC framework. However, if you're familiar with any web Model-View-Controller (MVC) framework (for instance Struts or WebWork), you should have no problem following along.

A basic knowledge of the Spring Framework and its guiding principles, such as the Inversion of Control pattern and dependency injection, is also assumed. You don't need to be a Spring expert to read this book, but you'll have an easier time if you have at least played around with Spring classes like `ApplicationContext` and `BeanFactory` and understand how Spring wires together beans.

Rather than bloating this book with a detailed description of Java web applications, Spring Web MVC, or even Spring in general, I refer you to the Apress books *Beginning Spring 2: From Novice to Professional* by Dave Minter (2005); *Pro Spring 2.5* by Jan Machacek, Jessica Ditt, Aleksa Vukotic, and Anirvan Chakraborty (2008); and *Pro Java™ EE Spring Patterns: Best Practices and Design Strategies Implementing Java EE Patterns with the Spring Framework* by Dhrubojyoti Kayal (2008). Find other Apress books at `http://www.apress.com`.

# Overview

This book provides both introductory material and in-depth coverage of Spring Web Flow. The following overview will help you focus on the chapters most relevant to you. You can also read this book from cover to cover, and I recommend doing so if you're new to Spring Web Flow. If you're already familiar with the framework, you can skip the first two chapters and head directly to Chapter 3.

### Chapter 1: Introducing Spring Web Flow

This chapter takes a high-level view and examines the problem Spring Web Flow was designed to solve. It will explain the context in which Spring Web Flow lives and give you a conceptual understanding of what exactly Spring Web Flow is.

### Chapter 2: Getting Started

After the broad introduction of Chapter 1, this chapter will help you to hit the ground running. It explains all the practical details to get started using and experimenting with Spring Web Flow. The environment setup in this chapter should enable you to easily follow along with the examples covered in later chapters and to *try things for yourself.*

### Chapter 3: Spring Web Flow's Architecture

Chapters 1 and 2 superficially touch on some of the Spring Web Flow concepts. Chapter 3 digs a little deeper. It explains the Spring Web Flow architecture, giving you a detailed understanding of the different subsystems involved and setting the stage for an in-depth study of the Spring Web Flow feature set in the following chapters.

### Chapter 4: Spring Web Flow Basics

This chapter covers basic Spring Web Flow features, needed in most, if not all, use cases. You'll learn how to design and implement a web flow using both the XML- and Java-based flow definition languages.

### Chapter 5: Advanced Web Flow Concepts

As a follow up to the basic concepts covered in Chapter 4, this chapter will detail more advanced functionality. It explains how to reuse flows as subflows from inside other flows, realizing Spring Web Flow's promise of modularity. Handling HTML form data is also covered.

### Chapter 6: Flow Execution Management

When working with Spring Web Flow, most of the development effort revolves around defining flows. Also very important, however, is understanding how Spring Web Flow manages flow executions and the associated data; these topics will be discussed in this chapter.

### Chapter 7: Driving Flow Executions

This chapter focuses on integrating Spring Web Flow into hosting frameworks like Spring Web MVC and JSF and driving flow executions from those environments. Developing views for a web flow will also be discussed.

### Chapter 8: Testing with Spring Web Flow

Unit testing Spring Web Flow applications is explained in this chapter. You'll learn how to perform integration tests with your flow definitions and how to test flow artifacts (such as actions) in isolation.

### Chapter 9: The Sample Application

To give you an example of a nontrivial application that combines both free browsing and controlled navigation situations, this chapter will document a sample application: Spring Bank. Spring Bank is a simple electronic banking application that allows users to do things such as manage their bank accounts or enter payments. Use cases of this application will be used throughout this book to help explain and illustrate Spring Web Flow's feature set.

### Chapter 10: Real-World Use Cases

This chapter covers some frequently asked questions related to use cases occurring in the real world. You'll learn about such things as securing your flows, tracking breadcrumbs, or stress testing Spring Web Flow applications.

### Chapter 11: Extending Spring Web Flow

The last chapter covers extending and customizing Spring Web Flow. You'll also learn how to build Spring Web Flow from the sources.

### Epilogue

To conclude this book, the epilogue leaves you with some parting thoughts and takes a look at what's new and improved in Spring Web Flow 2.

## Typographical Conventions

This book uses simple and easy-to-understand typographical conventions. All text to be interpreted in a literal sense, like Java class names, code fragments, file names, or XML elements uses a `fixed width font`. *Italics* indicate topics of particular importance, and new or important pieces of a code fragment are highlighted in `boldface fixed-width text`. Commands to be entered on the command line also use a **boldface font**.

Many of the program listings presented in this book have been formatted for read-ability and to make them fit nicely on the page. In some cases, additional line breaks had to be introduced. A backslash (\) line continuation marker is used whenever an extra line break had to be added.

## About the Examples

All the sample applications presented in this book use Java 5, Servlet API 2.4, and JSP 2.0. Make sure you have a Java 5 Development Kit (JDK) and an appropriate application server or Servlet engine installed on your computer (for instance, Tomcat 5 or Jetty 6).

Spring Web Flow 1.0.6, together with Spring 2.5.4, was used to develop the sample applications. Future Spring Web Flow 1.x and Spring 2.x versions will be compatible. Chapter 2 provides a detailed overview of setting up a build and development environ-ment you can use to run the sample applications.

The Spring Bank sample application, together with the other samples discussed in this book, can be found in the public Ervacon Subversion repository at `https://svn.ervacon.com/public/spring`. You can browse the source code by just pointing your browser at this address. Alternatively, you can check out the entire source tree using any Subversion client, for instance, TortoiseSVN (`http://tortoisesvn.tigris.org`) if you are using Microsoft Windows. The source code for this book is also available to readers at `http://www.apress.com` in the Downloads section of this book's home page. Please feel free to visit the Apress web site and download all the code there.

# CHAPTER 1

■■■

# Introducing Spring Web Flow

**E**nterprise applications, and more specifically web applications, form a large part of all applications developed using Java. Most Java developers have worked on a Java web application at one point or another in their careers. As such, it comes as no surprise that there is a large variety of so-called web model, view, controller (MVC) frameworks to choose from. Well known examples include the following:

- Struts from the Apache Software Foundation (`http://struts.apache.org`).

- Spring Web MVC, the web MVC framework built on top of the Spring Framework (`http://www.springframework.org`).

- WebWork, a web framework developed by the OpenSymphony project (`http://www.opensymphony.com/webwork`). WebWork was used as the basis for Struts 2, and its development continues under that umbrella.

In the last few years, these classic request-based frameworks have gotten more and more competition from component-based web MVC frameworks. Key players in this arena follow:

- JavaServer Faces (JSF), a framework developed by the Java Community Process (JCP) as Java Specification Requests (JSRs) 127, 252, and 314 (`http://java.sun.com/javaee/javaserverfaces/`)

- Tapestry from the Apache Software Foundation (`http://tapestry.apache.org`)

Request-based frameworks treat the HTTP request as a first-class citizen. Request handling is typically done by application actions or controllers and results in the rendering of a new page. Component-based frameworks, however, abstract the HTTP request and encapsulate application functionality in reusable components. This approach is very similar to the one taken by desktop graphical user interface (GUI) toolkits. Web application components react to events and manipulate their own internal state, leaving the rendering of a page up to the controlling framework.

Despite their differences, all of these frameworks use the *Model, View, Controller* (MVC) design pattern to structure web applications and make them easier to understand and maintain. MVC was originally developed in the Smalltalk community to structure the GUI of desktop applications. It has also proven to be very effective in web application development.

The MVC pattern tries to separate the concerns of the *view* (user interface) from those of the *model* (domain or business model) by introducing the *controller* as an intermediary. In web applications, the controller processes incoming requests by delegating to business components (for instance, a service layer) and preparing model data for rendering by a selected view. The view is typically implemented using a templating system such as JavaServer Pages (JSP) or Velocity.

---

■**Note** Web applications use a slight variation of the MVC design pattern sometimes called Model 2 architecture or web MVC. In the original MVC triad, the controller is not coupled to the view. Instead, the view acts as an observer of the model, receiving event notifications when the model is changed (Gamma et al 1995).

---

Most implementations of the MVC pattern in web applications introduce an additional component: the *front controller* (Fowler 2003). The front controller is technical in nature and coordinates request processing by enforcing a well defined request processing life cycle: it maps a request onto a particular controller and renders the view selected by that controller. The front controller can also manage common concerns like security and internationalization. Well known front controller implementations are the Struts `ActionServlet`, the Spring MVC `Dispatcher Servlet`, or the JSF `FacesServlet`. From the application's point of view, the controller is in the driver's seat. Once the front controller has selected the appropriate controller for a request, that controller decides how to interface with business components, which view to display, and the model data to render. This process is presented graphically in Figure 1-1.

Web MVC frameworks help us develop efficient, structured, and maintainable *web applications*: software applications that are usable on the World Wide Web (WWW). Such an application could, for instance, dynamically serve data coming from a database, in contrast to serving static HTML web pages.

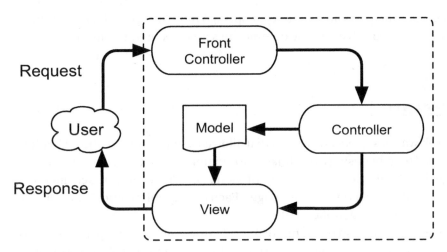

**Figure 1-1.** *Web MVC*

Web applications are pushing the boundaries of web technology. We have become accustomed to having complex conversations with these applications, requiring interactive dialogs spanning multiple requests. An airline ticket booking process is one example: you select a flight, indicate seating preferences, and enter payment information within the scope of an interaction with the application that spans several pages.

Java web application development based on the MVC design pattern is well understood. As always in the Java world, there is heated debate about the pros and cons of particular frameworks. The basics are agreed on by most people involved, however, and some of the older frameworks such as Struts have been used successfully in production deployments for several years. Given the enormous amount of effort that has already gone into the development of these frameworks, and the applications based on them, it comes as a huge surprise that not a single mainstream Java web application development framework offers a truly compelling way of implementing complex conversations.

Spring Web Flow aims to fill this void. It serves as a web application controller component focused entirely on the definition and execution of complex conversations in a web application. Instead of competing with the well established web MVC frameworks already available, Spring Web Flow integrates into those frameworks. It serves as the "C" in "MVC": a controller orchestrating interaction with business components, preparing model data, and selecting views (the role of Spring Web Flow as the controller has changed slightly in Spring Web Flow 2, which builds on top of Spring Web MVC).

To better understand the goals and benefits of Spring Web Flow, you must first understand the problems it tries to solve and the complexities involved in the solution. Let's investigate these next.

# Free Browsing

Historically, the Web was designed as a system that allowed users to browse through informational pages linked together using hyperlinks. Information is annotated using Hypertext Markup Language (HTML) to allow correct presentation in a browser and embed anchors that link the information to other resources or pages. Each page is uniquely identified in this web using a Uniform Resource Identifier (URI).

To keep the system scalable and efficient, the World Wide Web was set up as a stateless client-server environment. Client browsers retrieve information from web servers using the GET method defined by the Hypertext Transfer Protocol (HTTP). This simple setup allows caching of information both on the client side and on intermediary proxy servers. The web servers themselves can be easily scaled horizontally, adding additional systems to form a cluster, because they do not have to maintain information associated with individual users.

This simple stateless architecture was clearly a great success. The World Wide Web has scaled to unprecedented size, and millions of people are now familiar with its concepts. Browsers allow you to efficiently move between pages, offering navigational aides such as a browsing history with Back, Forward, and Refresh buttons. Users can directly type semantically meaningful URIs like `http://en.wikipedia.org/wiki/Plato` into their browsers and bookmark URIs to easily return to those pages at a later time. Browsing is not constrained in any way, and users surfing the World Wide Web are limited only by their own interests, time, and imagination.

The architecture of the World Wide Web is often called *RESTful*, since it follows the Representational State Transfer (REST) style of software architecture for distributed hypermedia systems, as originally formulated by Roy Fielding in his doctoral dissertation (2000):

> *Representational State Transfer is intended to evoke an image of how a well-designed Web application behaves: a network of web pages (a virtual state-machine), where the user progresses through an application by selecting links (state transitions), resulting in the next page (representing the next state of the application) being transferred to the user and rendered for their use.*

Many technical publications also use the term "RESTful" to describe applications using simple web technologies such as HTML, HTTP, and URIs. Furthermore, meaning-ful, user-readable URIs are often referred to as *REST-style URIs* or *URLs*.

When the World Wide Web was gaining momentum, designers quickly realized that it would be far more compelling if it allowed user interaction. To accommodate this new requirement, core World Wide Web standards were enhanced with interactive elements:

- HTTP was extended with additional request methods: POST allows information to be submitted to the server. PUT and DELETE allow clients to add resources to the server or remove them again.

- Elements allowing user interaction were added to HTML. The best known example is the HTML <FORM> tag, which allows you to include parameter key-value pairs in a request sent to the server (typically in a POST request).

- Using technology such as cookies, servers can track a user through an entire HTTP session spanning multiple requests, thus working around the stateless nature of HTTP and allowing servers to customize content for each user.

All of these techniques and enhancements combine to result in a system capable of supporting *web applications*: useful, interactive computer applications that leverage the ease of use and ubiquity of the World Wide Web while realizing important benefits, such as these:

- There's no need to install custom software on the client, making large-scale deploy-ment trivial.

- All clients always use the same, up-to-date version of the application.

- New subscription-based billing models are possible, opening up possibilities for new revenue streams.

- Users are familiar with the technologies involved—web browsers, HTML pages, and so on—often alleviating the need for training.

Of course, there is also a cost attached to these new possibilities:

- Having HTTP sessions makes scaling a web application more difficult than scaling a traditional web server. Simple solutions often cause *server affinity*, that is, require a user with an active session to always use one server from a cluster, thus preventing failover and effective load balancing. Still, this problem is on the server side, so it can be tackled by knowledgeable people, and the client browser can remain simple and lightweight.

- Web applications cannot offer the rich interactive user experience found in desktop GUI applications. This downside turned out to be somewhat of an advantage to users, since it forced web applications developers to create simple and intuitive interfaces for their applications.

With web developers, users, and businesses gaining more and more experience with web applications, the requirements of these applications become ever more challenging. Today we see web applications using techniques such as Asynchronous JavaScript and XML (AJAX) to offer a richer user experience. Web applications also go to great lengths to control a user's actions while interacting with the application. The next section explores this topic in detail.

# Controlled Navigation

Most modern web applications not only require free browsing but also have more demanding use cases requiring *controlled navigation*: the users' navigational freedom needs to be constrained to carefully guide them to the completion of a business process. There are many, well known examples of such controlled navigation use cases.

- One example is an airline ticket booking process, involving steps such as flight selection, seating preferences, frequent flyer policies, and payment information entry. Then too, most travel agencies allow you to book not only a flight but also an associated hotel room and rental car.

- Also, electronic banking has become commonplace in the last few years, allowing customers to use web applications to make payments, buy stock options, or manage their credit cards.

- Many governments are using web technology and web applications to allow citizens to perform tasks electronically, for instance, submitting tax declarations. Such processes are bound by legislation and are often extremely complex, requiring the user to follow an exact navigational flow corresponding to his or her situation.

These web applications potentially deal with sensitive user data or even the user's own money. It is therefore of utmost importance that the applications are very stable, secure, and robust. Users should feel comfortable interacting with the application, trusting it to do the right thing, even in situations where a user has accidentally used the browser's Back or Refresh buttons.

All of the Java web application frameworks discussed previously allow you to develop simple web applications with relative ease. Most use the HTTP session to manage state associated with a particular user and make it easy to work with pages containing HTML forms using techniques such as automatic data binding. However, they do not go beyond these abilities to provide support to tackle the difficult use cases where navigation needs to be controlled and users need to be carefully guided to the completion of a certain task.

This shortcoming is unfortunate, since correctly implementing a completely controlled navigation in a web application is a difficult problem to solve. Three key issues need to addressed:

- Navigational control

- State management

- Modularity

Let's investigate each of these topics in a little more detail.

## Navigational Control

The first question to be answered when implementing a controlled navigation in a web application is, "How do you control the user's navigational freedom?" As explained in the "Free Browsing" section, the World Wide Web was designed as a system promoting free browsing and unconstrained navigation. Browsers offer lists of favorite bookmarks, allowing a user to bookmark a page of particular interest and jump directly to that page again at later point in time. History lists maintained by browsers, and the Back, Forward, and Refresh buttons make it easy for users to go back to pages they visited earlier. A user can even open multiple browser windows or tabs at the same time to compare information, for instance.

You might think that all this functionality is just a convenience offered by modern browsers, but in reality, the free browsing spirit is engrained in the specifications of the core technologies powering the World Wide Web. The following extract from the HTTP 1.1 specification (section 13.13 of RFC 2616) suggests browsers should not reload a page from the server when the user accesses the browsing history, for instance, using the Back button:

> *User agents often have history mechanisms, such as navigation buttons and history lists, that can be used to redisplay an entity retrieved earlier in a session.*

*History mechanisms and caches are different. In particular, history mechanisms should not try to show a semantically transparent view of the current state of a resource. Rather, a history mechanism is meant to show exactly what the user saw at the time when the resource was retrieved.*

*By default, an expiration time does not apply to history mechanisms. If the entity is still in storage, a history mechanism should display it even if the entity has expired, unless the user has specifically configured the agent to refresh expired history documents.*

This definition suggests that the browser history is intended as a client-side navigational aid, enhancing the user's web surfing experience. At the time of this writing, most popular browsers, such as Mozilla Firefox (`http://www.mozilla.com/firefox`) and Microsoft Internet Explorer (`http://www.microsoft.com/ie`), do not strictly follow the specification and will use cache control settings to decide whether or not to reload a page from the history. The Opera browser (`http://www.opera.com`) is an example of a browser strictly complying with the specifications. When you click the Back button, Opera will redisplay the previous page exactly as it was shown before, without reloading it from the server.

It's clear that all of this free browsing support doesn't complement use cases requiring controlled navigation. Unfortunately, it is not generally possible to disable the browser's navigation history, its bookmarking capability, or its ability to open new windows or tabs. You are therefore forced to deal with the problem head-on: you must handle situations where the user uses free browsing conveniences when having a controlled conversation with a web application. Some of the situations that need to be handled follow:

- What happens when a user bookmarks a page in the middle of the conversation? We can't stop the actual bookmarking, but how should the application react when the user uses the bookmark to jump back into the conversation? In most cases, the answer will be that the application should produce an error informing the user that the conversation has expired or ended, possibly allowing the conversation to be restarted. The entry point into the conversation or task might be bookmarkable, but the internal pages typically are not. In other situations, it will be necessary to keep track of the conversation for a long period of time and allow users to jump back into it and continue where they left off.

- How does an application handle refresh requests or moving back or forward in the browsing history? Ideally, a refresh request is idempotent, not causing any side effects with repeated use and allowing the user to freely refresh pages. Handling back and forward navigation, however, is more difficult.

- A less common situation involves the user opening two browser windows on the same application, typically to compare results or evaluate alternatives. How does a web application deal with this? Care needs to be taken to avoid interference or double submits.

Applications can ignore these problems and just ask the user not to use the browser's Back button when starting a process requiring controlled navigation. This approach is obviously naive and brittle, as users are accustomed to surfing around the Internet, frequently clicking the Back or Refresh buttons. When a mistake is made, web applications should be able to handle it in a stable and predictable way.

Applications with a well known and controlled user group, like intranet applications, can sometimes avoid these problems altogether. By deploying a specialized or customized web browser, developers can completely disable all navigational aides. This is obviously not an option for web applications running on the Internet, where users use a wide variety of web browsers. Some Internet web applications try to simulate this by running the application in a special browser window that contains no button bar or other embellishments. This helps, but breaks easily, if for instance, the user presses the Backspace button or a special mouse button to navigate backward in the browser's history.

Incomplete navigational control and users accidentally using the navigational aids offered by the browser also cause another well known problem in web applications: the dangerous double submit.

## The Double Submit Problem

You have already seen the two central request methods supported by the HTTP protocol used on the World Wide Web. A request method indicates the intention of a request to the server.

The GET method allows a client to retrieve a resource (page) from the server. HTTP defines GET to be safe, meaning that it should only ever be used for information retrieval and does not change the state of the server. In other words, a GET request is idempotent and can be repeated (refreshed) any number of times, always producing the same result. GET was the first request method supported by HTTP and was originally the only one. It is still the most frequently used request method today.

The POST method, on the other hand, allows a request to submit data to the server for processing, possibly causing side effects such as updating records in a database. A user submitting a POST request is responsible for the changes caused to the state of the server. POST requests are not safe or idempotent and therefore cannot be refreshed or bookmarked. Historically, POST requests are initiated by clicking buttons on web pages, in contrast with textual links used for GET requests. Using buttons visually differentiates POST requests from GET requests, highlighting their sensitive nature to the user.

A user using the browser navigation history or Refresh button can accidentally repeat a POST request, causing server-side processing to occur twice. This repeat processing has the potential to result in incorrect or unwanted side effects and is known as the *double submit* problem. Imagine a user resubmitting a "confirm purchase" request, resulting in two purchases! Web browsers are aware of this problem and will display a warning to the user when they try to reissue a POST request, such as the following one from Internet Explorer:

In contrast, refreshing pages loaded using a GET request is allowed, and no warning will be shown. Although these warnings provide an extra layer of security, they will make an application feel brittle to the end user: accidentally clicking the Back button causes an unnerving message about possible duplicate transactions!

A real solution for the double submit problem is provided by the POST-REDIRECT-GET idiom (Jouravlev 2004). When a web application sends an HTML page in response to a POST request, that page will look like a normal web page to the user, causing the user to think it is bookmarkable and refreshable. Instead of sending the page data directly in reply to a POST request, the POST-REDIRECT-GET idiom states that a web application should issue a REDIRECT request in response to a POST request, causing a subsequent GET request. This is illustrated in Figure 1-2.

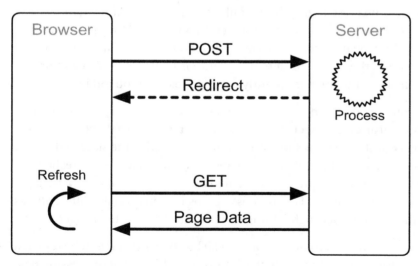

**Figure 1-2.** *The POST-REDIRECT-GET idiom*

A redirect instructs the web browser to look for the response elsewhere using a GET request. HTTP 1.1 defines result code 303, "See Other", for exactly this purpose (from section 10.3.4 of RFC 2616):

> *The response to the request can be found under a different URI and should be retrieved using a GET method on that resource. This method exists primarily to allow the output of a POST-activated script to redirect the user agent to a selected resource.*

For backward compatibility with older web browsers that do not support HTTP 1.1, many web applications don't use the 303 response and instead use the 302, "Found", code (from section 10.3.3 of RFC 2616):

> *The requested resource resides temporarily under a different URI.*

All web browsers in common use today react to the 302 code in exactly the same was as to the 303 code.

A browser receiving a redirect response will know that the requested resource is to be found at another location. As a result, it will not add the original request to its browsing history and instead add only the redirected GET request. This elegantly solves the double submit problem, since the redirected request can be safely refreshed (it's a GET request!). Furthermore, the navigational history will contain only idempotent GET requests, allowing the user to use the browser Back and Forward buttons or bookmark pages without causing alarming warning messages or side effects on the server.

The HTTP specification defines the semantics for GET and POST requests. Unfortunately, these semantics are enforced neither by the HTTP protocol nor by web servers. Because of this, many web sites and web applications abuse GET requests to submit data to the server and cause side effects. These compromises are often driven by visual requirements and a desire to make a web page look as beautiful as possible. JavaScript gives web developers a lot of freedom to post forms by clicking textual links or to get a resource from the server by clicking a button. Image buttons blur the presentational distinction between GET and POST requests even further, giving you complete visual freedom.

Since a GET request can also be used to submit data to the server for processing, possibly causing side effects, the POST-REDIRECT-GET idiom can be reformulated in a more general way as *redirect after submit*: a web application should issue a redirect in response to every submit, be it using a POST or a GET.

Redirecting after every submit allows you to build web applications that behave correctly even when the user accidentally uses functions such as the browser Back button. Another interesting problem is protecting the application against a malicious user trying to short-circuit a conversation with a web application.

## Short-Circuiting Conversations

Most complex conversations in web applications require a linear progression, typically working toward the completion of a business process, such as filling in a tax form. It is crucial that the user enters all the required data and does not jump ahead, skipping important information, or hack around sensitive checks. The server must carefully track a user's progression to ensure the task is completed as defined by the business requirements.

Having a client submit information about its location in a conversation is insufficient. A hacker could easily manipulate those request parameters to short-circuit the flow, possibly compromising the application and the data it manages.

Web applications have no control over the environment the client is using. Normal users will be using the popular browser variants. A malicious user, however, may be using other tools to craft special requests to trick the server into doing things it's not supposed to do. A well known rule among web application developers is that the server should always validate user input data, even when client-side (JavaScript) checks are used. This is also true of navigational control. The server needs to take responsibility and ensure the client follows the defined navigation rules.

In summary, controlling user navigation in a web application is clearly a hard problem to solve. The crux of the problem is the fact that we are trying to enforce navigational constraints in an environment that was explicitly designed for free browsing.

## State Management

Complex conversations within web applications not only mandate a controlled navigation but also involve state management. These subjects are often intertwined: a user accumulates state while progressing through the navigational flow prescribed by a particular business process. When the browser's navigational facilities are used, the application needs to handle the possible impact on the data associated with the conversation:

- When using the Back button, should the application undo (or forget) the edits already done on later pages, or should that information be retained for reuse when the user progresses again? Both alternatives are quite common.

- As browsers such as Opera do not contact the server at all when going back in the navigation history, how do we keep server state synchronized with the client? The client could be seeing stale data that is different from the current values managed by the server, which could lead to confusing situations or possibly even data corruption.

- An application needs to ensure that two browser windows for the same conversation do not interfere with each other, potentially overwriting data entered in one window with the data captured in the other window.

- When a conversation ends, associated data should be cleaned up to avoid memory leaks and prevent the same task from being completed multiple times.

Next to the actual application data, a web application also needs to maintain data structures that track a user's progress through a conversation. As explained earlier, this is necessary to avoid a malicious user short-circuiting a conversation. The application needs to have exact knowledge of the current position of a user in a conversation and the navigational options the user has from that location.

Most web application frameworks track user-related state in the HTTP session. This works well for data that needs to be available to an entire user session, such as user authentication credentials. It allows several users to interact with a web application without interfering with each other. The HTTP session, however, is too coarse grained to be used directly as a data storage medium for conversation-related data. For instance, if two browser windows participate in the same conversation, and conversational data is stored directly in the HTTP session, interference would typically be encountered, since both browser windows share the same HTTP session.

Instead of having multiple browser windows for a single conversation, a user could also be using multiple browser windows to run several conversations at the same time. A reasonable use case like concurrently executing more than one conversation in the same session should clearly be supported.

All data associated with a conversation also needs to be cleaned up. This obviously needs to happen when that conversation ends, but provisions should also be made for abandoned conversations to expire. Storing conversation- related data in the HTTP session helps, since a servlet engine will automatically expire the HTTP session after a configured idle period.

A design pattern traditionally used to control incoming requests, and work around some of these issues, is the synchronizer token, which is discussed in the next section.

## The Synchronizer Token Pattern

The Synchronizer Token is a well known design pattern that helps a web application developer avoid duplicate submissions (Alur 2003). This can, for instance, be used to prevent a user from submitting the same purchase multiple times on an e-commerce web site.

The Synchronizer Token pattern works as follows: When a conversation starts, the application generates a unique token that is stored in the HTTP session. The token is also embedded in each page generated during the conversation, and every request that is part of the conversation is required to include the token value. When a request arrives on the server, it compares the value of the token in the HTTP session with the value included in the request. If the two values match, the request is allowed to continue processing. If they don't match, an error is generated informing the user that the conversation has ended or was invalidated. The token is removed from the HTTP session when the conversation ends or the session expires.

Traditionally, the synchronizer token is used to guard single requests, not conversations spanning multiple requests. In this case, a new token value is generated and stored in the session for every request passing token validation, as illustrated in Figure 1-3.

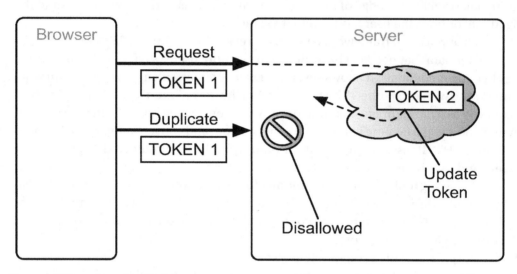

**Figure 1-3.** *Synchronizer Token pattern*

You might be wondering how this pattern relates to the POST-REDIRECT-GET idiom discussed earlier. Using POST-REDIRECT-GET avoids *accidental* double submits of a *single* request but does not help prevent a user from completing the same business process twice. Such a business process is typically composed of *multiple* pages spanning several requests. The Synchronizer Token pattern adds additional safety on top of the POST-REDIRECT-GET idiom by preventing a possibly intentional resubmit of a page or task. Both techniques should typically be combined to deliver a complete solution.

Some Java web application frameworks, noticeably Struts, come with built-in support for the Synchronizer Token pattern. However, this support is very low level, requiring the application developer to manually include token checks in application code.

In summary, the stateless design of the World Wide Web makes it far from trivial to implement a powerful, flexible, and easy-to-use state management system. Instead of leaving application developers to implement solutions to these common problems, a framework should step in to take away that burden.

## Modularity Concerns

Even if a development team were able to enhance its basic web MVC framework to adequately deal with navigational control and state management, the solution would still be likely to exhibit an important problem: it would be too fine grained. State management and navigational control code typically ends up being spread across several controllers or components, instead of being captured in a well defined application module.

Conversations have already been characterized as spanning multiple requests, guiding the user to the completion of a task or business process. A typical business process has low coupling with other processes and high internal cohesion, making it an ideal candidate for modularization. A supporting framework should make it easy to model a conversation as a coherent, self-contained module. Doing so has several important benefits:

- The navigational flow of a business process is readily available by looking at one module, typically defined in a single source code file. This makes it very easy to understand and visualize the process. Input from business experts in the form of flow or state charts can then directly be used when developing such a module without being obfuscated by a horde of technical details.

- Having coarse-grained, well defined, and self-contained modules promotes reuse. A module implementing a particular business process can easily be reused as a black box if it defines a clean input-output contract. One module can use another module as a submodule, allowing a very natural implementation of common usage scenarios, such as master-detail screens.

- Coarse-grained, reusable modules allow you to compose a larger application from manageable building blocks that can be understood in isolation. This approach promotes clean application structure and makes it easier to comprehend and maintain a large-scale application (Evans 2004).

The preceding sections should have made it painfully clear that implementing truly controlled navigation using classic web technology is very difficult. The free browsing spirit of the World Wide Web, and its stateless nature, make it difficult to control user navigation and manage conversational state. Homegrown solutions also tend to be too low-level and fine grained, making reuse and modularization difficult. Let's take a look at the approach typically taken to tackle the issues involved.

# Traditional Solutions

You probably have some awareness of the Struts web application framework and how it works. Struts has been around since 2000 and is still one of the more important request-based web MVC frameworks in use today. Without going into too much detail, this section will show you how a controlled navigation is typically implemented in a Struts application. A fictitious shopping basket checkout process is used in this example; the process is illustrated in the Unified Modeling Language (UML) state diagram in Figure 1-4.

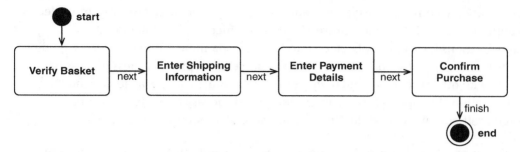

**Figure 1-4.** *A shopping basket checkout process*

In Struts, an Action controller handles a request. An action typically handles a single request, so a conversation spanning multiple requests needs to be decomposed into several actions. You could have a CheckBasketAction controller to verify the contents of the shopping basket, ShippingInfoAction to capture shipping information, PaymentInfoAction to deal with payment details, and finally, ConfirmationAction and MakePurchaseAction controllers to allow users to review entered data and submit their purchases. This covers the controllers in the MVC pattern. Struts uses an ActionForm object as the model, typically requiring an ActionForm subclass corresponding with each action, for instance, a PaymentInfoForm object used by the PaymentInfoAction controller. The views are normally implemented using JSP pages in a Struts application.

The struts-config.xml file allows you to associate an Action controller with an ActionForm object and its related views. Here is an excerpt from this application's struts-config.xml file:

```
<?xml version="1.0" encoding="iso-8859-1"?>
<!DOCTYPE struts-config PUBLIC
  "-//Apache Software Foundation//DTD Struts Configuration 1.2//EN"
  "http://struts.apache.org/dtds/struts-config_1_2.dtd">
<struts-config>
  <form-beans>
    <form-bean name="basketForm" type="com.ervacon.BasketForm"/>
    <form-bean name="shippingInfoForm"
      type="com.ervacon.ShippingInfoForm"/>

    ...
  </form-beans>
```

```
<action-mappings>
  <action path="/checkBasket"
    type="com.ervacon.CheckBasketAction"
    name="basketForm"
    scope="request"
    input="/checkBasket.jsp">
    <forward name="success" redirect="true" path="/shippingInfo.jsp"/>
  </action>

  <action path="/shippingInfo"
    type="com.ervacon.ShippingInfoAction"
    name="shippingInfoForm"
    scope="request"
    input="/shippingInfo.jsp">
    <forward name="failure" path="/shippingInfo.jsp"/>
    <forward name="success" redirect="true" path="/paymentDetails.jsp"/>
  </action>

  ...
</action-mappings>
</struts-config>
```

The ShippingInfoAction controller is configured to use the ShippingInfoForm object and display the paymentDetails.jsp view when shipping information is successfully processed. The paymentDetails.jsp view is displayed after a redirect, as suggested by the POST-REDIRECT-GET idiom (see "The Double Submit Problem"). In case of input validation errors or processing failures, the action displays the shippingInfo.jsp view again, showing the user any relevant error information.

Action implementation classes are independent of each other and are only wired together into a larger flow through the views. The CheckBasketAction controller will display the input form of the *next* action, shippingInfo.jsp, on successful completion. The shippingInfo.jsp view will contain a form submitting to the ShippingInfoAction controller using the /shippingInfo.do URL and continuing the process.

Several of these actions could also be combined into a single larger action, for instance, a Struts DispatchAction controller. This action would still force a view to submit information about its location in the overall process with URLs like /checkout.do?method=shippingInfo.

The end result is that the client drives the progression of the business process, triggering the next step by sending a request targeted at the next controller in the flow. Controllers will have to contain special code to verify that a malicious client is not trying to short-circuit the flow or complete the steps out of order. For instance, a hacker could send a request for /makePurchase.do after having entered shipping information, skipping the payment details altogether:

```java
public class MakePurchaseAction extends Action {
  public ActionForward execute(ActionMapping mapping, ActionForm form,
    HttpServletRequest request, HttpServletResponse response) {

    // make sure the client completed all steps
    if (shippingInfoCaptured() && paymentDetailsCaptured()) {
      if (makePurchase(...)) {
        return mapping.findForward("success");
      }
      else {
        // show purchasing failure to user
        ...
      }
    }
    else {
      // generate an error
      ...
    }
  }
}
```

All of this flow verification code can quickly become overwhelming. Introducing a synchronizer token to prevent duplicate submissions makes the code even more convoluted:

```java
public class MakePurchaseAction extends Action {
  public ActionForward execute(ActionMapping mapping, ActionForm form,
    HttpServletRequest request, HttpServletResponse response) {

    // make sure the client completed all steps
    if (shippingInfoCaptured() && paymentDetailsCaptured()) {
      if (isTokenValid(request)) {
        if (makePurchase(...)) {
          return mapping.findForward("success");

          // the process has ended
          resetToken(request);
```

```
      }
      else {
        // show purchasing failure to user
        ...
      }
    }
    else {
      // generate token error
      ...
    }
  }
  else {
    // generate an error
    ...
  }
 }
}
```

The only option Struts offers to accumulate information in a multistep process is using the HTTP session. The sample application would need to store the shopping basket, shipping information, and payment details in the session to make them available to the MakePurchaseAction controller. Once the purchase has been made, MakePurchaseAction is responsible for proper cleanup, adding still more code to the action.

To combat the overwhelming amount of plumbing code needed in each Action involved in the conversation, developers typically introduce an action superclass. The superclass handles some of the tasks automatically, such as token verification, and offers convenient helper methods to do things like session cleanup.

Modularity is not addressed at all by this solution. Although the actions are separate controllers handling a single request, they cannot easily be reused since they're implicitly connected to other controllers via the views. Without special care, the developed plumbing code quickly becomes process-specific and nonreusable.

The end result of all these efforts is an implementation that's still far from ideal:

- Navigation is only partially controlled with individual actions wired together through the views, giving an attacker a simple way to target the application. To prevent misuse, action code needs to duplicate the navigational rules in complex if-then-else structures.

- There is no special handling of the browser Back and Forward buttons, and it is unclear what the exact impact of using them could be. The POST-REDIRECT-GET idiom and Synchronizer Token pattern were employed to prevent accidental and intentional resubmissions, but using these techniques involved manual configuration and coding.

- The ad hoc state management leaves much to be desired. The lack of automatic cleanup opens the door for possible memory leaks or unintentionally using stale data from a previous execution in a new conversation. No measures were taken to avoid concurrent conversations running in the same HTTP session from interfering with each other's data.

- The navigational flow of the process, clearly outlined in the UML state diagram of Figure 1-4, is not at all apparent when looking at the code. Pieces of the overall process are scattered over several different implementation artifacts: the `Action` implementation code, the XML configuration, and the JSP views.

- With each action handling a single request, the solution is very request centric, ignoring the more coarse-grained concept of a business process or task, preventing any form of efficient reuse, and confusing the larger structure of the application.

- Lots of custom code has to be written, thus introducing an extra development and maintenance burden.

There must be a better solution to all of this? Luckily there is. It's called Spring Web Flow!

## Spring Web Flow

Spring Web Flow was specifically designed to help developers implement complex conversations in web applications. It solves all of the problems that have been discussed so far in a powerful, flexible, and elegant way, while keeping ease of use and testability as central goals. Let's glance at its feature set.

As a controller component in the MVC triad, Spring Web Flow integrates into hosting web MVC frameworks, serving as an application controller (Fowler 2003), handling screen navigation, and coordinating the flow of a business process. Adopting Spring Web Flow is easy; you can keep using your web application framework of choice and gain a new powerful tool in your toolbox.

Spring Web Flow captures business processes or conversations in modules called flows. A *flow* is a blueprint for the interaction a user can have with a web application; it reacts to user events to drive the process to completion. You can look at a flow as a simple manifestation of a finite state machine (FSM), consisting of a number of states that define the activities to execute while progressing through the flow. A state can allow a user to participate in the flow, or it can call business services. The flow can move from one state to another using transitions triggered by events.

**Note** In the remainder of this book, "conversation" and "flow" are used interchangeably as synonyms. Words such as "dialog" or "business process" cover similar ground.

As you have seen, business processes are commonly defined using UML state diagrams, and Spring Web Flow flow definitions use a similar model (Fowler 2000). The following screenshot shows a Spring Web Flow flow definition that mirrors the process definition in Figure 1-4:

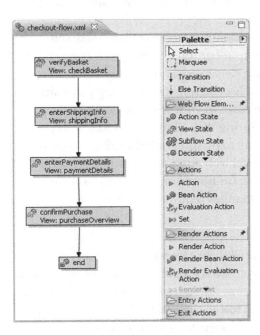

Flow definitions, such as the one preceding, can be made using a Domain Specific Language (DSL), for which both an XML and Java syntax exist. The fact that Spring Web Flow flow definitions map intuitively onto UML state diagrams fosters direct communication with nontechnical people like business experts and analysts.

Given the navigational rules set out in a flow definition, Spring Web Flow automatically takes care of navigational control. Using web continuations, Spring Web Flow can guarantee stable, predictable behavior of a web application even when the user uses the browser's Back, Forward, or Refresh buttons; revisits bookmarked pages; or opens multiple windows in the same conversation. The POST-REDIRECT-GET idiom will also be automatically applied, without any need for developer intervention.

Spring Web Flow manages a flow execution on behalf of a client, keeping track of the user's exact position in the flow. Using the flow definition, which provides a blueprint defining all possible navigational paths, Spring Web Flow can prevent users from short-circuiting flows. With their well defined life cycle, flow executions can also be observed by application code using an implementation of the Observer design pattern (Gamma et al 1995).

A flow execution tracks all data associated with an ongoing conversation, giving developers access to a set of well defined scopes. An advanced flow execution repository system automatically cleans up completed or expired conversations and ensures that concurrent conversations in the same HTTP session do not interfere with each other. Automatic flow execution management also makes double submissions impossible, without requiring any developer effort.

Conversations defined by Spring Web Flow flow definitions are well defined, self-contained modules declaring an explicit input-output contract. Spring Web Flow allows one flow to use another flow as a subflow, enabling easy reuse and modularization. Flows can capture anything from simple dialogs to complex conversations, giving you a single consistent technique to apply to many of the use cases in your web application.

On top of this already impressive feature list, Spring Web Flow also makes it very easy to unit test your flows, giving you an additional way to do integration testing. What's more, Spring Web Flow abstracts you from low-level web application artifacts, such as `HttpServletRequest`, allowing you to move a flow definition from a unit test environment to deployment in your web application, with no changes required.

---

■**Note**  Readers familiar with business process management (BPM) will have noticed the similarity between a flow definition and a more general work flow. Indeed, Spring Web Flow flow definitions are special, simple cases of such work flows; flow definitions lack advanced features such as splits and joins. Spring Web Flow does not leverage an existing BPM system but, instead, provides its own flow execution engine designed specifically to handle the challenge of controlling user navigation in a web environment, while remaining easy to use.

---

# Summary

This chapter introduced the complexities of building a conversation requiring controlled navigation in a web application. The heart of the problem is the fact that the World Wide Web was designed as a stateless environment promoting free browsing, making effectively controlling user navigation very difficult.

Well known design patterns and idioms help developers deal with some of the issues involved. The POST-REDIRECT-GET idiom avoids accidental double submits, while the Synchronizer Token pattern prevents duplicate transactions. Mainstream Java web application frameworks require a fair amount of development effort to correctly use these best practices.

Putting considerable time and effort into extending a base web MVC framework like Struts results in a solution that still leaves many questions unanswered. Having been designed specifically to tackle complex conversations in web applications, Spring Web Flow offers a powerful, elegant, and flexible solution that can be integrated into a base web framework of choice.

The rest of this book will provide an in-depth study of Spring Web Flow, describing its many features, explaining when to use particular functionalities (and when not to!), and illuminating best practices. Since doing is the best way of learning, let's get started by setting up an environment that allows you to easily experiment with Spring Web Flow.

# CHAPTER 2

■ ■ ■

# Getting Started

**N**ow that you have an idea of what Spring Web Flow is and a solid understanding of the problems it tries to solve, you're probably keen to get started and see it in action.

No programming book could ever be complete without a "Hello World" example. This chapter will introduce the simplest possible use of Spring Web Flow in a Spring Web MVC–based application. Since just displaying a message in a browser is a bit too simple, the classic "Hello World" application will be enhanced to introduce user interaction and demonstrate some of the power that Spring Web Flow offers you.

This chapter will also set you up for efficiently using and experimenting with Spring Web Flow. I will explain how to obtain the Spring Web Flow distribution and integrate Spring Web Flow into your application and its build system. Doing so requires a detailed understanding of Spring Web Flow dependencies. I will also illustrate how to set up a productive development environment using the Spring IDE.

## Downloading Spring Web Flow

The first thing to do is download the latest stable release of Spring Web Flow from the Spring Web Flow home page: http://www.springframework.org/webflow. The examples in this book are based on Spring Web Flow 1.0.6, but any later 1.x version should also work.

You can download and extract the Spring Web Flow distribution archive to any location on your computer. The examples in this book assume that it has been extracted to ~/swfbook/spring-webflow where the tilde (~) represents the user's home directory.

This is the ideal moment to take a bit of time to browse around the contents of the Spring Web Flow distribution archive. As you will see, it contains not only the Spring Web Flow JAR files but also extensive reference documentation, the complete source code of Spring Web Flow, and a number of sample applications illustrating Spring Web Flow features. You can use this wealth of information to your advantage when developing applications using Spring Web Flow. For instance, looking at the source code can be useful when you need a detailed understanding of how a particular feature works. The Spring Web Flow distribution even contains a flexible build system that you can leverage in your own applications, which is discussed in more detail in the "Spring Jumpstart" section.

# Runtime Requirements

To use Spring Web Flow, you need to be running at least Java 1.3 and Servlet API 2.3, as defined by the J2EE 1.3 specification. This means that it is possible to use Spring Web Flow in application servers, such as BEA WebLogic 6, IBM WebSphere 5, or the Tomcat 4 Servlet engine. Of course, you can also use more recent versions of these products.

Using XML-based flow definitions requires an XML parser that can handle XML schemas. Starting with Java 1.4, such a parser is included in the Java runtime environment. When using Java 1.3, you'll have to add an appropriate XML parser to your classpath, for instance, Xerces2 (http://xerces.apache.org/xerces2-j/).

When deploying on Java 1.3 or 1.4, you normally also want to add the util.concurrent library to your classpath (http://gee.cs.oswego.edu/dl/classes/EDU/oswego/cs/dl/util/concurrent/intro.html). Spring Web Flow will use the lock implementations provided by this library to do conversation locking. On Java 5, the lock implementations of java.util.concurrent will automatically be used. If no valid lock implementation can be found, Spring Web Flow will default to a no-op lock, resulting in no locking at all. In this case, a warning will be logged when the system starts up.

The only other common dependency of Spring Web Flow is the Spring Framework itself. You need at least Spring 1.2.7 to use Spring Web Flow. Some Spring Web Flow convenience features, in particular the configuration XML schema, are only available when using Spring 2.0 or later. As a general guideline, you should be using the latest stable point release of the major version of the Spring Framework you are using. For instance, when still using Spring 1.2.x, it is advised to use Spring 1.2.9, the latest stable Spring 1.2.x release at the time of this writing.

# Build System Integration

Spring Web Flow is a framework primarily intended for Java web application development. Building a web application is a nontrivial process involving steps such as compiling code, running unit tests, and creating a WAR (Web ARchive) file as specified by the Java Enterprise Edition (JEE) specification. Instead of executing these steps by hand, it's better to use a build system that does most of the grunt work for you.

This section explains how to make Spring Web Flow available to your application. You can either integrate it manually or use a dependency manager to retrieve all the libraries needed. Spring Web Flow does not require the use of any particular build system, and you should be able to easily integrate it into whatever build system your application is using.

# Manual Integration

If you're not using an automatic transitive dependency manager like Maven 2 or Ivy, you'll have to manually add a number of JARs to the classpath of your application. In a JEE web application, you typically add these JAR files to the `WEB-INF/lib` directory of your WAR file.

Spring Web Flow itself is composed of the two JAR files detailed in Table 2-1.

**Table 2-1.** *Spring Web Flow JAR Files*

| JAR File | Description |
| --- | --- |
| spring-webflow.jar | The Spring Web Flow implementation package, containing all the classes of the public API, as well as resources such as the Spring Web Flow XML schema |
| spring-binding.jar | The Spring Data Binding framework, a library used internally by Spring Web Flow |

These core JAR files have a number of external dependencies. Table 2-2 details the required dependencies needed for *all* Spring Web Flow usage scenarios.

**Table 2-2.** *Core Spring Web Flow Dependencies*

| JAR File | Description |
| --- | --- |
| commons-logging.jar | Jakarta commons logging is used for logging and is available at `http://jakarta.apache.org/commons/logging`. |
| ognl.jar | The Object Graph Navigation Language is the default expression language used by Spring Web Flow; it's available at `http://www.ognl.org`. |
| spring-beans.jar , spring-core.jar, spring-context.jar, and spring-web.jar | These are the required modules of the Spring Framework. Instead of adding each module individually, you can instead add the larger `spring.jar` file, which includes all of these modules. All these files are available at `http://www.springframework.org`. |

In addition to these core dependencies, Spring Web Flow has additional dependencies for particular usage scenarios. These dependencies are optional and need to be satisfied only when using Spring Web Flow in particular settings. Tables 2-3 to 2-7 will detail all groups of optional dependencies.

Unit testing is supported by the unit test dependency detailed in Table 2-3.

**Table 2-3.** *Spring Web Flow Test Support Dependency*

| JAR File | Description |
| --- | --- |
| junit.jar | This JAR file for the JUnit testing framework is needed only for unit testing and using the Spring Web Flow unit test support. It is available at `http://www.junit.org`. |

Integrating Spring Web Flow into the Spring Web MVC framework requires the JAR file in Table 2-4.

**Table 2-4.** *Spring Web MVC Integration Dependency*

| JAR File | Description |
|---|---|
| spring-webmvc.jar | The Spring Web MVC application framework is required only when integrating Spring Web Flow into a Spring Web MVC application, and it is available at http://www.springframework.org. |

Spring Web Flow can also be used from inside a JSR-168–compliant Portlet application. In that case, you need the JAR files listed in Table 2-5 in addition to the Spring Web MVC dependency mentioned previously.

**Table 2-5.** *Spring Portlet MVC Integration Dependency*

| JAR File | Description |
|---|---|
| spring-webmvc-portlet.jar | The Spring Portlet MVC application framework is needed only when using Spring Web Flow from inside a JSR-168/Spring Portlet MVC application. It is available at http://www.springframework.org. |

When you want to use Spring Web Flow from inside a classic Struts 1 application, you'll need to resolve the dependencies listed in Table 2-6.

**Table 2-6.** *Struts Integration Dependencies*

| JAR File | Description |
|---|---|
| struts.jar | The classic Struts 1 MVC framework is used by the integration of Spring Web Flow into the Struts 1 framework and is available at http://struts.apache.org/1.x. |
| spring-webmvc-struts.jar | This support code integrates the Spring Framework with a classic Struts 1 application and is available at http://www.springframework.org. |

Finally, Spring Web Flow can also be integrated into a JavaServer Faces (JSF) environment, in which case you need the dependencies listed in Table 2-7.

**Table 2-7.** *JSF Integration Dependencies*

| JAR File | Description |
|---|---|
| jsf-api.jar, and jsf-impl.jar | Any JSF 1 implementation, for instance, Apache MyFaces, which is available at http://myfaces.apache.org |

Consult the Ivy dependency descriptors (ivy.xml), included in the Spring Web Flow distribution, for exact details on which version of each of the JAR files mentioned in these tables is needed.

## Integration with Ivy

People using Ant (http://ant.apache.org) and the Ivy dependency manager (http://ant.apache.org/ivy) can integrate Spring Web Flow into their projects by simply adding a dependency to their ivy.xml file:

```
<dependency org="org.springframework" name="spring-webflow"
  rev="1.0.6" conf="default->mvc"/>
```

This will make the default configuration of the application depend on the mvc configuration defined by Spring Web Flow. An Ivy configuration is a set of dependencies required for a particular usage scenario, such as using Spring Web Flow in a Spring Web MVC application.

The Spring Web Flow Ivy dependency descriptor defines the configurations detailed in Table 2-8. Your application can depend on any of these configurations.

**Table 2-8.** *Ivy Configurations*

| Name | Description |
| --- | --- |
| Testing | Unit testing support using JUnit |
| Mvc | Integration with the Spring Web MVC framework |
| Portlet | Integration with the Spring Portlet MVC framework |
| Struts | Struts 1 integration |
| Jsf | Integration with JSF 1 environments |

Typically, you'll map the default configuration of your application to the Spring Web Flow configuration corresponding to your web application framework (e.g., JSF), and the unit test configuration of your application is mapped to the Spring Web Flow testing configuration, as follows:

```
<dependency org="org.springframework" name="spring-webflow"
  rev="1.0.6" conf="default->jsf"/>
<dependency org="org.springframework" name="spring-webflow"
  rev="1.0.6" conf="test->testing"/>
```

The default configuration is mvc, assuming Spring Web MVC integration. As you can see, these configurations map exactly with the groups of optional dependencies detailed in the "Manual Integration" section.

---

■**Note**  The Spring Web Flow Ivy dependency descriptor generally refers to the latest stable production release of the Spring Framework. Keep in mind, however, that you can use Spring Web Flow with Spring 1.2.7 and later.

---

Consult the Ivy documentation for more information on Ivy configurations and dependency management using Ivy in general.

## Integration with Maven

Users of the Maven 2 (http://maven.apache.org/) project management tool can make Spring Web Flow available to their applications by just declaring a dependency on it in the Project Object Model (POM) of their applications:

```
<dependency>
  <groupId>org.springframework</groupId>
  <artifactId>spring-webflow</artifactId>
  <version>1.0.6</version>
</dependency>
```

Maven does not allow you to define dependency configurations like Ivy does, so you must explicitly add <dependency> elements for the other JARs of the dependency group relevant for your deployment situation. For instance, when integrating with Spring Web MVC, you also need the following dependency:

```
<dependency>
  <groupId>org.springframework</groupId>
  <artifactId>spring-webmvc</artifactId>
  <version>2.5.4</version>
</dependency>
```

Normally, including this dependency should not be much of an issue, since you should already have the file if your application is using Spring Web MVC.

## Spring Jumpstart

The previous sections explained how to integrate Spring Web Flow into whatever build system your application is using. A build system is also needed for the sample applications used throughout this book. To keep things simple, we will reuse the build system used to build Spring Web Flow itself. This build system, called Spring Jumpstart, is included in the Spring Web Flow distribution, so you should already have it available on your computer. It resides in the projects/common-build directory.

Spring Jumpstart is based on Ant 1.6 or later and uses Ivy 1.3 or later for dependency management. You can download Ant from `http://ant.apache.org`. Installing Ant is trivial: just unpack the distribution in an appropriate directory. It's a good idea to add the Ant `bin` directory to your PATH, allowing you to directly type **ant** on the command line:

```
erwin@esther:~$ ant -version
Apache Ant version 1.6.5 compiled on June 2 2005
```

You don't need to install Ivy since it's included in the Spring Jumpstart build system. It goes without saying that you also need to have a JDK available on your machine.

A project built using Spring Jumpstart should follow a standardized directory layout, similar to the project structure of a Maven 2 project. Figure 2-1 shows the basic web application project structure.

**Figure 2-1.** *Basic web application project structure*

The root directory of your project, just called `project` in Figure 2-1, contains all sources in the `src` tree, along with a few files describing the project. Basic project properties are defined in a properties file, as shown in Listing 2-1.

Listing 2-1. Spring Jumpstart project.properties File

```
# properties defined in this file are overridable by a local
# build.properties in this project dir

# The location of the common build system
common.build.dir=/path/to/projects/common-build

# Do not publish built artifacts to the integration repository
do.publish=false

project.name=project
project.webapp.name=project
```

Edit the `common.build.dir` property to point to the location of the Spring Jumpstart common build system.

Spring Jumpstart is a modular build system. It contains modules dealing with tasks such as documentation generation or deployment on Tomcat. In the case of the sample applications in this book, we'll be using only the common targets provided by common-targets.xml. The Ant build script shown in Listing 2-2, which resides in the project directory, includes this module to make it available to the project.

Listing 2-2. Spring Jumpstart build.xml Ant Build Script

```xml
<?xml version="1.0"?>
<project default="dist">
  <property file="build.properties"/>
  <property file="project.properties"/>
  <property file="${common.build.dir} /build.properties"/>
  <property file="${common.build.dir} /project.properties"/>
  <property file="${user.home} /build.properties"/>

  <!-- this is a web application -->
  <property name="build.web" value="true"/>

  <import file="${common.build.dir} /common-targets.xml"/>
</project>
```

Finally, the ivy.xml Ivy dependency descriptor in the project directory declares the dependencies of the project. Listing 2-3 provides a template you can modify.

Listing 2-3. Spring Jumpstart ivy.xml Dependency Descriptor

```xml
<ivy-module version="1.1">
  <info organization="org.your" module="project"/>
  <configurations>
    <conf name="global" visibility="private"/>
    <conf name="buildtime" visibility="private"/>
    <conf name="test" visibility="private"/>

    <conf name="default" extends="global"/>
  </configurations>

  <dependencies defaultconf="global->default">
    <!-- insert dependencies here -->
  </dependencies>
</ivy-module>
```

The global, buildtime, and test configurations are recognized by Spring Jumpstart and will be used during the build process. The global configuration is intended for external usage through its public alias: default. The buildtime configuration can hold only build-time dependencies, while the test dependencies are used during unit testing. Both the buildtime and test configurations are private and only intended for internal use.

To find out about the functionality the Spring Jumpstart build system offers you, just run the ant -projecthelp command in the project directory:

```
erwin@esther:~/swfbook/project$ ant -projecthelp
Buildfile: build.xml

Main targets:
```

| | |
|---|---|
| clean | Scrub build, distribution, and test results directories |
| clean-all | Calls clean, but also cleans lib dir dependencies pulled down by Ivy |
| compile | Compile all source code |
| dist | Create all project distributables |
| ear | Create the enterprise application archive (.ear) |
| ear-stage | Create this enterprise application (.ear) in exploded format |
| gen | Generate code artifacts |
| jar | Create project jar containing code artifacts and other resources |
| javadoc | Create the project API documentation |
| publish | Publish this project in the ivy repository |
| report | Generates a dependencies report |
| resources | Force update of filterable resources (property config files, etc) needed at runtime and test time |
| retrieve | Retrieve all declared dependencies into the lib dir |
| run | Run a java application |
| run-with-arguments | Run a java application with arguments |
| statics | Copy static files before compile, replacing tokens as needed |
| test | Runs one local test using the value of the test.class property |
| test-resources | Force update of filterable resources (logging config files, etc) needed at test time |
| tests | Runs all tests, first local then server (if any) |

```
tests-dist          Run all tests after creating a project distribution
tests-local         Run all local tests
war                 Create the webapp in .war format
web                 Create this webapp in exploded format
Default target: dist
```

The basic functionality offered by Spring Jumpstart is all we need to build the sample applications, and explaining all of the available features is well beyond the scope of this book. Let's move on to seeing Spring Web Flow in action!

# Hello World

With all the technical lacing-up behind us, we can focus our attention back on Spring Web Flow itself and develop a simple "Hello World" application.

---

■**Note**  The sample applications documented in this book use Java 5, Servlet API 2.4, and JSP 2.0. You will need to use an application server or servlet engine adhering to these specifications, for instance Tomcat 5 or Jetty 6, to follow along with the examples.

---

Since this sample application will use the Spring Jumpstart build system, we start by creating a web application project directory structure as detailed in Figure 2-1. Let's call the project helloworld and make the necessary adjustments in project.properties:

```
# The location of the common build system
common.build.dir=~/swfbook/spring-webflow/projects/common-build

# Do not publish built artifacts to the integration repository
do.publish=false

project.name=helloworld
project.webapp.name=helloworld
```

The preceding properties assume Spring Web Flow is installed in ~/swfbook/ spring-webflow and reference the Spring Jumpstart build system at that location. The sample application resides in ~/swfbook/helloworld. Since this application will use Spring Web Flow (duh!), you need to add a dependency to ivy.xml:

```
<ivy-module version="1.1">
  <info organization="com.ervacon" module="helloworld"/>
```

```
<configurations>
  <conf name="global" visibility="private"/>
  <conf name="buildtime" visibility="private"/>
  <conf name="test" visibility="private"/>

  <conf name="default" extends="global"/>
</configurations>

<dependencies defaultconf="global->default">
  <dependency org="org.springframework" name="spring-webflow"
    rev="1.0.6" conf="global->mvc"/>
</dependencies>
</ivy-module>
```

As explained in the "Integration with Ivy" section, this dependency definition will make Spring Web Flow and Spring Web MVC available to the project. Run the ant retrieve command to retrieve all dependencies into the lib directory:

```
erwin@esther:~/swfbook/helloworld$ ant retrieve
Buildfile: build.xml

...

[retrieve.conf] :: retrieving :: [ com.ervacon | helloworld ]
[retrieve.conf]         confs: [global, buildtime, test]
[retrieve.conf]         9 artifacts copied, 0 already retrieved

retrieve.post:

retrieve:

BUILD SUCCESSFUL
Total time: 2 seconds
```

The helloworld project only has global dependencies, and the build system has copied nine JAR files into the lib/global directory of the project.

The next step to getting the "Hello World" application running is to configure Spring Web MVC and the DispatcherServlet in the web application deployment descriptor. Add the following web.xml file to helloworld/src/main/webapp/WEB-INF:

```
<?xml version="1.0" encoding="UTF-8"?>
<web-app version="2.4"
  xmlns="http://java.sun.com/xml/ns/j2ee"
  xmlns:xsi="http://www.w3.org/2001/XMLSchema-instance"
```

```
   xsi:schemaLocation="http://java.sun.com/xml/ns/j2ee
   http://java.sun.com/xml/ns/j2ee/web-app_2_4.xsd">

   <servlet>
     <servlet-name>dispatcher</servlet-name>
     <servlet-class>
        org.springframework.web.servlet.DispatcherServlet
     </servlet-class>
   </servlet>

   <servlet-mapping>
     <servlet-name>dispatcher</servlet-name>
     <url-pattern>*.html</url-pattern>
   </servlet-mapping>
</web-app>
```

This configures the Spring Web MVC `DispatcherServlet` to handle all *.html requests targeted at the application.

Recall that Spring Web Flow acts as a controller in a web MVC framework. The central point of integration between Spring Web MVC and Spring Web Flow is a controller implementation called `FlowController`. To actually integrate Spring Web Flow into Spring Web MVC, you need to add a bean definition for this controller to the application context file read by the `DispatcherServlet`: `dispatcher-servlet.xml`. Create the following `dispatcher-servlet.xml` file in the `helloworld/src/main/webapp/WEB-INF` directory:

```
<?xml version="1.0" encoding="UTF-8"?>
<beans xmlns="http://www.springframework.org/schema/beans"
  xmlns:xsi="http://www.w3.org/2001/XMLSchema-instance"
  xmlns:flow="http://www.springframework.org/schema/webflow-config"
  xsi:schemaLocation="
    http://www.springframework.org/schema/beans
    http://www.springframework.org/schema/beans/spring-beans-2.5.xsd
    http://www.springframework.org/schema/webflow-config
    http://www.springframework.org/schema/webflow-config/ \
      spring-webflow-config-1.0.xsd">

  <bean name="/flows.html"
    class="org.springframework.webflow.executor.mvc.FlowController">
    <property name="flowExecutor" ref="flowExecutor"/>
  </bean>
```

```
    <flow:executor id="flowExecutor" registry-ref="flowRegistry"/>

    <flow:registry id="flowRegistry">
      <flow:location path="/WEB-INF/hello-flow.xml"/>
    </flow:registry>
</beans>
```

The flow controller is configured to handle requests for /flows.html. In addition to FlowController itself, you also define two additional beans using the Spring Web Flow configuration schema: a flowExecutor bean that will handle flow execution on behalf of the client and a flowRegistry bean holding flow definitions.

A single flow definition is registered with the registry: /WEB-INF/hello-flow.xml. Let's create that flow definition file:

```
<?xml version="1.0" encoding="UTF-8"?>
<flow xmlns="http://www.springframework.org/schema/webflow"
  xmlns:xsi="http://www.w3.org/2001/XMLSchema-instance"
  xsi:schemaLocation="
    http://www.springframework.org/schema/webflow
    http://www.springframework.org/schema/webflow/spring-webflow-1.0.xsd">

  <start-state idref="sayHello"/>

  <view-state id="sayHello" view="hello.jsp"/>
</flow>
```

By just reading the flow definition, you can see that the flow will start in the sayHello state, rendering the hello.jsp view. The only thing left to set up is the hello.jsp view template in the helloworld/src/main/webapp/ directory:

```
<?xml version="1.0"?>
<!DOCTYPE html PUBLIC "-//W3C//DTD XHTML 1.0 Transitional//EN" \
  "http://www.w3.org/TR/xhtml1/DTD/xhtml1-transitional.dtd">
<html xmlns="http://www.w3.org/1999/xhtml">
  <head>
    <title>Hello World</title>
  </head>
  <body>
    <h1>Hello World</h1>
  </body>
</html>
```

We're now ready to build and run the application and say "Hello, World!" Type the **ant war** command to start the build and create a deployable WAR file:

```
erwin@esther:~/swfbook/helloworld$ ant war
Buildfile: build.xml

...

war.main:
  [mkdir] Created dir: ~/swfbook/helloworld/target/artifacts/war

    [jar] Building jar: ~/swfbook/helloworld/target/artifacts/war/ \
                        helloworld.war

war.post:

war:

BUILD SUCCESSFUL
Total time: 3 seconds
```

Finally, deploy the generated WAR file on the application server or Servlet engine you're using. In the case of Tomcat or Jetty, just copy the WAR file to the webapps directory, and start the server.

Once the server is up and running, access the /helloworld/flows.html?_flowId=hello-flow URI on the server (typically, the full URL will be http://localhost:8080/helloworld/flows.html?_flowId=hello-flow), and you'll see the famous message appear in your browser:

Looking at the URI, we can deduce from the configuration we did earlier that /helloworld/flows.html maps to the Spring Web MVC DispatcherServlet (since it ends with .html) and that the request is actually handled by the Spring Web Flow

FlowController handling /flows.html requests. By passing in the _flowId request parameter, we're instructing FlowController to launch hello-flow. The flow registry automatically assigned that ID to the web flow defined in WEB-INF/hello-flow.xml based on the file name.

This completes the classic "Hello World" implementation using Spring Web Flow. Don't worry if you don't yet fully understand all of the elements introduced in the sample application. Subsequent chapters will discuss these topics in much more detail.

---

**Note**  Some readers might believe the process of getting a basic "Hello World" application up and running to be a little complex. Keep in mind, however, that Spring Web Flow is targeted at the complex use cases in web applications. Saying "Hello World" is obviously not one of those; in a way, we're using a cannon to kill a fly. Furthermore, instead of just defining the hello-flow web flow, we also set up a Spring Web MVC application from scratch and integrated Spring Web Flow into it. In a real application, this set up would only have to be done once, and you could add new web flows by adding their flow definitions to the flow registry, making the overhead of adding a new flow to an existing application quite small.

Another thing to remember is that this simple sample application provides an excellent starting point for experimenting with Spring Web Flow.

---

# Spring Web Flow in a Development Environment

The previous section used a full-blown build system to build a deployable web application using Spring Web Flow. Such a build system is essential for performing repeatable, consistent builds that can be deployed in an acceptance or production environment. However, in a development environment, we want a shorter code-deploy-test cycle that makes developers productive and allows easy experimentation. This section explains how you can use the popular Eclipse IDE together with the Eclipse Web Tools Platform and the Spring IDE to set up such an environment.

## Installing an IDE

Eclipse is a modular IDE. The standard Eclipse installation includes the Java Development Tools (JDT) but does not provide support for working with web technologies like HTML and JSP. This functionality is provided by the Web Tools Platform (WTP), an Eclipse add-on including development tooling for standard web artifacts such as HTML, CSS, and JavaScript in the Web Standard Tools (WST) and JEE tooling for technologies such as JSP and servlets in the J2EE Standard Tools (JST).

To simplify this for end users, the Eclipse project started a release train initiative. Currently, the release train is called Europa (it was previously called Callisto). Europa releases

Eclipse and a number of accompanying add-ons simultaneously, ensuring compatibility and interoperability. You can find more information about Europa and downloads on the Europa web site: `http://www.eclipse.org/europa/`.

Once Eclipse has been downloaded, installation is very simple. All you need to do is unpack the Eclipse distribution and run the `eclipse` executable. With Eclipse up and running, additional features can be installed using the update manager. The update manager is available from the Help ➤ Software Updates ➤ Find and Install menu. Select to search for new features to install on the Europa Discovery Site, and Eclipse will present you with all available features:

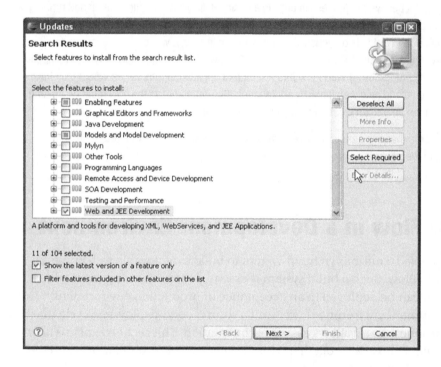

Select Web and JEE Development; click the Select Required button; and finish the installation. Once Eclipse has restarted, the WTP is ready for use.

---

■**Tip** The Eclipse Web Tools Platform has healthy memory requirements. It might be necessary to start Eclipse with special command line parameters to give it more room: `eclipse -vmargs -Xms128m -Xmx384m -XX:MaxPermSize=128m`.

---

If you're having troubling installing Eclipse or the WTP, check the installation guides you can find on the Europa home page (http://www.eclipse.org/europa). Those guides provide much more detailed installation instructions.

Before WTP can automatically deploy and run applications on your application server or Servlet engine, you have to configure that server. Open the Java EE perspective (Window ➤ Open Perspective), and add your server by right-clicking in the Servers view and selecting New ➤ Server. Eclipse will automatically prompt you to add a runtime environment for your server or Servlet engine. You're now set up to run your application server from inside Eclipse.

With WTP installed and configured, installing the Spring IDE is next. Spring IDE is another Spring subproject, just like Spring Web Flow, that provides advanced Spring tooling for Eclipse users. Since version 2.0, it also supports Spring Web Flow and offers a very nice graphical flow editor. The Spring IDE home page can be found at http://www.springide.org.

Spring IDE installation, like WTP's, is done using the Eclipse update manager. This time you will have to add a New Remote Site for the Spring IDE update site (http://springide.org/updatesite):

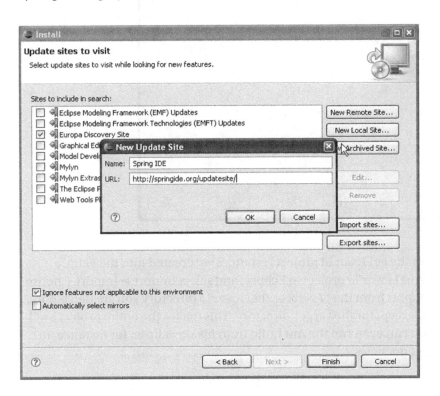

On the next screen, select the Spring IDE feature, and finish the installation.

You now have all Eclipse functionality available to efficiently develop Spring Web Flow applications. Let's import the "Hello World" application into Eclipse.

## "Hello World" in Eclipse

Start by creating a new helloworld Dynamic Web Project in Eclipse (select File ➤ New ➤ Project). Configure the project to use src/main/webapp as the content directory and src/main/java as the Java source directory, as shown in the following illustration:

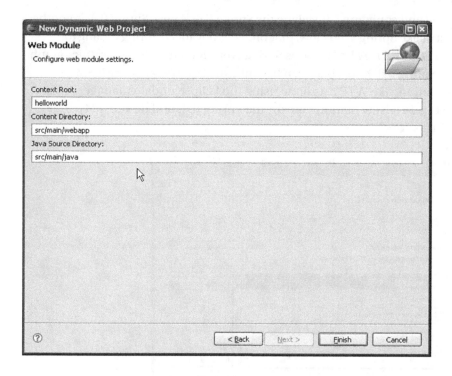

You can now import the helloworld project resources we created into the Eclipse project. Right-click the helloworld project in Eclipse, and select Import ➤ Import. Choose a general file system import from the ~/swfbook/helloworld directory you created before, and import everything except for the target directory. This makes the entire project available inside Eclipse. You can even run the Ant build from inside Eclipse, for instance, to retrieve additional dependencies.

The required JAR files are still located in the lib/global directory of the project. WTP expects them to be in WEB-INF/lib. Instead of copying them there, it is better to add the JAR files as J2EE Module Dependencies in the project properties (right-click the project, and select Properties). By keeping the JARs in the project lib directory, we can still use the build system to manage dependencies.

Before you can see if the project is running correctly, it needs to be deployed on the server you configured earlier. In the Servers view of the Java EE perspective, right-click your server, and select "Add and Remove Projects" to add the helloworld project to the server. Launch the server, and open the http://localhost:8080/helloworld/flows.html?_flowId=hello-flow URL in a browser:

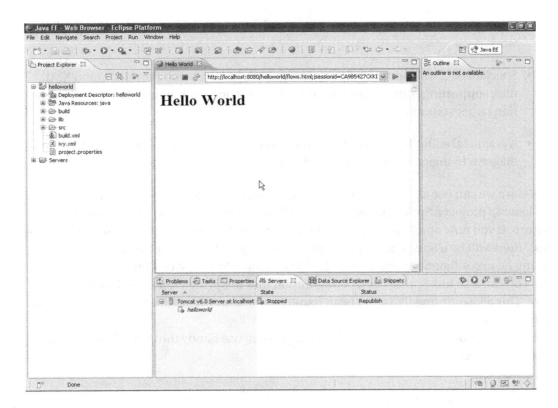

Excellent! The application is now running on the server, all from inside Eclipse. WTP will keep the server synchronized with the resources in your workspace. For instance, if you edit the index.jsp page and refresh the browser window, you will immediately see the results, without needing to rebuild the application or restart the server.

## Using Spring IDE

The Spring IDE provides advanced tooling for the Spring Framework and Spring Web Flow. It allows you to efficiently manipulate the configuration files required by these frameworks. Some of its more interesting features follow:

- Validation of Spring beans XML files and Spring Web Flow flow definition XML files to check things such as class names, property names, and bean references

- Graphical visualization of Spring beans XML configuration files showing bean relationships

- Easy navigation between related beans and searching for beans anywhere in the workspace

- Specialized XML editors for Spring beans XML files and web flow definition XML files, supporting content assist such as class and bean name completion and transition target state completion

- A graphical editor for Spring Web Flow flow definitions that can also export the flow diagram to image formats such as JPG or PNG

Before we can use all these great Spring IDE features, we first have to make the helloworld project a Spring project by right-clicking it and selecting Add Spring Project Nature. If you now open the project properties (right-click the project, and select Properties), there will be a Spring entry that you can use to add dispatcher-servlet.xml as a Spring bean configuration file and hello-flow.xml as a Spring Web Flow configuration file. You can also link Spring bean configuration files to Spring Web Flow flow definitions here. This allows Spring IDE to do bean name completion when editing a web flow definition XML file.

If you now open dispatcher-servlet.xml, you can use handy things such as command line completion:

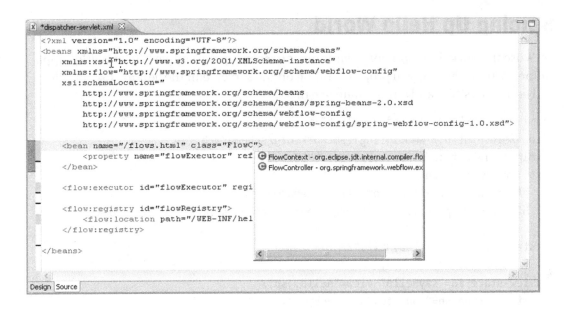

```
*dispatcher-servlet.xml
<?xml version="1.0" encoding="UTF-8"?>
<beans xmlns="http://www.springframework.org/schema/beans"
    xmlns:xsi="http://www.w3.org/2001/XMLSchema-instance"
    xmlns:flow="http://www.springframework.org/schema/webflow-config"
    xsi:schemaLocation="
        http://www.springframework.org/schema/beans
        http://www.springframework.org/schema/beans/spring-beans-2.0.xsd
        http://www.springframework.org/schema/webflow-config
        http://www.springframework.org/schema/webflow-config/spring-webflow-config-1.0.xsd">

    <bean name="/flows.html" class="FlowC">
        <property name="flowExecutor" ref      FlowContext - org.eclipse.jdt.internal.compiler.flo
    </bean>                                     FlowController - org.springframework.webflow.ex

    <flow:executor id="flowExecutor" regi

    <flow:registry id="flowRegistry">
        <flow:location path="/WEB-INF/hel
    </flow:registry>

</beans>
```

Design  Source

This saves a lot of typing and is much less error prone. You can also start to visually manipulate the simple `hello-flow` using the graphical Spring Web Flow editor:

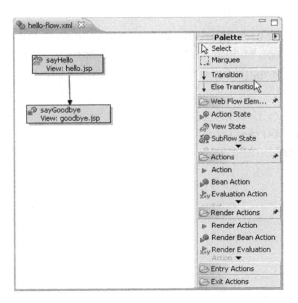

# Spicing Up Hello World

Let's use this slick development environment to spice up the simple "Hello World" application. With the `helloworld` project running on the server, edit the `hello-flow.xml` file, and add a transition and an end state like this:

```xml
<?xml version="1.0" encoding="UTF-8"?>
<flow xmlns="http://www.springframework.org/schema/webflow"
  xmlns:xsi="http://www.w3.org/2001/XMLSchema-instance"
  xsi:schemaLocation="
    http://www.springframework.org/schema/webflow
    http://www.springframework.org/schema/webflow/spring-webflow-1.0.xsd">

  <start-state idref="sayHello"/>

  <view-state id="sayHello" view="hello.jsp">
    <transition on="end" to="sayGoodbye"/>
  </view-state>

  <end-state id="sayGoodbye" view="goodbye.jsp"/>
</flow>
```

This captures the following intent: when the user signals the end event on the sayHello page, transition the flow to the sayGoodbye page, ending the flow in the process.

Let's edit the `hello.jsp` to allow the user to signal the end event:

```xml
<?xml version="1.0"?>
<!DOCTYPE html PUBLIC "-//W3C//DTD XHTML 1.0 Transitional//EN"
  "http://www.w3.org/TR/xhtml1/DTD/xhtml1-transitional.dtd">
<html xmlns="http://www.w3.org/1999/xhtml">
  <head>
    <title>Hello World</title>
  </head>
  <body>
    <h1>Hello World</h1>
```

```
    <form action="flows.html" method="post">
      <input type="hidden" name="_flowExecutionKey"
        value="${flowExecutionKey} "/>
      <input type="hidden" name="_eventId" value="end"/>
      <input type="submit" value="Goodbye"/>
    </form>
  </body>
</html>
```

We simply added an HTML form that posts to the flows.html URI and submits two values using hidden form fields when the Goodbye button is clicked:

- A request parameter named _eventId with a value end. This parameter is used to
  signal the end event. Spring Web Flow's FlowController will use the parameter value
  to trigger a transition in the hello-flow.

- A parameter called _flowExecutionKey, with a value obtained using the
  ${flowExecutionKey} JSP expression language (EL) expression. As will be
  explained in the next chapters, every request coming into an active flow
  execution needs to have a _flowExecutionKey parameter. The value of this
  parameter is used by Spring Web Flow to determine the conversation you are
  prticipating in.

Before you can try to click the new Goodbye button, you first need to add the
goodbye.jsp view referenced from the end state that was added to the flow:

```
<?xml version="1.0"?>
<!DOCTYPE html PUBLIC "-//W3C//DTD XHTML 1.0 Transitional//EN"
  "http://www.w3.org/TR/xhtml1/DTD/xhtml1-transitional.dtd">
<html xmlns="http://www.w3.org/1999/xhtml">
  <head>
    <title>Goodbye</title>
  </head>
  <body>
    <h1>Goodbye</h1>
  </body>
</html>
```

Refresh the "Hello World" page in your browser to give this a spin. You should see the new "Goodbye" button appear. Clicking it will lead to the "Goodbye" page.

Very interesting indeed! We've modified not just the JSP templates, but the flow definition of a running flow, and tested the results, all without restarting the server. Things get even more interesting when we refresh the "Goodbye" page. Doing that results in a nasty exception: "No conversation could be found with id '53AFCD68-7335-6374-FFFB-6762B9713883' -- perhaps this conversation has ended?". That's exactly what happened because the goodbye.jsp view was rendered by an end state. Spring Web Flow has been managing the conversation with the application and is preventing us from reentering a terminated conversation. As Chapter 1 explained, this kind of functionality prevents the well known double submit problem. Earlier, we could freely refresh the "Hello World" page, since that view was rendered by an active conversation, a conversation that had not yet ended. Launching a new conversation for the hello-flow is as simple as revisiting the /helloworld/flows.html?_flowId=hello-flow URI.

---

### A WORD ABOUT LOGGING

As discussed previously, Spring Web Flow uses the Jakarta commons logging library to produce logging output. Commons logging is just a wrapper on top of real logging systems such as Log4j or the standard Java logging facilities. As Spring Web Flow uses commons logging, it can adapt to whatever logging framework you're using in your application. In a Java 5 environment (as used in this book's examples), commons logging will automatically delegate to the Java logging facilities. You can switch to using Log4j (http://logging.apache.org/log4j) by adding an appropriate dependency in the ivy.xml file:

```
<dependency org="log4j" name="log4j" rev="1.2.15"/>
```

Putting a log4j.properties file on the classpath, for instance by placing the file in helloworld/src/main/webapp/WEB-INF/classes, allows you to configure Log4j. The following log4j.properties configuration will enable DEBUG-level logging for Spring Web Flow to the standard output stream:

```
log4j.rootCategory=WARN, stdout

log4j.appender.stdout=org.apache.log4j.ConsoleAppender
log4j.appender.stdout.layout=org.apache.log4j.PatternLayout
log4j.appender.stdout.layout.ConversionPattern=%-7p [%c{ 1} ] - %m%n

#Enable SWF debug logging
log4j.category.org.springframework.webflow=DEBUG
```

The result is verbose debug logging output like this:

```
DEBUG   [ViewState] - Entering state 'sayHello' of flow \
  'hello-flow'
DEBUG   [FlowExecutionImpl] - Paused to render redirect \
  and wait for user input
DEBUG   [SessionBindingConversationManager] - \
  Beginning conversation \
  [ConversationParameters@aa0877 name = 'hello-flow']; \
  unique conversation id = 3C3F9894-24BA-1C7C-1955-0554420F63B4
```

Looking at the logging output can be useful for understanding the processing that goes on inside of Spring Web Flow.

# Summary

This concludes the "Getting Started" chapter. I explained how you can obtain the Spring Web Flow distribution and how it can be integrated into the build system of your application. Spring Web Flow has well documented dependencies that vary with the usage context. Using a transitive dependency manager, such as Ivy or Maven 2, you can automatically pull in all required JAR files. I also explained how to manually incorporate the required libraries into your application.

To make experimenting with Spring Web Flow easier, we used the Spring Jumpstart build system (which also builds Spring Web Flow itself) to get a simple "Hello World" application up and running.

Finally, by setting up a well integrated development environment consisting of the Eclipse IDE, the Eclipse Web Tools Platform, and the Spring IDE, I showed an excellent way for developers to be very productive. This environment also gives you an easy way to experiment with Spring Web Flow while you work your way through this book. Furthermore, it proves that Spring Web Flow fits nicely into an agile environment requiring lightweight and productive tools and frameworks.

In the next chapter, we'll focus in on Spring Web Flow even more, and I'll explain its architecture and the different subsystems of which it is composed.

Starting in Chapter 3, this book will reference the Spring Bank sample application, which uses the Spring Jumpstart build system and can be imported into the Eclipse IDE as well. If you would like to see Spring Bank in action while you learn about its implementation details, skip ahead to Chapter 9. Once you have the application up and running, jump back to the start of Chapter 3.

# CHAPTER 3

■■■

# Spring Web Flow's Architecture

The previous chapters already discussed a number of Spring Web Flow–related concepts such as flow definitions, flow executions, and the flow executor. This chapter will detail the semantics of these concepts and their purposes in the Spring Web Flow framework.

Gaining a deep understanding of a concept or technology often hinges on grasping the broader context of the issues involved. Chapter 1 explained the complexities of controlling user navigation in a web application, providing you with a sense of the problems that need to be tackled, and why a framework like Spring Web Flow can be very useful. This chapter takes a similar approach, sketching the broader picture of Spring Web Flow's architecture to help you to understand key concepts such as flow definitions and flow executions *in context*.

Having a solid understanding of Spring Web Flow's architecture will help you grasp the details covered in later chapters. It will also help you leverage the full potential of Spring Web Flow, giving you ideas about and a context for possible extensions and customizations.

---

### ARCHITECTURAL ANALYSIS TOOLS

Designing a flexible, reusable, and maintainable architecture for a system or application can be very difficult. Luckily, there are tools that can help you analyze the structure of your application, highlighting problems and providing insights into how things can be improved. One such tool, JDepend (http://www.clarkware.com/software/JDepend.html), generates design-quality metrics by analyzing Java class files. JDepend is especially useful when you're trying to understand package dependencies, showing you things such as package dependency cycles. As open source software (under a BSD-style license), JDepend is a useful addition to any Java developer's toolbox.

Another very interesting tool to manage the architecture of your application is SonarJ (http://www.hello2morrow.com/en/sonarj/sonarj.php). SonarJ is a commercial product distributed by the German company hello2morrow (http://www.hello2morrow.com). It allows you to define the architecture of your application in terms of layers, vertical slices, and subsystems. You can then assign Java packages to subsystems and define the allowed dependencies between them. With these architectural definitions, SonarJ will analyze your class files, reporting any violations of the prescribed structure. The following screenshot shows SonarJ in action:

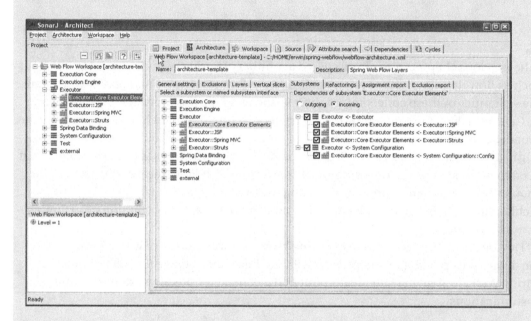

Spring Web Flow's architecture was designed with the help of SonarJ. The SonarJ architecture and workspace descriptions for Spring Web Flow are included in the projects/ directory of the Spring Web Flow distribution: webflow-architecture.xml and webflow-workspace.xml. You can open these files with SonarJ and study Spring Web Flow's structure.

# Language

Spring Web Flow was designed using a domain-driven design approach. In his excellent book *Domain-Driven Design: Tackling Complexity in the Heart of Software*, Eric Evans defines a *domain vision statement* as a short description (about one page) of the core domain and the value it will bring: the *value proposition* (2004). The domain vision statement ignores those aspects that do not distinguish this domain model from others, showing how the domain model serves and balances diverse interests. The classes, methods, and other design artifacts set up a language that can be used to talk about web conversations and the way Spring Web Flow manages them.

The rationale behind Spring Web Flow was explained in Chapter 1. Let's translate this into a domain vision statement, introducing Spring Web Flow's core domain and the key elements of its design language.

## Domain Vision Statement for Spring Web Flow

A domain vision statement for Spring Web Flow follows. It's a good idea to familiarize yourself with the italicized terms, since you'll see them again and again throughout this book (putting these words to music to make them easier to remember is an exercise I leave to you). Come back to this domain vision statement whenever you need a brief overview of Spring Web Flow's core domain and design and the value of the system.

Spring Web Flow helps developers implement use cases requiring controlled navigation in a web application. It captures the *definition* and manages the *execution* of user *conversations* within a web application.

A Spring Web Flow *flow definition* serves as a conversation blueprint, defining all possible navigational paths and the *actions* to take at particular *states* in the flow. A flow can react to *events*, triggering state *transitions* that guide the user to the completion of a business process. Flow definitions are self-contained, reusable *modules* with a well defined input-output contract. By registering a flow definition in a *flow definition registry*, it becomes eligible for execution.

A *flow execution* represents the execution of a flow definition on behalf of a single client. *Flow execution factories* create flow executions, while *flow execution repositories* manage storage and retrieval of active flow executions in between requests.

Spring Web Flow abstracts developers from the *external context* in which it is running, allowing it to be easily embedded in a wide range of hosting frameworks. Integration with those frameworks is handled by a *flow executor* front-end, which manages *launching*, *resuming*, and *refreshing* flow executions on behalf of clients.

It's clearly apparent that Spring Web Flow's central concepts relate closely to the three key issues of controlled navigation, as identified in the "Controlled Navigation" section in Chapter 1:

- *Navigational control*: A flow definition captures all the navigational rules of a conversation, allowing Spring Web Flow to enforce complete navigational control.

- *State management*: Flow executions manage conversational state, facilitating scoping, isolation, and cleanup.

- *Modularity*: Flow definitions are the unit of modularity, making it very easy to reuse one flow definition from another as a subflow.

Don't worry if all this seems a little bit abstract. The core concepts of this language set the stage for Spring Web Flow's overall structure, as detailed in the next few sections.

# Architectural Layers

Using carefully designed layers, Spring Web Flow's architecture isolates stable core domain concepts from more volatile implementation artifacts, as illustrated in Figure 3-1. The Execution Core layer serves as a stable foundation on which all other layers build.

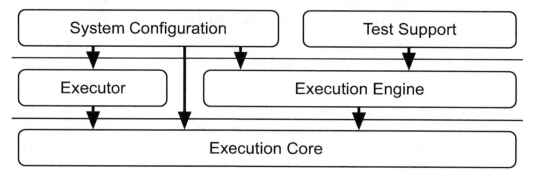

**Figure 3-1.** *Spring Web Flow's architectural layers*

The Execution Core layer is the most important layer in Spring Web Flow's architecture. It sets up the central concepts and their API, containing classes such as `FlowDefinition` and `FlowExecution`. The Execution Engine is an implementation of these core interfaces using a finite state machine. In theory, the engine could be replaced with another implementation, for instance one leveraging an off-the-shelf workflow framework. The engine implementation determines the available flow definitions formats (e.g., XML files) and how flow definitions are executed.

The Executor layer sits on top of the Execution Core, driving flow executions on behalf of clients. The Executor layer does not depend on the Execution Engine layer, however, so it could work with any implementation of the core API.

At the top level of the architectural layer diagram, we find the System Configuration and Test Support layers. The primary goal of both of these layers is *convenience*. The System Configuration layer makes it easy to configure Spring Web Flow, while the Test Support layer allows you to easily test your flow definitions. Since both the System Configuration and Test Support layers need to put all pieces of the puzzle together, they depend on all other layers of the system, requiring them to be top-level layers.

## Execution Core

As the core layer in Spring Web Flow's architecture, the Execution Core is by far the largest layer. It contains several well understood and stable core abstractions. Changes to these concepts are very unlikely, since such a change would impact Spring Web Flow's design and purpose. The Execution Core layer's internal structure is composed of several subsystems, as detailed in Figure 3-2.

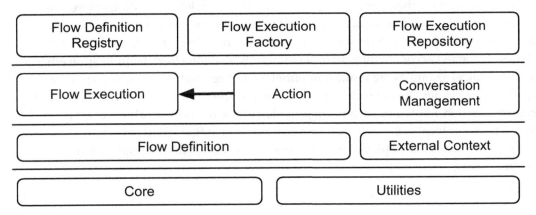

**Figure 3-2.** *Execution Core subsystems*

As the diagram shows, the subsystems of the Execution Core layer can themselves be divided into several layers, where the higher level layers depend on the lower level layers. Let's discuss these subsystems and how they relate to each other.

### Core and Utilities Subsystems

The Core and Utilities subsystems provide low-level utilities and abstractions used by all other subsystems of the Execution Core layer, and indeed by all of Spring Web Flow.

The Utilities subsystem, defined in Java package `org.springframework.webflow.util`, contains *general purpose* utilities used internally by Spring Web Flow. Among other things, it contains a globally unique identifier (GUID) generator (`RandomGuid`) and a class supporting URL-safe Base 64 encoding (`Base64`).

The Core subsystem (package `org.springframework.webflow.core`) provides central abstractions and classes used by all other layers and subsystems of the framework. The code in this subsystem differs from that in the Utilities subsystem in that it is not general purpose but *Spring Web Flow specific*. A key class provided by this subsystem is the `FlowException`, the superclass of all exceptions thrown by Spring Web Flow. The `org.springframework.webflow.core.collection` package contains a number of collection types that help Spring Web Flow abstract the hosting environment (such as HTTP servlets), while still providing a clear and type-safe API. For instance, the `ParameterMap` maps `String` keys to `String` values (similar to the request parameters of an `HttpServletRequest`) and the `AttributeMap` maps `String` keys to any `Object` value (just as the `HttpSession` does).

## External Context Subsystem

To make it easy to embed Spring Web Flow into a wide variety of hosting environments, the developer and the framework itself need to be shielded from that environment. This is the responsibility of the External Context subsystem. The `ExternalContext` interface allows abstracted access to information commonly available in web application environments. Typical examples are request parameters and request, session, and application attributes, for which the collection types defined by the Core subsystem are used. Four `ExternalContext` implementations are provided out of the box: `ServletExternalContext`, `PortletExternalContext`, `StrutsExternalContext`, and `JsfExternalContext`. These allow Spring Web Flow to be deployed into the most important Java web application environments.

**Note** Actually, there is a fifth `ExternalContext` implementation—`MockExternalContext`—that makes it possible to use Spring Web Flow in a test environment. This implementation resides in the Test Support layer and will be discussed in Chapter 8.

## Flow Definition Subsystem

This subsystem defines the elements of the Spring Web Flow domain language used to describe flow definitions (package `org.springframework.webflow.definition`). A `FlowDefinition` is a reusable, self-contained controller module that defines a blueprint for an executable user task. Flows typically orchestrate controlled navigations or dialogs within web applications to guide users through fulfillment of a business process or goal that takes place over a series of steps, modeled as states.

As previously discussed, the structure of a Spring Web Flow flow definition is similar to that of a finite state machine or UML state diagram. A `FlowDefinition` is composed of a set of `StateDefinition` instances. Some states, namely `TransitionableStateDefinition` ones, can transition the flow from one state to another using `TransitionDefinition`.

**Note** `Flow` and `FlowDefinition` are used interchangeably in the context of Spring Web Flow.

### Flow Execution and Action Subsystems

The Flow Execution and Action subsystems are logically related and were separated as a code structuring measure. The Action subsystem extends and depends on the Flow Execution subsystem, as indicated by the arrow in Figure 3-2.

The Flow Execution subsystem defines another central Spring Web Flow concept: the flow execution (package org.springframework.webflow.execution). FlowExecution is a runtime instance of FlowDefinition, managing execution of a flow on behalf of a single client. A useful analogy is the relationship between a class and an object in object-oriented programming: a FlowDefinition is similar to a class, defining structure, data, and behavior, while a FlowExecution corresponds to an object, a unique runtime instance of a class.

To prevent client code from being coupled to the flow execution system implementation (for instance, the one provided by the Execution Engine layer), FlowExecutionFactory is used. FlowExecutionFactory is a simple Abstract Factory pattern implementation, creating new FlowExecution objects while abstracting away instantiation details (Gamma et al 1995). Once created, flow executions follow a well defined life cycle. They can be started; events can be signaled; and the flow executions can be refreshed. All of these operations will result in a ViewSelection instance that provides callers with information about which page should be rendered and the data necessary to render it. Client code can observe the life cycle of a FlowExecution object using a FlowExecutionListener, a simple Observer pattern implementation (Gamma et al 1995).

A flow execution will execute Action implementations, as defined by the flow definition. The Action subsystem (package org.springframework.webflow.action) contains a number of useful actions, such as FormAction, which deals with input forms.

Client code, such as Action and FlowExecutionListener implementations, can interact with an ongoing flow execution using a RequestContext object. RequestContext provides all sorts of information about the current state of the flow execution and allows you to manipulate the data maintained in several different scopes (see the ScopeType class).

Flow executions are closely related to flow definitions, which stipulate the navigational rules to follow and the behavior to exhibit. Detailed coverage of both topics is provided in Chapters 4 and 5.

### Conversation Management Subsystem

The Java Servlet and Portlet specifications define requests, sessions, and applications but lack a conversation concept. The Conversation Management subsystem provides this missing link: ConversationManager manages Conversation instances. ConversationManager (package org.springframework.webflow.conversation) was designed to be independent of Spring Web Flow itself, so it uses only the Core, Utilities, and External Context subsystems. In theory, this subsystem could be moved into the Servlet API, where it really belongs, rather than being a Spring Web Flow feature.

The default Spring Web Flow `ConversationManager` implementation uses `HttpSession` (as defined by the Servlet API) to manage conversational state. This `SessionBindingConversationManager` class is discussed in more detail in Chapter 6. Writing your own conversation manager is illustrated in Chapter 11.

### Flow Definition Registry Subsystem

To be eligible for execution, flow definitions need to be registered with a flow definition registry. In the class-object analogy mentioned earlier, the flow definition registry corresponds to a package, scoping flow definitions and defining their visibility. The Flow Definition Registry subsystem (package `org.springframework.webflow.definition.registry`) declares a `FlowDefinitionRegistry` class and related artifacts.

Flow definition registries will be discussed in more detail in Chapter 4.

### Flow Execution Factory Subsystem

This subsystem provides a number of classes useful when implementing the `FlowExecutionFactory` interface, as defined by the Flow Execution subsystem (arguably, `FlowExecutionFactory` should have been in the Flow Execution Factory subsystem, instead of the Flow Execution subsystem where it is now defined). It resides in the `org.springframework.webflow.execution.factory` package.

### Flow Execution Repository Subsystem

Flow executions represent running flows, managing a user's conversation with a web application. Such a conversation typically spans several requests, requiring the flow execution to be paused and saved at the end of one request, and then restored and resumed with the next request. This is the responsibility of the flow execution repository, as defined by the Flow Execution Repository subsystem (package `org.springframework.webflow.repository`).

Besides the central `FlowExecutionRepository` class, this subsystem also provides several repository implementations that leverage the Conversation Manager subsystem for storing flow executions and related state information in between requests.

Chapter 6 discusses flow execution repositories and the implementations provided out of the box in much more detail.

## Execution Engine

The Execution Engine layer contains an implementation of the flow definition and execution systems defined by the Execution Core layer. To enable Spring Web Flow to evolve and innovate, the engine implementation needs to be able to change without impacting the stable abstractions defined by the Execution Core layer. This also avoids impact on applications using Spring Web Flow when improving its internal implementation details.

In short, the Execution Engine layer was designed to be more volatile than the stable and well understood Execution Core layer.

The implementation hosted by this layer is based on a Finite State Machine (FSM) (Finite State Machines, Wikipedia). It closely follows the flow definition domain language specified by the Execution Core, providing implementation classes such as `Flow` (implements `FlowDefinition`), `State` (implements `StateDefinition`), and `Transition` (implements `TransitionDefinition`). Several different state types are defined, allowing different kinds of behavior in each state. For instance, `ActionState` executes `Action` instances, typically interacting with business components, and responds to their results by triggering a transition. `ViewState` issues a response (page) to the user, soliciting user input and allowing the user to participate in the flow. All of the definition and execution artifacts offered by Spring Web Flow's default execution engine are described in Chapters 4 and 5.

The Execution Engine layer is composed of two subsystems:

- *Engine Implementation*: This subsytem contains the actual engine implementation classes, containing flow definition–related classes such as `Flow` and `ViewState`, as well as runtime artifacts like a `FlowExecution` implementation (`FlowExecutionImpl`) and a `RequestContext` implementation (`RequestControlContextImpl`). It resides in the package `org.springframework.webflow.engine`.

- *Flow Builder*: This subsystem provides classes that can assemble a Finite State Machine definition, which can be run by the execution engine, from external metadata (typically XML). This subsystem follows the classic Builder design pattern and is located in the `org.springframework.webflow.engine.builder` package, which declares among other things, the `FlowBuilder` class (Gamma et al 1995)

Flow builders will be discussed in Chapter 4.

## Executor

The Executor layer defines another key Spring Web Flow concept: the flow executor. A flow executor carries out flow executions on behalf of a client calling into Spring Web Flow. To be able to do this, it needs to combine three of the core concepts defined by the Execution Core layer: `FlowDefinitionRegistry`, `FlowExecutionFactory`, and `FlowExecutionRepository`. You can also look at a flow executor as a high-level Facade for driving Spring Web Flow flow executions (Gamma et al 1995).

When asked to launch a new flow execution, a flow executor will load an appropriate `FlowDefinition` instance from `FlowDefinitionRegistry` and create a new `FlowExecution` for this definition using `FlowExecutionFactory`. If the flow execution lives beyond a single request, the flow executor will use `FlowExecutionRepository` to persist the flow execution and retrieve it again in a subsequent request.

Besides being the subsystem declaring the FlowExecutor interface, the Executor layer also contains several flow executor front-end subsystems that integrate a flow executor into a hosting web MVC framework. For instance, FlowController integrates Spring Web Flow into the Spring Web MVC framework. The Executor layer and its subsystems reside in the org.springframework.webflow.executor package and its subpackages.

The flow executor itself will be discussed in Chapter 6. We'll cover more information about the flow executor front-end implementations provided by Spring Web Flow, and we'll discuss how to integrated them with a number of hosting frameworks in Chapter 7. Chapter 11 describes how to write your own flow executor front-end.

## Test Support

The Test Support layer, which resides in the package org.springframework.webflow.test, drives flow executions from unit test code, making it somewhat similar to the Executor layer. It defines a number of classes, such as AbstractXmlFlowExecutionTests, that allow you to easily test entire flows, providing an elegant way to do top-down integration tests of your web application.

Besides the flow execution test classes, the Test Support layer also contains a number of mocks or stubs (Fowler 2004), like MockRequestContext, allowing you to conveniently test flow-related artifacts like Action implementation classes *in isolation*.

Testing your flows and flow-related artifacts will be discussed in Chapter 8.

## System Configuration

The topmost layer of Spring Web Flow's architecture is the System Configuration layer (package org.springframework.webflow.config). As mentioned before, this layer serves purely as a convenience, making correctly configuring Spring Web Flow very easy.

Convenient and easy configuration is essential, as many Spring Web Flow subsystems need to work together to create a running framework. For instance, FlowExecutor needs to be configured with FlowDefinitionRegistry holding flow definitions understood by the flow executor's FlowExecutionFactory. This layer is responsible for hiding all of these details from the end user, while keeping the concepts themselves loosely coupled. In effect, the System Configuration layer allows Spring Web Flow to be both extremely flexible and easy to use.

# Summary

In this chapter, you learned about Spring Web Flow's architecture, gaining a broader context in which many of the Spring Web Flow concepts and classes can be understood.

The domain vision statement outlined in the "Language" section provides a succinct overview of Spring Web Flow's core domain and design language that sets the stage for understanding its architecture.

Spring Web Flow uses a layered architecture, with each layer composed of several subsystems. Well defined dependencies between the architectural layers and subsystems allow them to evolve independently and foster understanding. Defining clear, stable concepts in an Execution Core layer, separate from the more volatile implementation of those concepts in an Execution Engine layer, allows Spring Web Flow to evolve and be innovative without disrupting client applications. An Executor layer sits on top of the Execution Core, providing a higher level facade clients can use.

The many fine-grained abstractions defined by the layers and subsystems of Spring Web Flow are designed to be loosely coupled and have clear dependencies, making the framework extremely flexible. Users can customize the framework by extending classes or implementing key interfaces and plugging those into the system (Chapter 11, explains this further).

Having a lot of small, fine-grained classes can quickly lead to cognitive overload. The System Configuration and Test Support layers avoid this problem by allowing convenient and easy configuration and testing, taking care of all required low-level plumbing. The end result is a well designed, flexible, and easy-to-use framework.

Hopefully, this high-level architectural overview helps you understand the details discussed in the following chapters. Don't worry if the architecture still seems a bit vague at this point. The concepts introduced here will be elaborated on throughout this book. The next chapter dives back into code to show you Spring Web Flow in action and explains how to define and execute web flows.

# CHAPTER 4

■ ■ ■

# Spring Web Flow Basics

**T**he previous chapters explained the complexities of controlling user navigation in a web application, set up a convenient development environment, and provided an overview of Spring Web Flow's architecture. In this chapter, you'll leverage all of these things as we dive into the process of designing, building, and executing flows definitions.

When working with Spring Web Flow, most development effort is related to *flow definitions*. How do you design and implement a flow definition? How can it be deployed in your application? What actually happens at runtime? This chapter will answer these questions. It covers basic Spring Web Flow features necessary in almost all situations and details concepts such as these:

- Flow definitions

- Flow builders

- Flow executions

- Flow definition registries

Chapter 5 will continue with coverage of more advanced concepts. Both this chapter and the next will use the "enter payment" use case of the Spring Bank sample application to help introduce many of Spring Web Flow's concepts. Chapter 9 covers Spring Bank application in more detail.

# Designing Flows

*Flow definitions* are the primary development product when working with Spring Web Flow. They capture the structure of a conversation or business process, defining things such as the following:

- The states a process can enter into and the activities associated with those states, which include showing a page to the user or interacting with a business component

- The transitions, fired by events that reach the process, that take the process from one state to another

- The actions to be completed at particular points in the process

- When the process will start and end

Once you have developed your flow definition, Spring Web Flow will automatically manage the execution of that flow, requiring very little, if any, additional development effort.

That leads to an important question: how do you start to design a flow definition? State and transition diagrams provide an answer, fitting naturally with what a flow definition actually needs to capture.

State diagrams and data flow diagrams are very easy to understand. Most people, even nontechnical people such as business experts or analysts, are familiar with their concepts or can be brought up to speed in a matter of minutes. The state diagram allows direct, unambiguous communication between developers and business experts.

It's a good idea to take advantage of this fact when starting to design a flow definition. Together with a business expert, you can flesh out an informal sketch of your flow definition diagram, outline the overall flow of the process, and ask questions about the actions to take along the way. The following illustration shows the result of discussing the "enter payment" use case of the Spring Bank application with a business exert. Spring Bank is a simple electronic banking application (see Chapter 9 for more details).

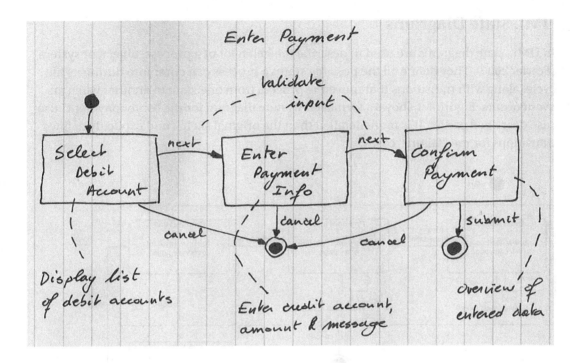

In the context of a web application, the states naturally correspond with pages or views. In the preceding illustration, the developer carefully noted the information that needs to appear on each page, the possible navigational paths, and the actions to take at particular steps of the flow.

As you will see later on in this chapter, an informal diagram like the illustration in this section is, in most cases, sufficient to get started with flow definition development, though it's useful to formalize this diagram as a UML state diagram to bring out a few more details. Many of Spring Web Flow's flow definition constructs correspond closely with the concepts supported by Unified Modeling Language (UML) state diagrams.

# UML State Diagrams

In UML, state diagrams are used to describe the behavior of a process, object, or system (Fowler 2000). They define all the possible states a process can enter into during its life cycle, along with transitions that move the process from one state to another when an event occurs. Figure 4-1 shows a formal UML state diagram for the "enter payment" use case described earlier. It is more detailed than the original sketch and explicitly defines transitions for the "failure" cases.

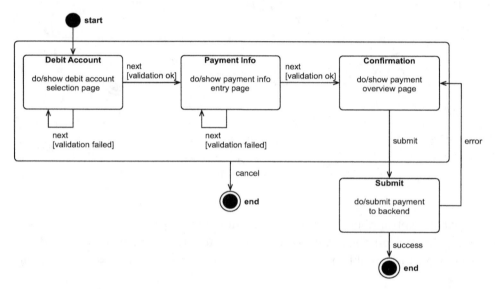

**Figure 4-1.** *The "enter payment" state diagram*

Let's discuss some of the UML state diagram functionality in a bit more detail. I will focus on the parts most relevant to page flow definitions.

State diagrams allow transitions to have *actions,* which are short, uninterruptible tasks executed when the transition fires. States on the other hand, can have associated activities, which potentially take longer.

---

**Note** As you will soon see, in Spring Web Flow, activities are implicitly defined by the state type. For instance, a `ViewState` executes the "show view" activity. Actions, however, can be explicitly defined.

---

The label of a transition in a state diagram has the following syntax: event [guard] / action. All three parts are optional, although most transitions have an associated event. When an event is signaled, transitions with a matching event label become eligible for execution. Guards, which are Boolean expressions, provide further control over transitions. A guarded transition will fire only if the guard evaluates to true. When an action is specified in the transition label, that action will be executed when the transition fires. The state diagram in Figure 4-1 does not specify any actions. In the next chapter, we will add more details to the diagram, adding transition actions dealing with web-application–specific requirements such as data binding and validation.

State activities are expressed in the state label using the do/activity syntax. Next to their main activity, states can also define entry actions and exit actions. *Entry actions* are executed whenever the given state is entered via a transition and occur before the activity defined for the state. *Exit actions* are executed every time the state is left via a transition. In the case of a *self-transition,* a transition that transitions back into its source state, the exit actions are executed first, followed by the transition actions, and finally the state entry actions. Figure 4-1 does not define any entry or exit actions.

UML state diagrams support a concept called *superstates*: substates of a superstate inherit all transitions defined on the superstate. This gives you a convenient way to define the cancel transition, avoiding the need to draw separate transitions from each state supporting the cancel event.

This detailed UML state diagram provides enough input to start creating a Spring Web Flow flow definition.

## Your First Flow Definition

Spring Web Flow provides a Domain Specific Language (DSL) that can be used to define flows. The constructs of this language correspond closely with the concepts of UML state diagrams. Expressiveness and ease of use were important design goals of the flow definition language. As a result, flow definitions are easy to read and understand, as shown in the flow definition in Listing 4-1.

**Listing 4-1.** *A Simple XML Flow Definition*

```
1   <?xml version="1.0" encoding="UTF-8"?>
2   <flow xmlns="http://www.springframework.org/schema/webflow"
3     xmlns:xsi="http://www.w3.org/2001/XMLSchema-instance"
```

```
 4    xsi:schemaLocation="
 5      http://www.springframework.org/schema/webflow
 6      http://www.springframework.org/schema/webflow/ \
 7        spring-webflow-1.0.xsd">
 8
 9    <start-state idref="showSelectDebitAccount"/>
10
11    <view-state id="showSelectDebitAccount">
12      <transition on="next" to="showEnterPaymentInfo"/>
13    </view-state>
14
15    <view-state id="showEnterPaymentInfo">
16      <transition on="next" to="showConfirmPayment"/>
17    </view-state>
18
19    <view-state id="showConfirmPayment">
20      <transition on="submit" to="submitPayment"/>
21    </view-state>
22
23    <action-state id="submitPayment">
24      <action bean="paymentAction"/>
25      <transition on="success" to="end"/>
26      <transition on="error" to="showConfirmPayment"/>
27    </action-state>
28
29    <end-state id="end"/>
30
31    <end-state id="endCancel"/>
32
33    <global-transitions>
34      <transition on="cancel" to="endCancel"/>
35    </global-transitions>
36  </flow>
```

Let's study this simple XML flow definition in more detail:

- *Line 2*: The root element of an XML-based flow definition is `<flow>`. A flow definition XML file contains one such flow definition, defining a single web flow. The Spring Web Flow XML schema reference indicates that this XML file adheres to the XML document type defined by the `spring-webflow-1.0.xsd` schema. If you use a schema-aware editor to edit your flow definitions, for instance, the flow definition editor included in Spring IDE, you will automatically get command line completion based on the syntax definitions contained in the schema.

## XML ECONOMY

The XML schema specification is to blame for the verbose and daunting way of referencing the schema used in an XML document (World Wide Web Consortium). The declaration at the top of the file is identical for all Spring Web Flow XML flow definitions. To avoid wasting valuable page space, listings in this book will leave out this declaration, simply specifying:

```
<flow>
  ...
</flow>
```

Of course, this truncated code is not technically valid, so you'll have to add in the XML schema reference when actually trying to run the examples.

- *Line 9*: Each flow has a single start state, identified using the required `<start-state>` element. A flow execution for this flow will start in the `showSelectDebitAccount` state.

- *Line 11*: A view state is one of several state types defined by Spring Web Flow. As its activity, a view state pauses the flow and selects a view that allows the user to participate in the flow. A user can signal an event by making a request into the application, for instance, by clicking a link or button. View states are defined using the `<view-state>` element.

Most view state definitions use the `view` attribute to indicate the logical name of the view to display. Listing 4-1 leaves this out to keep things concise. In the "View States" section of this chapter, I will revisit this concept in more detail.

- *Line 12*: A transition takes the flow from one state (the *source state*) to another state (the *target state*) on the occurrence of an event. The transition defined by this `<transition>` element moves the flow to the showEnterPaymentInfo state when the next event is signaled in the showSelectDebitAccount state.

- *Line 23*: An action state is another Spring Web Flow state type; it executes an action as its activity. In an XML flow definition, an action state is defined using the `<action-state>` element, and the action to execute is defined using a nested `<action>` element. Action states are typically used to interact with back-end services, for instance, those provided by the service layer of the application. They execute automatically and do not pause the flow execution.

  Spring Web Flow actions signal events. An action state can react to those events by transitioning to another state. In this case, the paymentAction can signal the success and error events. On success, the flow moves to the end state; on error, the flow transitions back to the showConfirmPayment view state to show an error message to the user.

- *Line 24*: An `<action>` element defines a single action to be executed. An action is backed by a piece of Java code, a class implementing the org.springframework. webflow.execution.Action interface. In this case, the action is defined as the paymentAction bean in a Spring application context.

  In addition to their use in action states, actions can also be associated with many other flow definition artifacts, for instance, transitions. Furthermore, there are a few syntactic variations to easily define particular types of actions. These topics will be discussed in the following sections and in the next chapter.

---

■**Note**  Spring Web Flow actions will be discussed in detail in the "Implementing Actions" section. For now, assume an action is a piece of Java code, executed in the context of a flow execution, that returns a result event. For instance, a PaymentAction could communicate with a mainframe system to submit a payment entered by the user, returning the success event if processing completes normally and error otherwise.

---

- Line 29: A flow can have any number of end states, defined using the `<end-state>` element. As its activity, an end state will terminate a flow execution (or more precisely, a *flow session*). When a flow transitions to an end state, the flow execution will end, and all associated resources will automatically be cleaned up.

  Having more than one end state is useful to distinguish between the different outcomes a flow can have. The "enter payment" flow can complete *normally* in the end state, while the endCancel state cancels the flow on user request. A web flow with no end states is also quite common. For instance, imagine a search process where the user can always start over.

---

**Tip** It's a good idea to name your states after the activity they perform, similar to the way you would define the activity in the `do-activity` label of a state in a UML state diagram. For instance, the `showSelectDebitAccount` view state will show (display) a view that allows the user to select a debit account. The action state `submitPayment` will submit the entered payment information to the back-end system, and the `end` end state will simply terminate the flow.

Spring Web Flow itself allows state IDs containing spaces, for instance, `do/show debit account selection page`. This is not possible using the XML flow definition format, however, because the `id` attribute is defined as an XML ID in the schema. The value of an XML ID cannot contain special characters like spaces or forward slashes. The benefit of using an XML ID is that XML editors and parsers will automatically enforce that all states in your flow have a unique ID. Another benefit is the fact that XML editors and parsers can check that the `idref` attribute of the `<start-state>` element refers to a valid state ID. The XML schema defines the `idref` attribute to be an XML IDREF, requiring it to reference an id defined in the same file.

---

- *Line 33*: Global transitions, as defined in the `<global-transitions>` element, are available from all state definitions in the flow. A global cancel transition allows the flow to be canceled from all states, as if an explicit cancel transition had been added to each and every state. Note that this is not completely in line with the flow defined in Figure 4-1, where the Submit state had no ability to cancel a transition.

The flow definition in Listing 4-1 uses the XML syntax for Spring Web Flow's flow definition language. Java syntax also exists. Before covering more flow definition constructs, it's a good idea to look at *flow builders*, which are the components that allow Spring Web Flow to support more than one type of syntax for its flow definition language.

# Flow Builders

Chapter 3, "Spring Web Flow's Architecture," explained Spring Web Flow's layered architecture. The execution engine layer contains an implementation of the stable concepts defined by the execution core layer. On the one hand, the engine implementation subsystem of the execution engine layer holds classes capable of capturing a flow definition in an object graph and then executing that flow definition. The flow builder subsystem, on the other hand, can construct such an *in-memory* flow definition object graph from an *external* representation, for instance, XML. The engine implementation subsystem defines the elements and constructs available in Spring Web Flow's flow definition language, while the flow builder subsystem determines the available syntax options.

As the name implies, the flow builder subsystem follows the classic Builder design pattern; the intent of this design pattern is to "separate the construction of a complex object from its representation," which precisely describes the subsystem's primary goal (Gamma et al 1995). Each of the participants identified by the builder design pattern is present in the execution engine layer:

- *Builder*: This is represented by the FlowBuilder interface, which defines methods to create the component parts of a flow definition.

- *Concrete builders*: Two concrete implementations of the FlowBuilder interface are provided: an XML-based XmlFlowBuilder and an AbstractFlowBuilder that allows flows to be defined in Java code.

- *Director*: The FlowAssembler serves as the director of the flow build process, coordinating FlowBuilder usage to create a flow definition.

- *Product*: The product produced by the build process is a Flow object. A Flow object implements the FlowDefinition interface, acting as in in-memory object representation of a flow definition.

The relationships and interactions between these participants are illustrated in Figure 4-2.

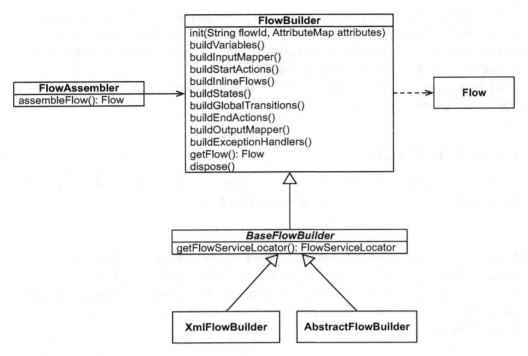

**Figure 4-2.** *Flow Builder subsystem structure*

You'll recognize some parts of the FlowBuilder interface; for instance, the buildStates() method is responsible for building state definitions, while buildGlobalTransitions() defines global transitions. The BaseFlowBuilder is an abstract base class for FlowBuilder implementations, providing common functionality and empty implementations for the optional parts of the build process.

Constructing a flow definition is easy with the help of a FlowBuilder and a FlowAssembler. Suppose that the flow definition in Listing 4-1 is stored in a file called enterPayment-flow.xml that is available on the classpath. You could construct a Flow object from this definition in just a few lines of code:

```
Resource file = new ClassPathResource("enterPayment-flow.xml");
FlowBuilder builder = new XmlFlowBuilder(file);
Flow flow = new FlowAssembler("enterPayment-flow", builder).assembleFlow();
```

Note that this example uses the resource abstraction provided by the Spring Framework (`org.springframework.core.io.Resource`). Normally, you will never have to write this kind of code yourself. Building a `Flow` object from its external definition is handled automatically by Spring Web Flow support code.

Let's take a closer look at the two `FlowBuilder` implementations Spring Web Flow provides out of the box.

## The XML Flow Builder

The `XmlFlowBuilder` reads flow definitions expressed using the XML syntax defined by the `spring-webflow-1.0.xsd` schema, as shown in Listing 4-1.

---

**Tip**  The Spring Web Flow flow definition schema contains lots of information about the semantics of the XML flow definition elements. You can reference this information if you're having trouble defining a flow. Since XML schemas, themselves, are XML documents, you can open the Spring Web Flow schema by simply pointing your browser to `http://www.springframework.org/schema/webflow/spring-webflow-1.0.xsd`.

---

Most people prefer the XML flow definition syntax, making it the most common variant. It has several important benefits:

- The XML flow definition syntax is clear and succinct. Experience shows that most people find it easy to work with XML, lowering the learning curve even more.

- XML-based flow definitions are *declarative* in nature: they describe what the flow looks like and not how to build it. As a result, they have a clear focus and do not contain any extraneous operational details, making it easy to mentally visualize the flow. Their declarative nature also allows a very direct mapping between UML state diagrams and XML flow definitions.

- Lots of frameworks use XML configuration files of some sort, so XML flow definitions are a familiar option.

- XML files are very toolable. Generic XML editors can be used to efficiently edit XML flow definition files, providing syntax highlighting, command line completion, and advanced validation using XML schema. Tools like Spring IDE can visualize XML-based flow definitions and allow graphical flow editing.

- Externalizing a flow definition in an XML file allows that flow definition to be reloaded at runtime, without needing to restart the application. You already saw this feature in action in Chapter 2, "Getting Started."

There are also a few downsides to consider:

- The declarative nature of XML flow definitions makes them very static. XML flow definitions cannot dynamically alter their flow building behavior when certain conditions arise at flow build time.

- Refactoring is more difficult when using XML-based flow definitions. For instance, when renaming method names on service objects, XML flow definitions will have to be updated to use the new method names. Tools such as the Spring IDE can help in this area.

- It's not Java. Some people dislike the fact that the flow definition uses a different syntax (XML) from the main code of the application.

- XML syntax is not very flexible. As a result, the XML flow builder supports all the standard features offered by Spring Web Flow but cannot elegantly leverage user customizations.

## The Java Flow Builder

You can define flows using Java by subclassing org.springframework.webflow.engine. builder.AbstractFlowBuilder. This will force you to implement the buildStates() method defined by the FlowBuilder interface. All other FlowBuilder methods have either been implemented for you (such as init(flowId, attributes)) or create optional flow definition artifacts. Let's take a look, in Listing 4-2, at a Java-based flow definition equivalent to the XML flow definition presented in Listing 4-1.

**Listing 4-2.** *A Simple Java Flow Definition*

```
1   public class EnterPaymentFlowBuilder extends AbstractFlowBuilder {
2
3     public void buildStates() throws FlowBuilderException {
4       addViewState("showSelectDebitAccount", null,
5           transition(on("next"), to("showEnterPaymentInfo")));
6       addViewState("showEnterPaymentInfo", null,
7           transition(on("next"), to("showConfirmPayment")));
8       addViewState("showConfirmPayment", null,
9           transition(on(submit()), to("submitPayment")));
10      addActionState("submitPayment",
11          action("paymentAction"),
12          new Transition[] {
13             transition(on(success()), to("end")),
14             transition(on(error()), to("showConfirmPayment")) } );
15      addEndState("end");
16      addEndState("endCancel");
17    }
18
19    public void buildGlobalTransitions() \
20        throws FlowBuilderException {
21      getFlow().getGlobalTransitionSet().add(
22          transition(on("cancel"), to("endCancel")));
23    }
24  }
```

You will notice quite a few interesting things in Listing 4-2:

- *Line 3*: Implementing the buildStates() hook method gives you the opportunity to define all the states of your flow.

- *Line 4*: Adding states to the flow can be done by a number of convenience methods offered by the AbstractFlowBuilder. In Listing 4-2, the addViewState(stateId, viewName, transition) method is used to add a view state to the flow. A null view name is used to make the example correspond exactly with the XML flow definition, which didn't specify the view attribute either. In most cases, you'll want to specify a view name. The AbstractFlowBuilder will automatically make the first state added to the flow the start state of the flow.

- *Line 5*: The transition passed into the addViewState(stateId, viewName, transition) method is created using a transition(matchingCriteria, targetStateResolver) convenience method, together with the on(transitionCriteriaExpression) and to(targetStateIdExpression) helper methods. The end result is an elegant and easy-to-read transition definition. This API style is sometimes referred to as a *fluent interface*, because it reads fluently, like a natural language (Fowler 2005).

- *Line 9*: The AbstractFlowBuilder defines several methods returning common event names. In this case, the submit() method is used, which returns the submit event. Using these convenience methods helps you maintain consistent event naming in all your flows.

- *Line 10*: An action state is added to the flow using the addActionState(stateId, action, transitions) helper method.

- *Line 11*: Action implementations can be looked up by ID using the action(id) method; calling this method will typically cause a bean to be looked up in a Spring application context.

- *Line 12*: Since the submitPayment action state has multiple transitions, we need to declare a transition array and pass that to the addActionState(stateId, action, transitions) method. Java 5 variable argument lists could make this code more elegant, avoiding the explicit array declaration. However, the Spring Web Flow API needs to be compatible with Java 1.3 and 1.4, ruling out use of Java 5 syntax.

- *Line 15*: Adding an end state is simple using the addEndState(stateId) method.

- *Line 19*: To add global transitions to the flow, a second hook method needs to be implemented: buildGlobalTransitions().

- *Line 21*: AbstractFlowBuilder does not provide convenience methods for adding global transitions to a flow. Instead, you have to use the getFlow() method of the flow builder to obtain a reference to the Flow object under construction and directly add the global transition to it.

## THE FLOWSERVICELOCATOR

One interesting object that is not shown in Listing 4-2 is `FlowServiceLocator`, which makes a flow service locator available to its subclasses, including `AbstractFlowBuilder`. Using the methods defined by the `FlowServiceLocator` interface, a flow builder can look up and create all sorts of flow services. Several types of flow services are available from the flow service locator:

- Externally managed objects used by the flow definition, such as actions

- A factory to create actual flow definition artifacts, such as states and transitions

- Infrastructural services, such as a Spring `BeanFactory`, an expression parser, or a type conversion service

As will be illustrated later in this chapter and in the next chapter, Java flow builders often use the flow service locator (available via `getFlowServiceLocator()`) to look up required service objects. Many of the convenience methods provided by the `AbstractFlowBuilder` class internally delegate to the flow service locator. For instance, `action(id)` just calls `getFlowServiceLocator().getAction(id)`.

Like using the `XmlFlowBuilder`, using the `EnterPaymentFlowBuilder` to build a flow is straightforward:

```
FlowBuilder builder = new EnterPaymentFlowBuilder();
Flow flow = new FlowAssembler("enterPayment-flow", builder).assembleFlow();
```

Listing 4-2 already hints at some of the flexibility offered by Java-based flow definitions. Having complete control over the `AbstractFlowBuilder` subclass means you could define constructors that take arguments used during the build process. As I will discuss in Chapter 10, "Real-World Use Cases," this provides an elegant way to parameterize a flow builder.

Some of the benefits of using Java to define your flows follow:

- Java all the way! Java-based flow definitions allow you to use a single language for your entire system and allow IDEs to present all the code of an application in a consistent, well integrated fashion. For instance, you can navigate directly from an action implementation class referenced by your flow builder to the declaration of that class.

- Refactoring is easy, as all modern Java IDEs have very impressive refactoring features.

- Building your flows in Java provides much more control over the build process and gives you greater power and flexibility than the XML flow builder offers. For instance, you can easily use custom state implementations or elegantly parameterize a flow builder with Java constructor arguments or getters and setters.

  More generally, you can leverage the full power of the Java language from your flow builders. Java inheritance can be used to create flow definition hierarchies, where concrete flow builder implementations complete template flows defined by abstract superclasses. Another possibility is to define your own base flow builder superclass (which subclasses `AbstractFlowBuilder`), adding convenience methods to deal with flow definition constructs common in your application.

On the other hand, there are some consequences to keep in mind:

- Java-based flow definitions are *imperative*: they describe the steps needed to build a flow. The imperative nature of Java-based flow definitions tends to make them harder to understand. Dealing with low-level issues like typing, object construction, and exception handling can confuse the overall structure of the flow. In most cases, you'll find that you need to *read* a Java-based flow definition to visualize it in your mind.

- Visual editing and other types of specialized tooling support are much more difficult to provide with Java than with the XML flow builder.

## Choosing an Appropriate Flow Builder

The XML and Java flow builders have the same expressive power and allow you to define the same flows. Choosing one is a matter of taste (XML versus Java) and of following a few rules of thumb:

- The majority of static web flows are most naturally expressed using the XML flow definition syntax.

- When you want more dynamic aspects in the flow build process, for instance, parameterizing flow definitions, the Java-based flow definition syntax is best.

A single application can use more than one type of flow definition syntax, allowing you to mix and match. Both XML- and Java-based examples will be shown when I discuss the flow definition constructs offered by Spring Web Flow in the rest of this book.

---

**■Caution**  When selecting a flow builder, keep in mind that Spring Web Flow 2 does not currently support a Java flow definition builder. As a result, using Java-based flow definitions will make migrating to Spring Web Flow 2 more difficult.

---

# Defining Flows

Now that you know how to go about designing a flow and the syntax options you have to express your design, let's look in detail at the basic constructs offered by the Spring Web Flow flow definition language: flows, states, and transitions.

## Flows

The engine implementation subsystem class used to model a web flow is `org.springframework.webflow.engine.Flow`, an implementation of the `FlowDefinition` interface defined by the execution core layer. The `FlowDefinition` interface, shown in Listing 4-3, defines the key functions that every flow definition implementation should have.

**Listing 4-3.** *The FlowDefinition Interface*

```
package org.springframework.webflow.definition;

public interface FlowDefinition extends Annotated {

  public String getId();
  public StateDefinition getStartState();
  public StateDefinition getState(String id)
    throws IllegalArgumentException;
}
```

A `Flow` object maintains references to all other objects that are part of the flow definition, serving as the root of the flow definition object graph.

An XML flow definition represents a `Flow` object with the `<flow>` tag, the root tag of the flow definition XML file:

```
<flow>
  ...
</flow>
```

Java flow builders automatically create an empty `Flow` instance in the `init(flowId, attributes)` method of the `FlowBuilder` interface. The created `Flow` object is available to subclasses by calling the `getFlow()` method, as illustrated in Listing 4-2. When the build process is in progress, `getFlow()` will return a `Flow` object that is still under construction and not yet ready for use.

As required by the `FlowDefinition` interface, a `Flow` object manages three core pieces of information: an ID, a set of states indexed by ID, and a reference to the start state of the flow. Next to these core properties, `Flow` objects also have a number of extra fields, representing optional flow definition constructs, such as a set of global transitions. Most optional parts of a flow definition will be covered in the next chapter.

## Flow IDs

Each flow is identified by an ID, which will typically be unique among all flows in an application. You can use the ID when asking Spring Web Flow to launch a new flow execution for a particular flow. In Chapter 2, you saw URLs of the form `/helloworld/flows.html?_flowId=hello-flow` referring to a flow using its ID.

Assigning an ID to a flow is the responsibility of a flow definition registry. This explains why there was no ID defined in the XML or Java flow definitions covered earlier. The flow definition language provides no constructs to define the ID of a flow. Flow definition registries will be discussed in more detail in the "Flow Definition Registries" section.

## Flow States

A `Flow` object is a representation of a finite state machine, containing a set of states (`StateDefinition` implementations). Each state has a unique ID in the owning flow.

You can add states to your flow definition by declaring state elements in the flow definition XML file, for instance:

```
<view-state id="showEnterPaymentInfo">
  ...
</view-state>
```

The Java flow builders have access to a number of convenience methods to add states to the flow:

```
addViewState("showEnterPaymentInfo", ...);
```

Java flow builders can also directly instantiate state objects and add them to the flow. This allows you to add custom state types to your flow, for instance:

```
MyFormState formState = new MyFormState(getFlow(), stateId, ...);
formState.getTransitionSet().add(someTransition);
formState.setSomeProperty(...);
```

Instantiating a state object will automatically add it to the flow passed into the constructor; we'll explore this in greater detail in the "States" section.

### The Flow Start State

One of the states in the flow is identified as the start state of the flow, where flow executions will begin.

When using the XML syntax, the start state is identified using the `<start-state>` element, referencing the state to use as the start state:

```
<start-state idref="showSelectDebitAccount" />
```

When using Java-based flow builders, the first state added to the flow will automatically become the start state. You can also explicitly set the start state:

```
getFlow().setStartState("showSelectDebitAccount");
```

The state with the provided ID should already have been added to the flow before `setStartState(stateId)` is called. Instead of using a magic constant to refer to the start state, you can also code this in a richly typed way:

```
State showSelectDebitAccountState =
  addViewState("showSelectDebitAccount", ...);
getFlow().setStartState(showSelectDebitAccountState);
```

## States

The central state implementation artifact offered by the execution engine layer is the `org.springframework.webflow.engine.State` class, an implementation of the `StateDefinition` interface. Each state has a unique ID, identifying it in the owning flow. As discussed earlier, states execute an activity, and thus make something happen at a particular point in the flow. Some state types have activities that result in the flow transitioning to another state. Those state types subclass the `org.springframework.webflow.engine.TransitionableState` class, an implementation of the `TransitionableStateDefinition` interface, and maintain a collection of transitions. The class diagram for all state implementations provided by Spring Web Flow is shown in Figure 4-3, and the core state types will be explained in the "Basic State Types" section. Chapter 5 covers DecisionState and SubflowState.

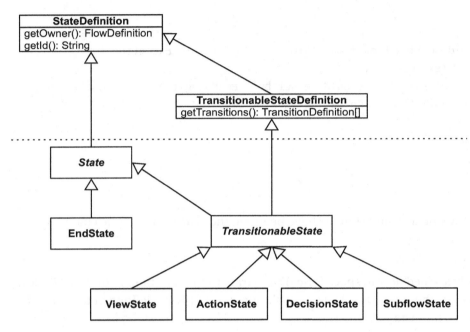

**Figure 4-3.** *State class diagram*

One important thing to understand is that a flow is a composition of states. A state may belong to only one flow and will cease to exist when the flow dies. To enforce that design, the State class defines a single constructor requiring both a reference to the owning flow and a state ID as arguments. This constructor will automatically add the newly created state to the specified flow:

```
package org.springframework.webflow.engine;

public abstract class State extends AnnotatedObject
    implements StateDefinition {

  ...

  protected State(Flow flow, String id) throws IllegalArgumentException {
    setId(id);
    setFlow(flow);
  }
```

```
  private void setId(String id) {
    Assert.hasText(id, "This state must have a valid identifier");
    this.id = id;
  }

  private void setFlow(Flow flow) throws IllegalArgumentException {
    Assert.hasText(getId(),
      "The id of the state should be set before adding the state to a flow");
    Assert.notNull(flow, "The owning flow is required");
    this.flow = flow;
    flow.add(this);
  }
```

...

Once the owning flow and state ID have been set, they can no longer be changed.

### State IDs and Transitions

You've already learned how to specify the ID and transitions of a state. With the XML flow definition syntax, the state ID and state transitions can simply be defined in the state definition element, for instance:

```
<view-state id="showConfirmPayment">
  <transition on="submit" to="submitPayment"/>
</view-state>
```

Java flow builders can pass the state ID and transitions into the convenience methods for adding states to the flow:

```
addViewState("showConfirmPayment", null,
    transition(on(submit()), to("submitPayment")));
```

### Entry and Exit Actions

Just like the states of a UML state diagram, Spring Web Flow State objects can have entry actions that will be executed every time the flow enters into the state. Entry actions will be executed *before* the state performs its inherent activity.

TransitionableState objects maintain a list of transitions that can take the flow out of the current state and into the next one. When a transition fires, the source state exits, and any defined exit actions will be executed before the flow enters into the next state, the target state of the transition.

Entry and exit actions can be defined in XML using the <entry-actions> and <exit-actions> elements, respectively.

```
<view-state id="myViewState">
  <entry-actions>
    <action bean="myEntryAction"/>
  </entry-actions>
  ...
  <exit-actions>
    <action bean="myExitAction"/>
  </exit-actions>
</view-state>
```

When defining flows using Java, you can pass the entry and exit actions directly into the convenience methods for adding states to the flow. Alternatively, you can specify the entry and exit actions for a state after it has been added to the flow:

```
ViewState myViewState = (ViewState)addViewState("myViewState", ...);
myViewState.getEntryActionList().add(action("myEntryAction"));
myViewState.getExitActionList().add(action("myExitAction"));
```

Use entry actions for things you want to do or check *every time* the flow enters into a state. Example usages of entry actions could be security checks, verifying preconditions, or preparing data needed by the state. Likewise, exit actions can be used to check post-conditions or perform cleanup activities before leaving a state. Implementing actions will be covered in the "Implementing Actions" section.

## Transitions

The last core flow definition construct to discuss is the transition. A *transition* takes a flow from one state of the flow, the source state, to another state of that same flow, the target state. The execution engine layer contains an org.springframework.webflow.engine. Transition class, implementing the TransitionDefinition interface. The interface in Listing 4-4 requires all transition implementations to have an ID and identify a target state.

**Listing 4-4.** *The TransitionDefinition Interface*

```
package org.springframework.webflow.definition;

public interface TransitionDefinition extends Annotated {

  public String getId();
  public String getTargetStateId();
}
```

Note that there is no mention of a source state. In general, the source state is not known at flow definition time. Recall the global cancel transition of the "enter payment" web flow that was discussed in the "Your First Flow Definition" section. Such a global transition has no statically defined source state. The actual source state will become apparent only at runtime.

### Transition Matching Criteria and Target States

The ID of a transition is typically the event used to match the transition, and the target state ID identifies the state of the flow to transition into. Using the XML flow definition syntax, the ID of the transition is specified using the on attribute of the <transition> element, while the target state ID is defined using the to attribute:

```
<transition on="next" to="showConfirmPayment"/>
```

Java flow builders use similar on(transitionCriteriaExpression) and to(targetStateIdExpression) factory methods, whose result can be passed into the transition(matchingCriteria, targetStateResolver) method:

```
Transition t = transition(on("next"), to("showConfirmPayment"));
```

As illustrated in Figure 4-4, the implementation of a Transition object does not define an *event* field but instead maintains a TransitionCriteria object as matchingCriteria. It is the responsibility of the *matching criteria* to decide if the transition is eligible for execution, typically by matching it with the last event signaled in the ongoing flow execution. An EventIdTransitionCriteria class implements exactly this behavior. Similarly, a Transition object does not directly reference the target state or its ID. Instead, a TargetStateResolver implementation will calculate the target state of the transition at runtime. The default implementation will look up the target state *by ID*. The next chapter will explain more advanced transition criteria and dynamic target state resolvers.

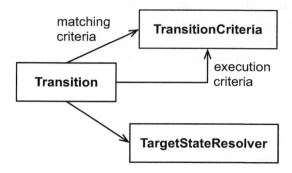

**Figure 4-4.** *Transition class diagram*

## Transition Execution Criteria

Transitions in a UML state diagram can have guards. The Spring Web Flow equivalents of guards are the execution criteria of a Transition object. Once a transition has been selected (matched) as eligible for execution, the execution criteria of the transition decide whether the transition can complete execution, moving the flow into the target state, or whether it should roll back, causing the flow to reenter the source state. Execution criteria are also expressed in terms of a TransitionCriteria object, similar to the matching criteria. Figure 4-5 summarizes the transition execution process.

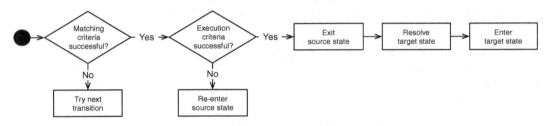

**Figure 4-5.** *Transition execution*

Implementing execution criteria using actions is common; in that case, you're basically combining the guard and action of a UML state diagram transition into a single concept. The ActionTransitionCriteria implementation does exactly this, checking the outcome of action execution and turning it into a Boolean result. A success event will be interpreted as true, with all other events being interpreted as false.

The XML flow builder allows you to define the execution criteria of a transition by adding actions to the <transition> element:

```
<transition on="event" to="targetState">
  <action bean="myAction"/>
</transition>
```

In the case of the Java flow builder, you can either pass the execution criteria to the transition(matchingCriteria, targetStateResolver, executionCriteria) convenience method or explicitly configure them for a transition already added to the flow:

```
Transition t = transition(on("event"), to("targetState"));
t.setExecutionCriteria(ifReturnedSuccess(action("myAction")));
```

The ifReturnedSuccess(action) factory method creates an ActionTransitionCriteria object. With the Java flow builder, you can, of course, also directly instantiate a TransitionCriteria implementation class and use the resulting object in your transitions.

Using actions as execution criteria provides an elegant way of adding behavior to a flow that should prevent the flow from continuing when the actions fail. A classic example detailed in the next chapter is input validation. If the validation of user-input data fails, the flow should not continue on to the next state but instead reenter the source state to display relevant error messages to the user.

---

### FINE-GRAINED FLOW CONTROL

You can always rewrite a state containing a transition with action execution criteria as a state with a normal transition transitioning into an extra action state. For instance, the following state definition:

```
<view-state id="myViewState">
  <transition on="event" to="targetState">
    <action bean="myAction"/>
  </transition>
</view-state>
```

is equivalent to the combination of these two states:

```
<view-state id="myViewState">
  <transition on="event" to="myActionState"/>
</view-state>

<action-state id="myActionState">
  <action bean="myAction"/>
  <transition on="success" to="targetState"/>
  <transition on="error" to="myViewState"/>
</action-state>
```

Moving an action into its own action state is useful if you want to have explicit control over the transitions and the routing decisions they make in the flow.

---

## Global Transitions

Besides transitions defined in a particular state, a flow can also have global transitions. On the occurrence of an event, if Spring Web Flow cannot find any matching transitions in the current state of the flow, it will try to find a matching global transition. Global transitions are implemented using normal Transition objects, so they can also have execution criteria (guards).

XML flow definitions define global transitions using the `<global-transitions>` element:

```
<global-transitions>
  <transition on="cancel" to="endCancel" />
</global-transitions>
```

Since global transitions are an optional part of a flow definition, Java-based flow builders have to implement the optional `buildGlobalTransitions()` hook method:

```
public void buildGlobalTransitions() throws FlowBuilderException {
  getFlow().getGlobalTransitionSet().add(
      transition(on("cancel"), to("endCancel")));
```

## Flow Definition Structure

The basic flow definition constructs offered by the Spring Web Flow execution engine layer, shown in Figure 4-6, illustrate the central flow definition classes and their relationships. The interfaces above the dotted line are part of the execution core layer. They present an abstract view of the structure of a flow definition: a flow definition is composed of a number of state definitions, some of which are transitionable and can contain transition definitions. Below the dotted line you can find the concrete implementations of these interfaces, as defined by the execution engine layer.

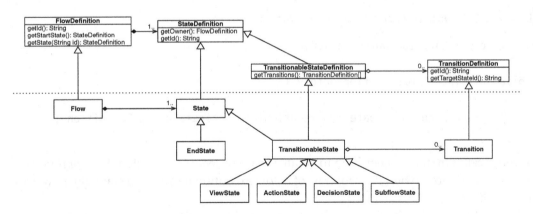

**Figure 4-6.** *Flow definition class diagram*

At this point, actions have already been mentioned numerous times. You've seen how they are executed in an action state or as part of transition execution. Although actions are referenced from static flow definition constructs such as states and transitions, they will only play an active role at flow execution time. To understand how to implement actions and what they can do, you must first grasp the basics of Spring Web Flow's flow execution management.

# Flow Executions

When Spring Web Flow is asked to launch a new execution of a particular flow definition, it will create a new FlowExecution object for the identified FlowDefinition (Chapter 6, "Flow Execution Management," will explain this in much more detail). While a flow definition captures the static structure of the flow, FlowExecution tracks runtime information *on behalf of a single client.* If you have ten users interacting with your web application, all running the same flow, there will be ten independent FlowExecution objects for a single FlowDefinition object, because FlowDefinition objects are *singletons* (Gamma et al 1995). As discussed previously, this is similar to the way an object is an instantiation of a class in object-oriented programming. Flow executions and flow definitions work together to build a system capable of supporting *conversations* within a web application.

The life cycle of a FlowExecution object starts when it is created using a FlowExecutionFactory, which is shown in Listing 4-5.

**Listing 4-5.** *The FlowExecutionFactory Interface*

```
package org.springframework.webflow.execution;

public interface FlowExecutionFactory {

  public FlowExecution createFlowExecution(FlowDefinition flowDefinition);
}
```

The FlowDefinition object used to create the FlowExecution is called the *root flow* of that flow execution. When the root flow of a flow execution hits an end state, the flow execution will end and be discarded.

Once a FlowExecution object has been created, calling code can manipulate it using the core flow execution life cycle methods; the FlowExecution interface is shown in Listing 4-6.

**Listing 4-6.** *The FlowExecution Interface*

```
1   package org.springframework.webflow.execution;
2
3   public interface FlowExecution extends FlowExecutionContext {
4
5     public ViewSelection start(MutableAttributeMap input,
6       ExternalContext context) throws FlowExecutionException;
7     public ViewSelection signalEvent(String eventId,
8       ExternalContext context) throws FlowExecutionException;
9     public ViewSelection refresh(ExternalContext context)
10      throws FlowExecutionException;
11  }
```

The following lines in Listing 4-6 are of particular interest:

- *Line 5*: Calling start(input, context) will begin the flow execution by entering the start state of the root flow of that flow execution. Processing continues from the start state on, until the flow pauses to render a view. At that moment, a view selection will be made. A ViewSelection object identifies the view to be rendered and contains all model information available to the view. View selections will be explained in more detail in the next chapter. An attribute map containing input for the new flow execution can be passed into the start(input, context) method.

- *Line 7*: A paused flow execution can be resumed by calling signalEvent(eventId, context). This will signal the specified event in the current state of the flow execution. The flow will resume processing by firing a transition matching the signaled event. Once event processing is complete, the flow execution will return the resulting view selection.

- *Line 9*: An *active* flow execution, one that has started but not yet ended, can always be refreshed by invoking refresh(context). Refresh is an idempotent operation that can be safely called to reconstitute the last view selection.

All methods defined by the FlowExecution interface receive an ExternalContext argument. An ExternalContext object provides abstracted access to the environment that called into the flow execution. Since Spring Web Flow is a system targeted at web applications, the operations defined by the ExternalContext interface are web oriented, as shown in Listing 4-7.

**Listing 4-7.** *The ExternalContext Interface*

```
package org.springframework.webflow.context;

public interface ExternalContext {

    public String getContextPath();
    public String getDispatcherPath();
    public String getRequestPathInfo();
    public ParameterMap getRequestParameterMap();
    public MutableAttributeMap getRequestMap();
    public SharedAttributeMap getSessionMap();
    public SharedAttributeMap getGlobalSessionMap();
    public SharedAttributeMap getApplicationMap();
}
```

If you're familiar with the Servlet API, you will immediately see the correspondence between these methods and their counterparts in the Servlet API.

---

■**Note** An ExternalContext instance is a *single-threaded* object, specific to one invocation of a FlowExecution method.

---

## Flow Sessions

Starting a flow execution creates and activates a new FlowSession for the root flow. A *flow session* maintains all information and data related to running a particular flow definition in the context of a flow execution. In the next chapter, you'll see that a single flow execution can have multiple flow sessions, in particular when one flow spawns another flow as a *subflow*. A flow execution maintains a stack of flow sessions to accommodate this. The flow session at the top (or bottom, depending on how you look at it) of the stack is the active flow session, as illustrated in Figure 4-7.

Flow sessions have a well defined life cycle, illustrated in Figure 4-8.

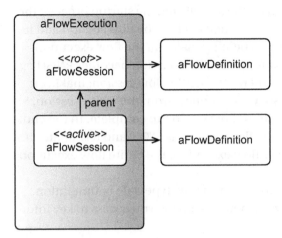

**Figure 4-7.** *Flow executions and flow sessions*

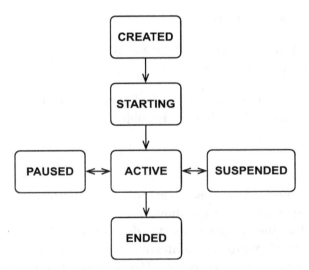

**Figure 4-8.** *Flow session life cycle*

Initially, a flow session is CREATED, waiting to be started. During the startup process, the session is STARTING, and finally, it becomes ACTIVE. When ACTIVE, the flow session and its associated flow definition actively process events being signaled in the flow execution. When the flow execution pauses to solicit user input, the flow session becomes PAUSED. The next event signaled in the flow execution will reactivate the flow session, making it ACTIVE once more. When the flow execution spawns a subflow from the active session, that session becomes SUSPENDED, waiting for the subflow session to complete. In the end, the flow will enter an end state, which marks the flow session as ENDED and terminates it. If the flow session is the root flow session of the flow execution, the entire flow execution will end at this point.

These life cycle states are defined by the FlowSessionStatus type-safe enumeration. The FlowSession interface declares the following methods, giving you access to key information related to the session:

- getDefinition() returns the FlowDefinition of the session.

- getStatus() returns the current FlowSessionStatus.

- isRoot() returns true if the session is the root session of the governing flow execution. If not, getParent() returns the parent flow session.

- The currently active state of the flow definition running in the flow session can be retrieved using getState(), which returns a StateDefinition object.

## The Flow Execution Context

If you're an attentive reader, you probably noticed the FlowExecutionContext interface mentioned in the declaration of the FlowExecution interface shown earlier.

While the FlowExecution interface defines the operations used to drive the flow execution life cycle, the FlowExecutionContext interface provides contextual information about the flow execution. Client code that only has access to a FlowExecutionContext reference is not intended to manipulate the flow execution. Instead, it can only query runtime information related to the flow execution, using the methods defined by the FlowExecutionContext interface shown in Listing 4-8.

**Listing 4-8.** *The FlowExecutionContext Interface*

```
1  package org.springframework.webflow.execution;
2
3  public interface FlowExecutionContext {
4
5    public boolean isActive();
6    public FlowSession getActiveSession()
```

```
 7         throws IllegalStateException;
 8
 9     public FlowDefinition getDefinition();
10
11     public MutableAttributeMap getConversationScope();
12
13     public AttributeMap getAttributes();
14 }
```

Here are the pertinent details from Listing 4-8:

- *Line 5*: The active flow session can be retrieved using getActiveSession(). This will throw an exception if the flow execution is not yet or is no longer active. You can test whether or not a flow execution is active using the isActive() method.

- *Line 9*: The root flow definition of the flow execution is available as getDefinition(). If the active flow session is the root flow session, this method will return the same FlowDefinition object as getActiveSession().getDefinition().

- *Line 11*: As will be explained in the next section, conversation scope is shared by an entire flow execution and all sessions inside it. So naturally, conversation scope is available from the flow execution context.

- *Line 13*: A flow execution can have associated metadata attributes, potentially influencing the flow execution. This will be discussed in Chapter 6.

## The Request Context

The FlowExecution interface, together with FlowSession and FlowExecutionContext, provides a view of a flow execution geared towards external clients. Recall how the key methods defined by the FlowExecution interface all received an ExternalContext instance as an argument. Objects such as action implementations live *inside* the flow execution and need a different interface to work with (they are *internal* rather than *external*). The request context fulfills this role.

The RequestContext interface acts as a facade, giving flow artifacts such as actions, access to their execution context, namely, the governing flow execution. As the name suggests, a request context is tied to a single request into a flow execution. It is a *single-threaded object*: it's local to the thread handling the request. RequestContext objects are internal to a flow execution and are never exposed to external code. A FlowExecution implementation will create a new request context for every call into the flow execution, be it to start the execution, signal an event, or just refresh it. When the call into the flow execution returns, the RequestContext object goes out of scope and is discarded, as illustrated in Figure 4-9.

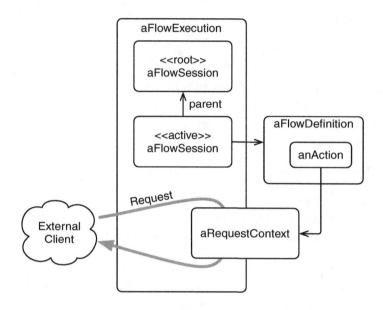

**Figure 4-9.** *The request context*

The operations defined by the RequestContext object do not allow direct manipulation of the flow execution. This makes sense, since an object living inside a flow execution is managed by that flow execution and not the other way around. An action, for instance, should not be able to do things such as refreshing the flow execution, which would have been possible had the action been given direct access to the FlowExecution object.

Since the RequestContext is accessible to most, if not all, flow artifacts discussed in this book, it is a good idea to study it in depth (see Listing 4-9).

**Listing 4-9.** *The RequestContext Interface*

```
1   package org.springframework.webflow.execution;
2
3   public interface RequestContext {
4
5     public FlowExecutionContext getFlowExecutionContext();
6
7     public FlowDefinition getActiveFlow()
8       throws IllegalStateException;
9     public StateDefinition getCurrentState()
10      throws IllegalStateException;
11
```

```
12     public MutableAttributeMap getRequestScope();
13     public MutableAttributeMap getFlashScope();
14     public MutableAttributeMap getFlowScope();
15     public MutableAttributeMap getConversationScope();
16
17     public ExternalContext getExternalContext();
18     public ParameterMap getRequestParameters();
19
20     public Event getLastEvent();
21     public TransitionDefinition getLastTransition();
22
23     public AttributeMap getAttributes();
24     public void setAttributes(AttributeMap attributes);
25
26     public AttributeMap getModel();
27  }
```

Here are the most important aspects of Listing 4-9:

- *Line 5*: It comes as no surprise that the request context provides access to its flow execution context, through the FlowExecutionContext interface, as discussed in "The Flow Execution Context" section. Flow artifact code can use this to obtain information about the ongoing flow execution, for instance, the active flow session (FlowExecutionContext.getActiveSession()).

---

■**Tip** Using getFlowExecutionContext().getActiveSession().isRoot(), you can find out whether or not the active flow is running as a top-level root flow of a flow execution or as a subflow of another flow. This is useful when you want a flow to have slightly different behavior in both cases.

---

- *Line 7*: Querying the currently active flow and the current state of that flow is possible using getActiveFlow() and getCurrentState(). getActiveFlow() is equivalent to getFlowExecutionContext().getActiveSession().getDefinition(), while getCurrentState() is shorthand for getFlowExecutionContext(). getActiveSession().getState().

- *Line 12*: Spring Web Flow defines four scopes you can use to store conversational data: request scope, flash scope, session scope, and conversation scope. These scopes will be discussed in detail in the next section.

- *Line 17*: You can access the external context describing the request coming into the flow execution from an external caller, using getExternalContext(). The ExternalContext object returned by this method is essentially the reason this RequestContext object exists. getRequestParameters() provides convenient access to the request parameters included in the current web request (typically, an HttpServletRequest as defined by the Servlet API), and is equivalent to getExternalContext().getRequestParameterMap().

- *Line 20*: The request context itself tracks the last event signaled and the last transition that fired during the current request. The last event is represented using an Event object, containing the event ID (for instance, next) and potential payload attributes.

- *Line 23*: A request context maintains a set of attributes, which are local to the current request context. These attributes can impact the behavior of flow artifacts. For instance, an action implementation might check these attributes to decide whether or not to validate user input *for the current request*. The request context attributes can be manipulated using the setAttributes(attributes) method.

---

**Note**  Don't confuse the request *context attributes* with the request *scope*. The request context attributes are technical in nature, potentially influencing the flow execution, but do not contain application-related data. That data should instead be stored in the request scope (or any of the other provided data scopes).

---

- *Line 26*: The getModel() method returns the model (the "M" from MVC) implied by the current status of the flow execution. The model returned by this method will be included in the ViewSelection object the flow execution returns to the external caller and will be exposed to the selected view for rendering. It contains the union of all data in the request, flash, flow, and conversation scopes.

### Flow Execution Scopes

Spring Web Flow's flow execution system provides four well defined scopes for use by application developers. These scopes complement the three scopes defined by the Servlet specification, namely:

- Request scope, as implemented by the request attributes of an HttpServletRequest

- Session scope, modeled by the HttpSession attributes

- Application scope, managed by the attributes of ServletContext

Previous chapters already discussed how the Servlet request scope is too fine grained for use in web conversations, while the session scope and application scope are too coarse grained. Spring Web Flow alleviates this problem by providing scopes better suited for web conversations. Let's look at each of the scopes Spring Web Flow defines.

### Request Scope

As the name suggests, the request scope is tied to the `RequestContext` object, scoped at the level of a single request into the flow execution. Each and every request coming into the flow execution will start with a new and empty request scope.

Request scope is *not* linked to flow sessions. Consequently, a request moving a flow execution from a parent flow to a subflow (or vice versa) always sees the same request scope.

You can use the request scope to store objects only required while processing the current request. Objects that are cheap to create or load can also be put in the request scope, because they can be re-created or reloaded every time they are needed. Objects stored in the request scope are *not* required to be serializable.

---

**Note**  Spring Web Flow's request scope is similar in scope to the Servlet request scope. In Spring Web Flow applications, these two scopes are essentially equivalent. Spring Web Flow defines its own request scope to avoid being tied to external environments providing such a scope. Spring Web Flow offers convenient ways to access the `RequestContext` request scope, making it the preferred choice.

---

### Flash Scope

Flash scope attributes persist until the next event is signaled in a flow execution, using `FlowExecution.signalEvent(eventId, context)`. This is particularly useful to support flow execution refreshes, which do not signal an event, and as a result will always see the same flash scope. You can think of the flash scope as a kind of request scope that survives a flow execution refresh.

The flash scope is linked with the flow session. It is accessible from the request context using either `getFlashScope()` or `getFlowExecutionContext().getActiveSession().getFlashMap()`. All objects put into the flash scope are required to be serializable.

Storing objects in the flash scope is particularly useful for objects that cannot easily be re-created and should be available for every refresh of the current view selection, for instance, input validation errors. Objects stored in the flash scope typically support view rendering.

■**Caution** The fact that the flash scope is tied to the flow session has an unintuitive side effect when launching subflows. A subflow has its own flow session, separate from the parent flow session. As a consequence, a request that causes a subflow to spawn will *switch* flash scopes along the way! As soon as the subflow session becomes active, a new flash scope will be in effect, separate from the flash scope associated with the parent flow session. Figure 4-10 illustrates this.

### Flow Scope

The scope of flow scope is a *flow session*. Each flow running in the context of a flow execution has its own flow session, and as a result, its own flow scope. This means that an attribute placed in the flow scope by a parent flow will *not* be accessible from the flow scope of a subflow of that flow.

The flow scope is accessible via the getFlowScope() method of the RequestContext interface. Alternatively, you can access it directly on the flow session object using getFlowExecutionContext.getActiveSession().getScope(). Objects stored in the flow scope must be serializable.

Use the flow scope to store objects that should be available for the entire flow session. Objects in the flow scope are mostly related to the application and the functionality it implements, for instance, domain object instances manipulated by the flow. As an example, imagine a Payment object created and populated by the "enter payment" web flow.

■**Note** Since FlowSession provides access to the parent flow session (if any), you can access the flow scope of the parent flow using getFlowExecutionContext().getActiveSession().getParent(). getScope(). However, it is unlikely you will ever need to do that.

### Conversation Scope

The conversation scope is scoped at the level of an *entire conversation*. You can think of a flow execution as a representation of a logical conversation a user has with the application. Attributes in the conversation scope are available to the whole flow execution and all flow sessions contained within it. In contrast to the flow scope, an attribute placed in conversation scope by a parent flow will be available from inside a subflow of that flow.

You can access the conversation scope using the getConversationScope() method of the RequestContext interface. This is basically a shortcut for using getFlowExecutionContext(). getConversationScope().

Just like the flow scope, the conversation scope mostly stores application-related objects. Use the conversation scope if those objects should be available for the entire flow execution, rather than a single flow session. If your flow does not use subflows, the conversation scope and the flow scope are semantically equivalent.

**Caution** Be careful when storing large objects in flow scope or conversation scope. These scopes have relatively long life spans, meaning that the data stored in them needs to be maintained for a prolonged period of time. This puts additional stress on server resources. As an alternative to storing large objects in the flow or conversation scope, consider reloading those objects for every request and storing them in request scope.

The data model for a view, as prepared by RequestContext.getModel(), is the union of all scopes. The attributes in the data model will typically be exposed to the view using request attributes (request scope as defined by the Servlet specification).

**Tip** Sometimes, accessing the scopes defined by the Servlet specification from inside a web flow is useful. A typical example is exchanging data with a native controller of the hosting framework (for instance, a Spring Web MVC Controller). The HTTP session is most useful for these cases. All of the scopes defined by the Servlet specification are available through RequestContext. The HttpServletRequest attributes are returned by getExternalContext().getRequestMap(); the HttpSession can be found using getExternalContext().getSessionMap(); and the application scope is accessible via getExternalContext().getApplicationMap().

The different scopes defined by Spring Web Flow, and their respective *scope*, are summarized in Figure 4-10.

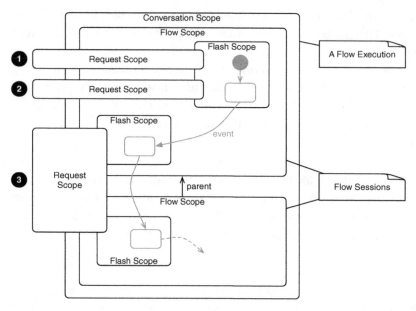

**Figure 4-10.** *Flow execution scopes*

The first request in the figure, step 1 in Figure 4-10, launches a new flow execution. As a result, new conversation, flow, and flash scopes will be set up. Each request, of course, also has its own request scope. The second request, step 2 in Figure 4-10, is a refresh of the first request. It sees the same flash scope but gets its own request scope. A third request, step 3 in Figure 4-10, signals an event causing the flow to move to another state, launching a subflow in the process. Since it signals an event, the third request does not share the flash scope of the first two requests. Also note how the flash scope is tied to the flow session for the third request, causing the request scope to be the same for the entire request, while a new flash scope appears once the subflow session is activated.

With all this background on Spring Web Flow's flow execution system covered, you are ready now to start developing some actions for the "enter payment" web flow.

# Implementing Actions

Action implementations are the workhorses of a flow definition. An action is a piece of Java code embedded in a flow definition, typically delegating to the service layer to perform business operations. You already saw actions used to execute behavior in the context of an action state or as part of transition execution. Actions bridge the web tier and middle tier of your application, allowing web flows to interact with business modules.

All actions referenced by a Spring Web Flow flow definition need to implement the org.springframework.webflow.execution.Action interface in Listing 4-10.

**Listing 4-10.** *The Action Interface*

```
package org.springframework.webflow.execution;

public interface Action {

  public Event execute(RequestContext context) throws Exception;
}
```

There is only one method to implement: execute(context). An action implementation receives a RequestContext object as an argument to the execute(context) method, giving it access to the governing flow execution (as discussed in the section called "The Request Context"). When action execution completes, an Event is returned (signaled). This event describes the outcome of action execution, for instance, success, error, moreResultsAvailable, or any other meaningful identifier. An event object can also carry along any payload attributes, such as an exception object in an error event.

---

**Note**  Note that actions are not controllers in the MVC triad. Web MVC controllers not only interact with service layer components but also select views. Actions do not do that, and they just signal a logical event outcome the flow will react to. In Spring Web Flow, the flow *is* the controller.

---

Although it is clearly possible to directly implement the Action interface, Spring Web Flow offers a few action base classes you can subclass. The basic Action hierarchy is shown in Figure 4-11.

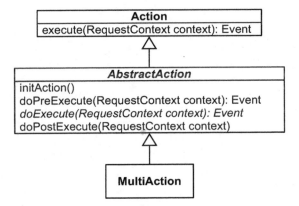

**Figure 4-11.** *Action class diagram*

# AbstractAction

AbstractAction is an abstract base class for action implementations, offering common convenience functionality.

The first thing AbstractAction does is define a number of hook methods that allow subclasses to extend its behavior:

- Actions can override the initAction() hook method to implement action initialization logic.

- AbstractAction implements the execute(context) method defined by the Action interface, providing more fine-grained hook methods. AbstractAction will first call the optional doPreExecute(context) hook method. If this hook method returns a non-null event object, action execution will be interrupted, and the result of doPreExecute(context) will be returned to the caller. When doPreExecute(context) returns null, doExecute(context) will be called, followed by doPostExecute(context) (which is again an optional hook method).

  Using doPreExecute(context) and doPostExecute(context), you can add precondition and postcondition checking code to your actions. This also allows you to add interceptor style aspects to actions, without resorting to true aspect-oriented programming (AOP).

---

**Caution** AbstractAction implements the InitializingBean interface defined by the Spring Framework to receive an initialization callback. As a result, the initAction() hook method will only be called if the action is deployed in a Spring application context! See the "Deploying Actions" section for more details.

---

Second, `AbstractAction` defines a number of event factory methods creating `Event` objects with common event identifiers. These factory methods automatically set the source of the created event object to be the calling action.

- Using `success()`, `error()`, `yes()`, and `no()`, you get events with the corresponding ID. You can also add a payload object to a `success` event using `success(result)`. The result object will be indexed as `result` in the event payload attributes. Similarly, an exception object can be added to an `error` event using `error(exception)`, causing the exception object to be indexed as `exception` in the event payload attributes.

- The `result(booleanResult)` method will return the yes or `no` event, depending on the Boolean argument.

- More general purpose `result` methods create events with custom IDs and an arbitrary payload.

Instead of using these event factory methods, you can, of course, also directly instantiate `Event` and return the resulting object.

The event factory methods make it very easy to consistently use the same event IDs in your action implementation code, without littering that code with magic constants, for instance:

```
public class PaymentAction extends AbstractAction {

  protected Event doExecute(RequestContext context) throws Exception {
    try {
      // submit payment to back-end
      return success();
    }
    catch (PaymentProcessingException ex) {
      return error(ex);
    }
  }
}
```

---

**Note** The execute(context) method defined by the Action interface and the hook methods provided by AbstractAction all declare that they throw Exception. This means action implementation code is not forced to handle possible exceptions. On the other hand, if you want to signal a specific event when a particular exception occurs, you can do that by catching the exception. The PaymentAction example shown in this section illustrates this. In the next chapter, other techniques to deal with exceptions occurring in a flow execution will be explained.

---

## MultiAction

In many cases, it is natural to put several action execution methods on a single class. A classic example is a CRUD action with methods to create, read, update, and delete some object. The MultiAction class allows you to do exactly this.

The doExecute(context) implementation provided by MultiAction investigates the request context to decide which action execution method to delegate to. Action execution methods must adhere to the following signature:

```
public Event methodName(RequestContext context) throws Exception;
```

This corresponds with the execute(context) method defined by the Action interface, except that the method name can be freely chosen. As an example, you can rewrite the PaymentAction shown earlier like so:

```
public class PaymentAction extends MultiAction {

  protected Event submitPayment(RequestContext context) throws Exception {
    try {
      // submit payment to back-end
      return success();
    }
    catch (PaymentProcessingException ex) {
      return error(ex);
    }
  }
}
```

A MultiAction class can have any number of action execution methods, and the appropriate one will be chosen by a MethodResolver implementation, which returns the name of the method to invoke, as shown in Listing 4-11.

**Listing 4-11.** *The MethodResolver Interface*

```
public interface MethodResolver {

  public String resolveMethod(RequestContext context);
}
```

The default MethodResolver implementation, unimaginatively named DefaultMultiActionMethodResolver, uses the following algorithm to determine the action execution method name:

1. If the currently executing action has a method attribute defined, the value of that attribute is used as the method name.

2. Otherwise, the ID of the current state of the flow is used as a fallback. This state will normally be the action state invoking this action.

Explicitly specifying the method attribute is the preferred option. When using the XML flow definition syntax, you can specify the method to use using the method attribute of the <action> element:

```
<action bean="paymentAction" method="submitPayment"/>
```

Java flow builders can use the invoke(methodName, multiAction) helper method. You can load a MultiAction instance using the action(id) utility shown earlier. Of course, the referenced action is expected to be a MultiAction:

```
invoke("submitPayment", action("paymentAction"))
```

---

■**Tip** Unless you have good reasons not to, you should normally subclass MultiAction when developing actions. This allows you to combine the functionality offered by AbstractAction and the flexibility of MultiAction.

---

## Deploying Actions

You now know how to implement actions, but how do you make them available for use in your flow? The <action> element of an XML flow definition refers to the action using a bean ID. This bean ID is expected to correspond with the ID of a bean defined in a Spring application context.

Deploying an action to make it usable by a flow definition simply involves defining the action as a bean in a Spring application context. A flow definition can reference all actions (and other beans) available from the application context hosting the flow definition registry defining that flow definition (see the "Flow Definition Registries" section for more information).

The fact that actions are defined as normal beans in a Spring application context also means that you can leverage the full power of Spring to configure those actions, injecting dependencies or wrapping them in proxies to apply infrastructural aspects like transaction management.

---

**Note** Actions are typically singletons, like most beans defined in a Spring application context. When implementing singleton actions, you have to make sure your actions are thread safe, since they can potentially be invoked concurrently in multiple different threads. Although Spring Web Flow does not require actions to be singletons, it is uncommon to see prototype actions.

---

We can now finish the implementation of the PaymentAction used by the "enter payment" web flow; see Listing 4-12.

**Listing 4-12.** *PaymentAction*

```
public class PaymentAction extends MultiAction {

  private PaymentProcessingEngine engine;

  public void setEngine(PaymentProcessingEngine engine) {
    this.engine = engine;
  }

  protected Event submitPayment(RequestContext context) throws Exception {
    try {
      Payment payment =
        (Payment)context.getConversationScope().get("payment");
      engine.submit(payment);
      return success();
    }
    catch (PaymentProcessingException ex) {
      return error(ex);
    }
  }
}
```

An engine property was added to express the dependency of this action on a PaymentProcessingEngine. Also notice how the action obtains the Payment object populated by the flow from the conversation scope and submits it for processing. Recall that the flow was referencing this action as follows:

```
<action bean="paymentAction" method="submitPayment"/>
```

The only thing left to do is define the paymentAction bean in a Spring application context:

```
<?xml version="1.0" encoding="UTF-8"?>
<beans xmlns="http://www.springframework.org/schema/beans"
  xmlns:xsi="http://www.w3.org/2001/XMLSchema-instance"
  xsi:schemaLocation="
    http://www.springframework.org/schema/beans
    http://www.springframework.org/schema/beans/spring-beans-2.5.xsd">

  <bean id="paymentProcessingEngine"
    class="com.ervacon.springbank.domain.PaymentProcessingEngineImpl"/>

  <bean id="paymentAction"
    class="com.ervacon.springbank.web.PaymentAction">
    <property name="engine" ref="paymentProcessingEngine"/>
  </bean>
</beans>
```

## Flow-Local Bean Definitions

Defining all beans referenced from a flow definition in the application context that contains the flow definition registry, which defines that flow definition, quickly becomes unmanageable. There are two reasons for this:

- If you have many flows in a flow registry, all the bean definitions related to those flow definitions confuse and bloat the application context file.

- A bean definition referenced by a flow is typically specific to that one flow definition. Since other flow definitions do not reference the bean, *localizing* it (making it private to the flow) is better.

To tackle this problem, Spring Web Flow allows you to associate a Spring application context file with a flow definition. The beans defined in that flow-local application context are private to the flow definition and not visible to other parts of the system. The

XML flow builder uses the `<import>` element to import a bean definition resource and set up a flow-local application context:

```
<import resource="enterPayment-context.xml"/>
```

A flow can reference any number of bean definition resources. The value of the resource attribute is a path to a bean definition XML file, relative to the referencing flow. In the example, the enterPayment-context.xml file is expected to be in the same directory as the enterPayment-flow.xml flow definition.

Spring application contexts can form a hierarchy. Beans defined in a parent context can be referenced from beans in a child context, but not vice versa. The flow-local application context will be a child context of the application context containing the flow definition registry defining the flow.

In the "enter payment" use case, the paymentAction is a bean directly supporting the "enter payment" flow definition. It does not serve any other purpose and belongs in the flow-local application context. The paymentProcessingEngine bean, on the other hand, is more general, possibly being referenced from several actions in different flows. To make that possible, it needs to reside in a higher level application context.

---

**Tip** It's a good idea to follow a naming convention when naming your flow definition files and their associated application contexts. For instance, use a -flow suffix for flow definition files and a -context suffix for the associated application context file. The paymentAction example uses this convention: the enterPayment-flow.xml flow definition uses the enterPayment-context.xml application context. Since these two files are closely coupled, it's best to keep them in the same directory.

---

The Java flow builder does not provide any direct support for flow-local application contexts. That's not a big problem, since it's easy to set up something similar directly from inside your AbstractFlowBuilder subclass:

```
public class EnterPaymentFlowBuilder extends AbstractFlowBuilder {

  private GenericApplicationContext localContext;

  protected void initBuilder() {
    // setup flow local application context
    localContext = new GenericApplicationContext();
```

```java
    new XmlBeanDefinitionReader(localContext).loadBeanDefinitions(
        getFlowServiceLocator().getResourceLoader().getResource(
          "classpath:enterPayment-context.xml"));
    localContext.getBeanFactory().setParentBeanFactory(
        getFlowServiceLocator().getBeanFactory());
    localContext.refresh();
  }

  protected Action localAction(String id) {
    return (Action)localContext.getBean(id, Action.class);
  }

  public void buildStates() throws FlowBuilderException {
    addViewState("showSelectDebitAccount", null,
        transition(on("next"), to("showEnterPaymentInfo")));
    addViewState("showEnterPaymentInfo", null,
        transition(on("next"), to("showConfirmPayment")));
    addViewState("showConfirmPayment", null,
        transition(on(submit()), to("submitPayment")));
    addActionState("submitPayment",
        invoke("submitPayment", localAction("paymentAction")),
        new Transition[] {
          transition(on(success()), to("end")),
          transition(on(error()), to("showConfirmPayment")) } );
    addEndState("end");
    addEndState("endCancel");
  }

  public void buildGlobalTransitions() throws FlowBuilderException {
    getFlow().getGlobalTransitionSet().add(
        transition(on("cancel"), to("endCancel")));
  }
}
```

This code defines a `localAction(id)` method that tries to obtain the referenced action in a local application context. The `initBuilder()` hook method is used to initialize the local application context and link it to the parent application context containing the flow definition registry defining this flow (available as `getFlowServiceLocator().getBeanFactory()`). This kind of code would typically reside in a Java flow builder superclass used in your project.

---

**Caution** Flow builder initialization code cannot be put in the constructor of your Java flow builder. When the flow builder is instantiated, the correct flow service locator (returned by `getFlowServiceLocator()`) will not yet be available. Use the `initBuilder()` hook method to initialize your Java flow builder.

---

The next chapter will cover additional action-related syntax supported in Spring Web Flow flow definitions and the specialized action implementations backing that syntax. A number of reusable action implementations offered out of the box will also be discussed.

### A Test Drive

Before covering more flow definition details, let's take some time to test drive the "enter payment" flow definition constructed so far. An easy way to do that is to modify the "Hello World" sample application created in Chapter 2; we'll plug in `enterPayment-flow.xml`.

Copy the `enterPayment-flow.xml` file and associated `enterPayment-context.xml` application context file to the `WEB-INF/` directory of the "Hello World" application. Then modify the definition of the flow registry in `dispatcher-servlet.xml`, adding the "enter payment" flow:

```
<flow:registry id="flowRegistry">
  <flow:location path="/WEB-INF/hello-flow.xml"/>
  <flow:location path="/WEB-INF/enterPayment-flow.xml"/>
</flow:registry>
```

Of course, you will also have to plug in a dummy `PaymentProcessingEngine`, which is referenced by the `PaymentAction`.

If you start the application and open the `/helloworld/flows.html?_flowId=enterPayment-flow` URI, a nice HTTP 404, "Not Found," error will appear. The problem is, of course, the fact that no views (JSP pages) have been implemented so far! Let's take an explicit look at view states and developing views for a web flow, along with Spring Web Flow's other core state types: action states and end states.

# Basic State Types

The three core states types defined by Spring Web Flow were already illustrated in the "enter payment" flow. As you will see, most flow definitions define states of these types. Let's investigate them in detail.

## View States

The quintessential state type of a web flow is the view state, implemented by
the `org.springframework.webflow.engine.ViewState` class, a subclass of
`TransitionableState`. A view state *pauses* flow execution and renders a response,
returning control to the user and allowing the end user to participate in the flow
execution. The flow execution resumes when the user signals an event in the view state.

Response rendering is typically done by a view template (for instance a JSP page), and
not by the view state itself. A view state identifies the view template to be used. Recall that
Spring Web Flow is a controller technology using the MVC pattern, so this use of the view
state fits with the design. In exceptional cases, it is useful for the flow (the controller) to
directly issue a response, instead of referencing a view template. An example could be a
view state that loads a PDF from a database and sends it to the client. How this is done
depends on the framework with which Spring Web Flow is integrated, and the process will
be explained in Chapter 10.

Using the XML flow definition syntax, you can define a view state using the
`<view-state>` element. A view state is *transitionable*, meaning it can contain nested
`<transition>` elements and define transitions. In addition to the required `id` attribute,
the optional `view` attribute identifies the view template to be used:

```
<view-state id="showSelectDebitAccount" view="selectDebitAccount">
  <transition on="next" to="showEnterPaymentInfo" />
</view-state>
```

When no `view` attribute is specified, Spring Web Flow assumes the view state (or
flow) has generated the response itself. Java flow builders can use the overloaded
`addViewState(. . .)` methods to add a view state to the flow:

```
addViewState("showSelectDebitAccount", "selectDebitAccount",
    transition(on("next"), to("showEnterPaymentInfo")));
```

Passing in `null` as the view name is equivalent to not specifying the `view` attribute in the
XML syntax.

---

**Tip** Try to relate your view name to the ID of the view state rendering the view. In the example in this section, the `showSelectDebitAccount` view state shows the `selectDebitAccount` view as its activity.

---

As with any other transitionable state type, a view state supports entry and exit actions. Additionally, a view state can also have *render actions*, actions executed in preparation of view rendering. In an XML flow definition, render actions are specified using the `<render-actions>` element:

```
<view-state id="showEnterPaymentInfo" view="enterPaymentInfo">
  <render-actions>
    <action bean="formAction" method="setupForm"/>
  </render-actions>
  <transition on="next" to="showConfirmPayment" />
</view-state>
```

When using the Java flow builder, you can look up the render action using the `action(id)` helper, as explained in the "Implementing Actions" section, and pass it to the relevant `addViewState(. . .)` variant:

```
addViewState("showEnterPaymentInfo", "enterPaymentInfo",
    invoke("setupForm", action("formAction")),
    transition(on("next"), to("showConfirmPayment")));
```

Alternatively, you can explicitly add render actions to a view state that has already been added to the flow:

```
ViewState viewState = (ViewState)addViewState(
    "showEnterPaymentInfo", "enterPaymentInfo",
    transition(on("next"), to("showConfirmPayment")));
viewState.getRenderActionList().add(
    invoke("setupForm", action("formAction")));
```

This makes the code a little bit more explicit.

Render actions are only executed when a view will actually be rendered by the current request into the flow execution. To understand the need for render actions, you must understand the Spring Web Flow request life cycle.

## Request Life Cycle

Chapter 1's "The Double Submit Problem" section explained the POST-REDIRECT-GET idiom. By default, Spring Web Flow will automatically apply this idiom to every request using a feature called always redirect on pause (Chapter 6 will explain how to configure this).

Using the POST-REDIRECT-GET idiom implies that a single *logical* request is decomposed into two *physical* requests. First, there is the POST request that causes the actual processing to take place, followed by a redirected GET request to show the results. The GET request is idempotent and can be refreshed any number of times. Spring Web Flow follows this logic and identifies an event-processing phase and a render phase. When "always redirect on pause" is enabled, the event-processing and render phases happen in separate physical requests.

To illustrate this in a little bit more detail, consider the following flow definition fragment, part of the "enter payment" web flow:

```
<view-state id="showSelectDebitAccount" view="selectDebitAccount">
  <transition on="next" to="showEnterPaymentInfo" />
</view-state>

<view-state id="showEnterPaymentInfo" view="enterPaymentInfo">
  <render-actions>
    <action bean="formAction" method="setupForm"/>
  </render-actions>
  <transition on="next" to="showConfirmPayment" />
</view-state>
```

Let's investigate the exact processing that takes place when the next event is signaled in the showSelectDebitAccount view state, the currently active state in the flow execution (Figure 4-12 illustrates this graphically).

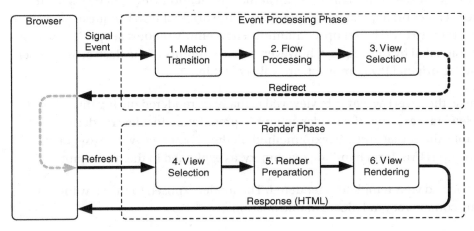

**Figure 4-12.** *Spring Web Flow request life cycle*

Event processing follows these steps:

1. When the first request, typically a POST request, arrives in the flow execution, the first thing that happens is matching the event embedded in the request with a transition defined in the view state that paused the flow. In this example, the next transition will match, and the flow will try to transition to the showEnterPaymentInfo state. Every new request into the flow execution, including this one, will cause a new RequestContext instance to be created, with a new empty request scope. Since this request signals an event, the flash scope will be reinitialized and cleared.

2. The matched transition executes, causing the execution criteria to be evaluated (none in this case). The flow exits the showSelectDebitAccount view state, executing any exit actions (none in the example) and enters the showEnterPaymentInfo state. On entering the target state, any state entry actions are executed (none in this example). The processing that happens between two view states in a flow can, of course, be arbitrarily complex; for instance, it can involve action states. This example just transitions directly from one view state to the next.

3. The showEnterPaymentInfo view state selects a view to be rendered. Since Spring Web Flow assumes that it should always redirect on pause, the view state will issue a redirect response, causing a client side redirect.

4. The second request, a redirected GET request, arrives in the flow execution, causing a flow execution refresh. The showEnterPaymentInfo view state again makes a view selection. This time, an actual application view will be selected. Since this second request is independent of the original POST request, a new RequestContext will be set up, containing a new empty request scope. No event is being signaled by this request, however, so the contents of the flash scope, as set up by the original POST request, are still available.

5. Because the enterPaymentInfo view will actually be rendered during this request, the view state executes the render actions in preparation for view rendering. In the example, the setupForm(context) method on the formAction will be executed, setting up HTML form handling machinery, as explained in the next chapter.

6. The selected view template is rendered. The model exposed to the view for rendering contains several pieces of information:

   - The union of all attributes in the request, flash, flow, and conversation scopes

   - The unique ID of the governing flow execution, indexed as flowExecutionKey

   - A FlowExecutionContext object, providing access to flow-execution-related information, indexed as flowExecutionContext

Notice that a flow execution refresh does not *reenter* the current view state! A refresh request causes processing to start at step 4. Consequently, state entry actions will not be reexecuted. Using render actions, you still have a way to plug in custom view preparation logic. Render actions *should* be idempotent, causing no noticeable side effects. However, Spring Web Flow does not enforce that.

---

**■Tip** Render actions are ideally suited for use in combination with the request scope. A render action executes in the request that renders the view. As a result, render actions can store information in the request scope to make it available to the view for rendering. Entry actions or actions executed by an action state cannot generally do this, since they run during the event processing phase, typically in a separate request, with a separate request scope.

Storing data in the request scope avoids prolonged storage of that data. Flash, flow, and conversation scopes need to be maintained across requests, but the request scope does not. If the data that you need to render can be cheaply reloaded, load it from a render action, and store it in request scope. A typical example is a list of search results obtained by a search action.

---

## Implementing views

As a controller component in a hosting web MVC framework, Spring Web Flow does not decide the view technology used. As a result, view implementation details differ from one deployment context to the next: when using JSF, you code views using JSF components, while you use classic HTML and JavaScript when using Spring Web MVC or Struts. Chapter 7, "Driving Flow Executions," will provide more details on this subject.

Still, it is useful to quickly revisit Spring Web Flow view development. Chapter 2 already showed a few simple examples of Spring Web MVC–based views participating in a web flow. Such views are required to submit two special request parameters:

- _flowExecutionKey: This is the unique key identifying the flow execution in which the user is participating. Recall that a flow execution manages the execution of a flow definition *on behalf of a particular user*. Each flow execution receives a unique ID that is available as flowExecutionKey in the model exposed to the view.

  All requests coming into Spring Web Flow need to contain a flow execution key to identify the relevant flow execution. The exceptions are requests that launch a new flow execution of a particular flow. Such requests only need to contain the _flowId request parameter.

- _eventId: This is the event to signal in the current state of the flow: the view state that paused the flow execution and rendered the view. The event will be used as grounds to drive the next state transition.

### Continuing the Test Drive

Let's use this knowledge to implement some views for the "enter payment" web flow. The first view state (showSelectDebitAccount) renders the selectDebitAccount view. With the simple setup of the "Hello World" sample application, this view name is mapped to the selectDebitAccount.jsp in the webapp/ directory of the project structure. To submit the next event leading to the showEnterPaymentInfo state (as discussed in the "Request Life Cycle" section), you can use an HTML anchor like this, adding it to the selectDebitAccount.jsp:

```
<a href="flows.html?_flowExecutionKey=${flowExecutionKey} &_eventId=next">
  Next
</a>
```

Alternatively, you can use an HTML form:

```
<form action="flows.html">
  <input type="hidden" name="_flowExecutionKey"
    value="${flowExecutionKey}"/>
  <input type="hidden" name="_eventId" value="next"/>
  <input type="submit" value="Next"/>
</form>
```

Except for _flowExecutionKey and _eventId, Spring Web Flow views are in no way different from normal views in a Spring Web MVC application. They are resolved by the installed ViewResolver and can use the Spring Web MVC–specific tag libraries, such as the Spring binding or Spring form tag libraries, as well as third-party tag libraries like Displaytag (http://displaytag.sourceforge.net).

Adding selectDebitAccount.jsp, enterPaymentInfo.jsp, and confirmPayment.jsp to the sample application, along with HTML anchors and forms to signal the necessary next and submit events, allows you to navigate through the "enter payment" web flow. Give it a try!

## Action States

Action states execute one or more actions. Actions are typically used to interact with business components or call into the service layer, as detailed in the "Implementing Actions" section. An action state is modeled using the org.springframework.webflow.engine. ActionState class, a subclass of TransitionableState.

Since action states are transitionable, they can contain any number of transition definitions. An action state will match the events returned by action implementations to find a transition eligible for execution. Both local and global transitions are considered. When a matching transition is found, action execution is interrupted and the transition executes.

Figure 4-13 illustrates the action execution process used by action states. You could look at this as an implementation of the Chain of Responsibility pattern (Gamma et al 1995).

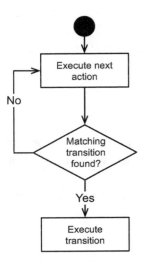

**Figure 4-13.** *Action state action execution*

If the action list is exhausted before a matching transition is found, an exception will be raised.

To give you more control over the events matching particular transitions, you can give an action a name, turning it into a *named action*. The result event of a named action will be prefixed with the action name. For instance, a success event returned by an action named paymentAction will be turned into paymentAction.success. The qualified event is then used to find a matching transition. You can use this technique to ignore certain events returned by actions.

An example will prove useful here. It is very common, even a best practice, for action implementations to return the success event in case of successful execution, and this practice can cause some unexpected consequences. Suppose you have a sampleAction MultiAction, with two action execution methods: foo(context) and bar(context), which both signal either success or error. If you coded an action state like this:

```
<action-state id="sample">
  <action bean="sampleAction" method="foo"/>
  <action bean="sampleAction" method="bar"/>
  <transition on="success" to="successState"/>
  <transition on="error" to="errorState"/>
</action-state>
```

the bar(context) action would never be invoked, because the flow will find a transition matching either the success or error event signaled by the foo(context) action, causing it to interrupt action execution and transition to the next state. Instead, you'll have to change the action state definition to the following:

```
<action-state id="sample">
  <action bean="sampleAction" name="foo" method="foo"/>
  <action bean="sampleAction" method="bar"/>
  <transition on="foo.error" to="errorState"/>
  <transition on="success" to="successState"/>
  <transition on="error" to="errorState"/>
</action-state>
```

The preceding code will cause the foo.success event to be ignored, while the foo.error event will still move the flow to the error state. The bar(context) action will execute after foo(context) and will move the flow along as usual.

As illustrated previously, XML flow definitions can specify the name of a named action using the name attribute of the <action> element:

```
<action bean="sampleAction" name="foo" method="foo"/>
```

Java flow builders can use the name(name, action) convenience method:

```
name("foo", invoke("foo", action("sampleAction")))
```

## End States

The last core state type to be discussed is the end state. An end state terminates the active flow session. If that flow session is the root flow session of the ongoing flow execution, the entire flow execution will end. When the session is a subflow session, processing will resume in the parent flow. The next chapter will explain the relationship between end states and subflow states. End states are implemented by the org.springframework. webflow.engine.EndState class, a subclass of State.

Notice that end states are *not* transitionable. This makes sense since an end state represents a final point in the flow, from which you cannot continue.

A flow can have any number of end states. It is not uncommon for a flow to have no end states, for instance, with a repetitive process such as searching (where you typically have a Search Again button). Having multiple end states is also common, one for each *logical* outcome of the flow.

An end state can optionally reference a view. Such a view can be used to confirm flow processing ended successfully and is typically called a *confirmation view*. The view referenced by an end state will only be rendered when that end state terminates the entire flow execution. If the end state ends a subflow session, view selection is the responsibility of the resuming parent flow. If an end state that terminates the entire flow execution does not specify a view, the flow is assumed to have generated a response directly, for instance, using an action. This is equivalent to what was discussed for view states.

> ■**Caution**  End state views cannot be rendered after a redirect, as prescribed by the POST-REDIRECT-GET idiom, because flow execution ends during the event processing phase when an end state is entered, cleaning up any associated resources. As a result, that flow execution cannot be refreshed in a subsequent render phase, because it no longer exists. In other words, when an end state renders a view, the render phase for that view will always occur in the same physical request as the event processing phase.
>
> Consequently, confirmation views cannot be refreshed, and trying to refresh them will produce an error informing you the governing flow execution is no longer available (Chapter 2 already illustrated this). Instead of rendering a confirmation view from an end state, it is better to use an end state to redirect to a stable *external* URL. This is an explicit variation on the POST-REDIRECT-GET idiom. The next chapter will explain how to do this.

End states can be added to an XML flow definition using the `<end-state>` element. Just like in the case of a view state, the `view` attribute can be used to specify the confirmation view:

```
<end-state id="endAndShowConfirmationView" view="confirmationView"/>
```

When using a Java flow builder, use one of the provided `addEndState(. . .)` variants:

```
addEndState("endAndShowConfirmationView", "confirmationView");
```

# Flow Definition Registries

The flow definition constructs discussed so far in this chapter already allow you to define a lot of useful web flows. Before those web flows can be run, however, you need to deploy them in a flow definition registry, making them eligible for execution. This section will discuss flow definition registries.

> ■**Note**  The terms "flow definition registry," "flow registry," and "registry" are used interchangeably, just like "flow definition" and "flow."

As the name implies, a *flow definition registry* is a registry containing flow definitions, indexed by ID. The flow definition registry is responsible for assigning a flow ID to a particular flow definition. A single flow definition can be registered multiple times in the same registry using different IDs. Likewise, a single flow definition could also be registered with the same (or different) IDs in multiple registries.

---

**Tip** Registering the same flow definition multiple times, with different flow IDs, in the same registry is useful if the flow definition is parameterized differently in each case. This will be illustrated in Chapter 10.

---

The structure of the Flow Definition Registry subsystem of the execution core layer is detailed in Figure 4-14.

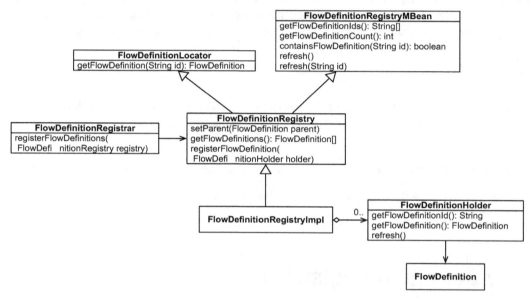

**Figure 4-14.** *Flow definition registry class diagram*

A flow definition registry is an implementation of the org.springframework. webflow.definition.registry.FlowDefinitionRegistry interface, defining a registerFlowDefinition(holder) method that can be used to add a flow definition to the registry. If all you want to do is look up a FlowDefinition by ID, you can use the getFlowDefinition(id) method defined by the FlowDefinitionLocator interface, a parent interface of the FlowDefinitionRegistry.

Populating a flow definition registry with flow definitions is the responsibility of a FlowDefinitionRegistrar. Flow definition registrars know where to find flow definition resources and how to load them. For instance, XmlFlowRegistrar loads XML flow definitions and creates corresponding FlowDefinition objects using the XML flow builder, as discussed in the "The XML Flow Builder" section. Notice that a flow definition registrar will not directly register the FlowDefinition with the registry. Instead, it registers a FlowDefinitionHolder wrapping the FlowDefinition and associating it with a flow ID. The level of indirection provided by the FlowDefinitionHolder allows the flow definition registry to lazily load flow definitions or refresh them at runtime.

Since the details of locating flow definition resources (for instance XML files) and building corresponding FlowDefinition objects are encapsulated inside FlowDefinitionRegistrar implementations, Spring Web Flow can provide a single generic flow definition registry implementation: the FlowDefinitionRegistryImpl. Here is a code example directly using the FlowDefinitionRegistryImpl and XmlFlowRegistrar:

```
FlowDefinitionRegistry registry = new FlowDefinitionRegistryImpl();

ApplicationContext context =
  new ClassPathXmlApplicationContext("enterPayment-context.xml");
FlowServiceLocator serviceLocator =
  new DefaultFlowServiceLocator(registry, context);
XmlFlowRegistrar registrar = new XmlFlowRegistrar(serviceLocator);
registrar.addLocation(new ClassPathResource("enterPayment-flow.xml"));
registrar.registerFlowDefinitions(registry);

FlowDefinition flow = registry.getFlowDefinition("enterPayment-flow");
```

Notice that the code passes a FlowServiceLocator object into the XmlFlowRegistrar. This service locator will be used during the flow build process to locate action beans, sub-flow definitions, and other flow-related services.

---

**Note** If you're familiar with Spring's bean definition loading system, you will see that the way various FlowDefinitionRegistrar implementations populate a generic FlowDefinitionRegistry is similar to Spring BeanDefinitionReader implementations registering bean definitions with a BeanDefinitionRegistry.

---

You normally don't need to directly use the FlowDefinitionRegistry or FlowDefinitionRegistrar APIs. Instead, Spring Web Flow provides Spring factory beans that make it easy to set up an XML flow definition registry containing flows loaded by an XML flow builder or a Java flow definition registry holding flow definitions loaded using a Java flow builder.

## XML Flow Definition Registries

XmlFlowRegistryFactoryBean allows convenient configuration of a flow definition registry containing flows loaded from XML flow definition files. Internally, XmlFlowRegistryFactoryBean will use the XmlFlowRegistrar to populate a FlowDefinitionRegistry.

## Spring 2 Configuration

Spring Web Flow provides a Spring 2 configuration schema that allows you to elegantly set up an XML flow definition registry. Here is typical example:

```
1    <?xml version="1.0" encoding="UTF-8"?>
2    <beans xmlns="http://www.springframework.org/schema/beans"
3      xmlns:xsi="http://www.w3.org/2001/XMLSchema-instance"
4      xmlns:flow="http://www.springframework.org/schema/ \
5        webflow- config"
6      xsi:schemaLocation="
7        http://www.springframework.org/schema/beans
8        http://www.springframework.org/schema/beans/ \
9          spring-beans-2.5.xsd
10       http://www.springframework.org/schema/webflow-config
11       http://www.springframework.org/schema/webflow-config/ \
12         spring-webflow-config-1.0.xsd">
13
14     <flow:registry id="flowRegistry">
15       <flow:location path="/WEB-INF/hello-flow.xml"/>
16     </flow:registry>
17   </beans>
```

The following points are key in the preceding listing:

- *Line 4*: By referencing the spring-webflow-config-1.0.xsd schema and associating it with the flow: namespace, you can use the custom tags defined by that schema to configure XML.

- *Line 14*: The <flow:registry> tag defines a bean of type FlowDefinitionRegistry. There is only one attribute: the id of the defined bean.

- *Line 15*: Nested <flow:location> tags define the locations to load flows from. You can specify any number of locations, causing flows from all of those locations to be loaded into a single flow definition registry.

The path attribute of the <flow:location> element specifies the XML flow definition resources to load. The preceding example identified a single flow definition XML file: /WEB-INF/hello-flow.xml, loaded from the WEB-INF/ directory of a Java web application. You can also use Ant-style patterns matching several flow definition XML files, for instance:

```
<flow:location path="/WEB-INF/flows/**/*-flow.xml"/>
```

This is a very typical definition that will match all XML files ending with the `-flow` suffix, in the `/WEB-INF/flows` directory or any of its subdirectories. Table 4-1 summarizes Ant-style wildcard patterns.

**Table 4-1.** *Ant-Style Wildcards*

| Symbol | Meaning |
| --- | --- |
| * | Matches zero or more characters |
| ? | Matches exactly one character |
| ** | Matches zero or more directories |

The value of the `path` attribute is interpreted as a Spring resource specification (`org.springframework.core.io.Resource`). Consequently, you can also reference flow definition XML files on the classpath, for instance:

```
<flow:location path="classpath:enterPayment-flow.xml"/>
```

It is even possible to reference a flow definition on another server, although that's not generally useful:

```
<flow:location path="http://my.flow.server/enterPayment-flow.xml"/>
```

At this point, you might be wondering how an ID gets associated with a flow definition, particularly when referencing multiple flow definitions in a single location path. The `XmlFlowRegistrar` used by the `XmlFlowRegistryFactoryBean` will automatically assign a flow ID equal to the flow definition XML file name minus the `.xml` extension. For instance, a flow defined in `enterPayment-flow.xml` will get the `enterPayment-flow` ID *by convention*.

---

**FLOW DEFINITION RESGISTRY CONFIGURATION**

It is a good idea to favor *convention over configuration* in the case of flow IDs. If you set up a reasonable naming convention, it minimizes configuration overhead. For instance, configuring your flow registry as follows:

```
<flow:registry id="flowRegistry">
  <flow:location path="/WEB-INF/flows/**/*-flow.xml"/>
</flow:registry>
```

will allow you to put all flows of your web application in the `/WEB-INF/flows` directory. You can freely organize those flows in subdirectories, and use the file name to specify the flow ID.

Alternatively, you can deploy your flows on the classpath. This has the advantage of allowing consistent and easy access to your flow definition resources from anywhere in the application code or unit tests. The downside of this is that you will have to explicitly identify each flow definition XML file in your registry configuration (because Java does not allow classpath listing).

XML flow definition registries support runtime reloading of flow definitions. This was already demonstrated in Chapter 2. When you edit a flow definition XML file, the registry will automatically reload and rebuild that flow definition the next time it is retrieved from the registry. This is particularly useful in development environments.

### Finishing the Test Drive

Changing the flow registry definition (in `dispatcher-servlet.xml`) in the modified "Hello World" sample application allows you to experiment with the different ways of referencing flows. For instance, using the following definition will give exactly the same result as explicitly referring to the `hello-flow.xml` and `enterPayment-flow.xml` flow definition XML files:

```
<flow:registry id="flowRegistry">
  <flow:location path="/WEB-INF/*-flow.xml"/>
</flow:registry>
```

### Classic Bean Configuration

When you are still using Spring 1, you cannot use the Spring 2–specific `webflow-config` schema. Instead, you'll have to directly configure the `XmlFlowRegistryFactoryBean` using generic bean definitions. Even when using Spring 2, direct configuration can be useful. The `<flow:registry>` element only supports the very common configuration options. Directly configuring the `XmlFlowRegistryFactoryBean` gives you more power and flexibility, at the cost of a little verbosity.

Here is a simple example, directly configuring the registry using the `org.springframework.webflow.engine.builder.xml.XmlFlowRegistryFactoryBean`:

```
<bean id="flowRegistry"
  class="org.springframework.webflow.engine.builder.xml. \
    XmlFlowRegistryFactoryBean">
  <property name="flowLocations" value="/WEB-INF/flows/**/*-flow.xml"/>
</bean>
```

The `flowLocations` property corresponds with the `<flow:location>` element and accepts exactly the same values (using Ant-style patterns). Using `flowLocations` will cause convention-based flow IDs to be used. If you want to explicitly specify the flow ID, use the `flowDefinitions` property:

```
<bean id="flowRegistry"
  class="org.springframework.webflow.engine.builder.xml. \
    XmlFlowRegistryFactoryBean">
```

```
<property name="flowDefinitions">
  <value>
    enterPayment=classpath:enterPayment-flow.xml
    helloWorld=/WEB-INF/hello-flow.xml
  </value>
</property>
</bean>
```

The defined value will be converted into a `java.util.Properties` object by Spring's `PropertyEditor` machinery. Each property key specifies the flow ID, while the property value identifies the XML flow definition file.

## Java Flow Definition Registries

Setting up Java flow definition registries focuses on using *Java*, just like in the case of `AbstractFlowBuilder`-based Java flow builders. Currently, you cannot directly define a Java flow definition registry using Spring XML bean definitions. Instead, you'll have to subclass `AbstractFlowBuilderFlowRegistryFactoryBean` and implement the `doPopulate(registry)` hook method. Here is a simple example:

```
public class SpringBankFlowRegistry extends
    AbstractFlowBuilderFlowRegistryFactoryBean {

  protected void doPopulate(FlowDefinitionRegistry registry) {
    registerFlowDefinition(registry, "enterPayment-flow",
        new EnterPaymentFlowBuilder());
  }
}
```

The `AbstractFlowBuilderFlowRegistryFactoryBean` provides a few `registerFlowDefinition(. . .)` convenience methods that you can use to populate the registry with flow definitions. Notice how the preceding code directly instantiates the flow builder. This means that you have complete control over flow builder instantiation and configuration. You could define a constructor taking parameters used to parameterize the flow builder or provide any other means of configuration (for instance, setter methods). As mentioned before, this gives Java flow builders flexibility beyond what XML flow builders can deliver, leveraging the full power of Java.

Once you have your `AbstractFlowBuilderFlowRegistryFactoryBean` subclass implemented, you can define it as any other bean in a Spring application context:

```
<bean id="flowRegistry"
  class="com.ervacon.springbank.web.SpringBankFlowRegistry"/>
```

## Combining Flow Definition Registries

The flow definition registries set up by the XmlFlowRegistryFactoryBean and AbstractFlowBuilderFlowRegistryFactoryBean determine the visibility of the contained flow definitions. One flow definition can see and use only another flow definition (as a subflow) if that flow definition resides in the same flow registry. To extend this visibility concept and make it more powerful, flow definition registries can form a hierarchy. Notice the setParent(parent) method of the FlowDefinitionRegistry in Figure 4-14. A flow can reference other flows defined by the parent flow definition registry.

Specifying the *parent* of a flow definition registry is not possible when using the Spring 2 webflow-config schema. Instead, you'll have to use a classic Spring bean definition for the XmlFlowRegistryFactoryBean or for your AbstractFlowBuilderFlowRegistryFactoryBean subclass to be able to configure the parent property:

```
<bean id="globalFlowRegistry"
  class="org.springframework.webflow.engine.builder.xml. \
    XmlFlowRegistryFactoryBean">
  <property name="flowDefinitions">
    <value>
      fooFlow=classpath:/flows/foo-flow.xml
      barFlow=classpath:/flows/bar-flow.xml
    </value>
  </property>
</bean>


<bean id="flowRegistry"
  class="org.springframework.webflow.engine.builder.xml. \
    XmlFlowRegistryFactoryBean">
  <property name="flowLocations" value="/WEB-INF/flows/**/*-flow.xml"/>
  <property name="parent" ref="globalFlowRegistry"/>
</bean>
```

Using the parent property, you can combine XML flow definition registries and Java flow definition registries, referencing a Java-based flow definition from an XML flow, or vice versa. Spring Web Flow has no out-of-the-box support for heterogeneous flow definition registries. This is simple enough to implement, however, by directly registering your flow definitions in a generic FlowDefinitionRegistryImpl, as shown earlier.

# Summary

This chapter introduced you to basic Spring Web Flow usage. It detailed how to go about designing web flows, taking a state-diagram–inspired approach, and showed you how this high-level design translates naturally into a Spring Web Flow flow definition.

Using a flow builder system, Spring Web Flow can provide several different syntax options for its core flow definition language: a Domain Specific Language (DSL) targeted at the domain of page flows. The XML flow builder interprets XML flow definitions adhering to a custom XML schema. Java flow builders use plain old Java to build a flow definition.

The core flow definition constructs flows, states and transitions were detailed in the "Defining Flows" section. A flow definition is a static conversation blueprint. Executing flows and the concept of a flow execution were introduced in the "Flow Executions" section. While the FlowExecution interface provides a façade that external client code can use to drive a flow execution, the RequestContext gives flow definition artifacts access to the flow execution in which they are running. Using the RequestContext, objects like action implementations can access the different scopes defined by Spring Web Flow: request scope, flash scope, flow scope, and conversation scope.

Actions and the Action interface are the key extension point in Spring Web Flow, allowing you to plug code into your flows that interacts with business components (for instance, residing in the service layer). Actions are deployed as normal Spring beans in a Spring application context and can leverage all of Spring's power, benefiting from dependency injection or declarative services.

Almost all flow definitions employ the three core state types provided by Spring Web Flow. A view state pauses the flow and displays a view, allowing users to participate in the flow execution. An action state executes actions, bridging the web and application tier, and finally, an end state terminates a flow session.

This chapter concluded with a discussion of flow definition registries. When a flow definition is deployed into a flow registry, it becomes eligible for use in a flow execution or reuse as a subflow of another flow.

Using the core flow definition constructs presented in this chapter, you were able to define a basic web flow for the "enter payment" use case of the Spring Bank sample application. This web flow currently looks as follows:

```
<?xml version="1.0" encoding="UTF-8"?>
<flow xmlns="http://www.springframework.org/schema/webflow"
  xmlns:xsi="http://www.w3.org/2001/XMLSchema-instance"
  xsi:schemaLocation="
    http://www.springframework.org/schema/webflow
    http://www.springframework.org/schema/webflow/spring-webflow-1.0.xsd">
```

```
<start-state idref="showSelectDebitAccount"/>

<view-state id="showSelectDebitAccount">
  <transition on="next" to="showEnterPaymentInfo"/>
</view-state>

<view-state id="showEnterPaymentInfo">
  <transition on="next" to="showConfirmPayment"/>
</view-state>

<view-state id="showConfirmPayment">
  <transition on="submit" to="submitPayment"/>
</view-state>

<action-state id="submitPayment">
  <action bean="paymentAction" method="submitPayment"/>
  <transition on="success" to="end"/>
  <transition on="error" to="showConfirmPayment"/>
</action-state>

<end-state id="end"/>

<end-state id="endCancel"/>

<global-transitions>
  <transition on="cancel" to="endCancel"/>
</global-transitions>

<import resource="enterPayment-context.xml"/>
</flow>
```

In this chapter, you learned about the basic web flow for the "enter payment" use case of the Spring Bank sample application. This next chapter continues with more advanced flow definition constructs, and we'll complete the "enter payment" web flow along the way.

# CHAPTER 5

■ ■ ■

# Advanced Web Flow Concepts

This chapter continues in the same trend as the previous one but covers more advanced topics. The basic flow definition artifacts explained in the previous chapter are essential to most flow definitions. In this chapter, you'll learn about additional functionality that will give you more power and flexibility when expressing your flows. Some of the subjects covered follow:

- OGNL, Spring Web Flow's default expression language

- Data binding and validation

- Reusing flow definitions as coarse-grained application modules with the help of subflow states

The previous chapter set up the foundation of the "enter payment" use case of the Spring Bank sample application. This chapter will complete the flow definition, filling in the missing parts.

Let's start with an investigation of OGNL, an expression language leveraged by Spring Web Flow.

## OGNL

Object Graph Navigation Language (OGNL) is Spring Web Flow's default expression language and is available at http://www.ognl.org. OGNL gets and sets properties of Java objects. Along with basic object graph navigation and bean property access, OGNL also supports powerful advanced features such as projections and list selections.

Using OGNL expressions from inside a flow definition avoids writing boilerplate Java code that takes care of trivial tasks such as getting or setting values in one of Spring Web Flow's scopes. For instance, an Action implementation like this

```
public class ExampleAction extends MultiAction {

  public Event setFoo(RequestContext context) throws Exception {
    String bar = context.getRequestParameters().get("bar");
    Foo foo = (Foo)context.getFlowScope().get("foo");
    foo.setBar(bar);
    return success();
  }
}
```

can be reformulated in terms of a reusable set action and two OGNL expressions (the set action will be explained in more detail later):

```
<set attribute="${foo.bar} " scope="flow"
  value="${requestParameters.bar} "/>
```

In this example, ${foo.bar} and ${requestParameters.bar} are OGNL expressions. The value expression will be evaluated against RequestContext, like most expressions in Spring Web Flow, and translates to RequestContext.getRequestParameters().get("bar"). The attribute expression will be evaluated against the flow scope attribute map, as indicated by the specified scope, making it equivalent to ((Foo)AttributeMap.get("foo")). setBar(. . .). Notice how OGNL shields you from low-level details such as type casts. In many cases, this makes simple property access easier and much more readable.

---

### OGNL EXPRESSION DELIMITERS

In the ${foo.bar} example, the OGNL expressions are delimited using ${. . .}. This is only necessary if Spring Web Flow does not know whether or not something is an expression. In the case of a set action, the value expression and attribute expression are always interpreted as OGNL expressions, so the example could have been coded as follows:

```
<set attribute="foo.bar" scope="flow"
  value="requestParameters.bar"/>
```

A typical example where the use of ${. . .} delimiters is required is embedding expressions into a larger string. For instance

```
externalRedirect:http://www.google.be/search?q=${flowScope.queryString}
```

can obviously not be rewritten as

```
externalRedirect:http://www.google.be/search?q=flowScope.queryString
```

which would be interpreted as one big constant string (this example is taken from the "View Selections" section).

A comprehensive guide to all of the features supported by the OGNL expression language can be found on the OGNL web site: http://www.ognl.org. Instead of reproducing that material here, I will only illustrate those OGNL functionalities most relevant to Spring Web Flow. Refer to the OGNL language reference for more details.

---

■**Caution**  OGNL is very powerful and even allows simple programming constructs like variable or function declarations. Don't abuse these features to start *programming in XML*. Cases requiring nontrivial logic are better implemented using Java and a custom action invoked from your flow definition.

One important issue to keep in mind is refactoring. The more "code" you have in OGNL expressions, the harder the expression becomes to refactor. For instance, IDEs currently do not update an OGNL expression like foo.bar when you would rename the bar property of Foo to something else.

---

## OGNL by Example

Let's study OGNL's more interesting functionality by looking at some simple examples. Consider the Java class in Listing 5-1.

**Listing 5-1.** *A Person POJO*

```java
public class Person {

  private String firstName;
  private String lastName;
  private Person friend;

  public String getFirstName() {
    return firstName;
  }

  public void setFirstName(String firstName) {
    this.firstName = firstName;
  }

  public String getLastName() {
    return lastName;
  }
```

```
  public void setLastName(String lastName) {
    this.lastName = lastName;
  }

  public Person getFriend() {
    return friend;
  }

  public Person setFriend(Person friend) {
    this.friend = friend;
  }

  public String sayHello() {
    return "Hello " + getFirstName() + " " + getLastName() + "!";
  }

  public void rename(String firstName, String lastName) {
    setFirstName(firstName);
    setLastName(lastName);
  }
}
```

Accessing the firstName property of a Person object can be done using a simple
${firstName} expression. Most OGNL expressions can be used to both get (read)
and set (write) a property value. When getting the value, the ${firstName} expression
is equivalent to getFirstName(), while it translates into setFirstName(firstName)
when updating the value. OGNL also supports direct access to the public fields of
an object, avoiding the need for getters and setters. You can chain together property
names using the . (dot) operator. For instance, ${friend.firstName} translates to
getFriend().getFirstName() or getFriend().setFirstName(firstName), depending on
whether you're reading or writing the property.

---

■**Caution** Unlike some other expression languages, for instance the JSP expression language, OGNL does
not silently ignore null values. Consider the case where the friend property of a Person object is null;
evaluating the ${friend.firstName} expression against that object would result in an exception.

OGNL has another little quirk you should be aware of. When you try to set the value of a property to an object
that cannot be coerced into the type of that property, OGNL will fail silently and set the property value to null.
For instance, trying to set the friend property to a java.util.Date object will result in the friend property being set to null. Strangely enough, and inconsistent with Object typed properties, OGNL will generate
an exception when a value cannot be converted to a primitive type number (e.g., int or long).

---

When evaluating an OGNL expression against a map, the property name is taken to be the key of an entry in the map. So ${person.firstName} evaluated against a map set up like this

```
Person person = ...;
Map map = new HashMap();
map.put("person", person);
```

would return the value of the firstName property of the person object in the map.

OGNL also allows indexed access to elements in arrays or lists using the [] syntax. For instance, ${list[0].firstName} would resolve to the firstName property of the first Person object in the following list:

```
Person person = ...;
List list = new LinkedList();
list.add(person);
```

OGNL can also be used to invoke *public* methods on objects. To invoke a method, simply add parentheses to the method name. The expression ${sayHello()} invokes the sayHello() method defined by the Person class. Method arguments can be specified in between the method parentheses. For instance, ${rename(friend.firstName, friend.lastName)} calls the rename(firstName, lastName) method, passing in the name of the friend property. Static methods can also be called using the following format: @class@method(args), for instance ${@java.lang.Math@random()}.

From time to time, it is useful to express a constant value in an OGNL expression. OGNL supports the following constants:

- Using null resolves to the Java null literal.

- String literals can be placed between either single or double quotes, for instance, ${rename('John', 'Doe')}. They support Java character escaping using a backslash (\).

- Character literals can be specified using single quotes. Using Java character escapes is again supported.

- The Boolean values true and false are recognized.

- Numeric constants (integers, floats, etc.) can be defined using the same syntax as in Java. OGNL also supports two extra possibilities however. Using the B suffix creates a BigDecimal (e.g., 13.4B), while the H (huge) suffix results in a BigInteger.

New objects can be created in an expression as usual, using the new operator. There is one caveat with this, however: you have to specify the fully qualified class name. Constructor arguments can be passed in just like in a normal method invocation.

OGNL has special syntax to allow easy construction of collection types such as arrays, lists, and maps, for instance:

```
${ { new com.ervacon.sample.Person(), new com.ervacon.sample.Person() }  }
```

This creates a `java.util.List` containing two `Person` objects. Note the extra curly braces, indicating *collection construction syntax*. Similarly, you can also create arrays and maps, as in this example:

```
${new int[] {1, 2, 3 }  }
${#{"person" : new com.ervacon.sample.Person() }  }
```

The first line creates an integer array with three elements: 1, 2, and 3. The second line instantiates a `java.util.Map` containing a single `Person` object indexed as `person`.

Most Java operators are supported by OGNL, including the ternary conditional operator. Here are a few examples:

```
${age > 18 ? "adult" : "minor" }
${order.shippingRequired or (order.weight gt 100) }
${firstName == "John" and lastName != "Doe" }
${firstName.equals("John") }
${firstName not in {"John", "Jack" }  }
```

Of particular interest are the or, and, lt, gt, lte, gte, and not synonyms for ||, &&, <, >, <=, >=, and !, making OGNL expressions XML friendly. OGNL also has a convenient in operator that you can use to test whether or not an object is contained in a collection.

Now that you have a good idea of what OGNL expressions are capable of, let's see how Spring Web Flow leverages them in flow definitions.

## OGNL in Action

Both the XML and Java flow definition syntax allow you to use OGNL expressions. The XML flow builder will automatically parse an expression string into an `Expression` object. The `AbstractFlowBuilder` superclass used by Java flow builders offers `expression` (expressionString) and `settableExpression(expressionString)` methods that create appropriate `Expression` objects. A *settable expression* is an expression that can be used to set the value of a property, for instance:

```
RequestContext context = ...;
Expression e = expression("flowScope.person.sayHello()");
String helloMessage = (String)e.evaluate(context, null);
```

```
SettableExpression se =
  settableExpression("flowScope.person.firstName");
se.evaluateToSet(context, "Bob", null);
```

Notice that the expression strings in this example do not use the optional ${. . .} delimiters. The entire strings will be interpreted as OGNL expressions.

---

**Note** The expression(expressionString) and settableExpression(expressionString) methods use the ExpressionParser available from the flow service locator (as getFlowServiceLocator().getExpressionParser()) to parse the expression strings.

---

## Transition Matching Criteria

As a first example of using OGNL expressions in a flow definition, let's take a look at transition matching criteria. The previous chapter explained that a TransitionCriteria object is responsible for matching a transition as eligible for execution. The TransitionCriteria interface is very simple (see Listing 5-2).

**Listing 5-2.** *The TransitionCriteria Interface*

```
package org.springframework.webflow.engine;

public interface TransitionCriteria {

  public boolean test(RequestContext context);
}
```

So far, I have only illustrated the EventIdTransitionCriteria, which matches on the last event that occurred in the flow, available as RequestContext.getLastEvent(). Spring Web Flow also supports a number of other TransitionCriteria types, as detailed in Table 5-1.

**Table 5-1.** *Transition Criteria Encodings*

| Encoded | Description |
| --- | --- |
| eventId | This encoding is converted into an EventIdTransitionCriteria object matching the last event that occurred in the flow, as returned by RequestContext.getLastEvent(). |
| * | This WildcardTransitionCriteria matches on everything: it always returns true. Not specifying any transition criteria is equivalent to using wildcard transition criteria. |

**Table 5-1.** *Transition Criteria Encodings (Continued)*

| Encoded | Description |
| --- | --- |
| ${. . .} | This encoding will be converted into a BooleanExpressionTransitionCriteria object that evaluates the specified expression against the RequestContext. The result of the expression should be of Boolean type and will be returned to the caller.<br><br>The expression can use the #result shorthand notation to refer to the ID of the last event that occurred. So #result is equivalent to RequestContext.getLastEvent().getId(). |
| bean:id | This encoding will obtain and use the identified TransitionCriteria bean from the Spring application context defining the flow definition. This allows you to easily plug in custom TransitionCriteria implementations.<br><br>The bean:id form is mainly targeted at XML flow builders. Java flow builders always have the option of directly instantiating a TransitionCriteria implementation of choice and using that. |

Notice that using ${. . .} is required in the case of transition criteria expressions, to distinguish them from the default eventId criteria.

The value of the on attribute of the <transition> element of an XML flow definition supports all the encoded forms mentioned in Table 5-1, for instance:

```
<transition on="next" to="showConfirmPayment"/>
<transition on="${#result=='next' and flowScope.person.minor} "
  to="showMinorWarning"/>
<transition on="*" to="nextState"/>
<transition to="nextState"/>
<transition on="bean:myCriteria" to="nextState"/>
```

Likewise, the on(transitionCriteriaExpression) method of the AbstractFlowBuilder also supports all of these encoded forms:

```
transition(on("next"), to("showConfirmPayment"))
transition(on("${#result=='next' and flowScope.person.minor} ",
  to("showMinorWarning"))
transition(on("*"), to("nextState"))
transition(on("bean:myCriteria"), to("nextState"))
```

Using OGNL expressions to express transition criteria gives you a lot of flexibility defining transitions that are only matched in particular situations. The expression can take any information available in the request context into account. For instance, the ${#result=='next' and flowScope.person.minor} expression illustrated previously looks at a Person object in flow scope. The transition criteria expressed by this OGNL expression could also have been coded directly in Java as follows:

```
public class SampleTransitionCriteria implements TransitionCriteria {

  public boolean test(RequestContext context) {
```

```
    String result = context.getLastEvent().getId();
    Person person = (Person)context.getFlowScope().get("person");
    return result.equals("next") && person.isMinor();
  }
}
```

This implementation can be deployed into a Spring application context and referenced using the bean:id notation.

---

**Tip** Remember that transition criteria expressions are evaluated against the RequestContext.

---

## Target State Resolvers

OGNL expressions can also be used to specify the target state of a transition. As the previous chapter already mentioned, a Transition uses a TargetStateResolver strategy to determine the state to transition to *at flow execution time*. The TargetStateResolver interface is simple and defines only a single method (Listing 5-3).

**Listing 5-3.** *The TargetStateResolver Interface*

```
package org.springframework.webflow.engine;

public interface TargetStateResolver {

  public State resolveTargetState(Transition transition,
      State sourceState, RequestContext context);
}
```

Besides the RequestContext, a TargetStateResolver also has access to the transition for which it is resolving the target state and the source state of that transition.

Be default, the target state will be looked up by ID, but several other encoded forms are also supported, as detailed in Table 5-2.

**Table 5-2.** *Target State Resolver Encodings*

| Encoded | Description |
| --- | --- |
| stateId | This statically identifies the state to transition to *by ID*. |
| ${...} | This encoder calculates the ID of the target state of the transition at flow execution time by evaluating a given OGNL expression against the RequestContext. The expression should return a String, the ID of the target state. |
| bean:id | This loads a TargetStateResolver bean from the Spring application context defining the flow definition. It allows you to plug in custom TargetStateResolver implementations. |

Using ${. . .} delimiters is again required to distinguish an OGNL expression from a static state ID.

XML flow definitions can use these encoded forms in the value of the to attribute of the `<transition>` element:

```
<transition on="next" to="showConfirmPayment"/>
<transition on="next" to="${flowScope.nextStateId} "/>
<transition on="cancel" to="bean:cancelStateIdCalculator"/>
```

Java flow builders can do the same thing using the `to(targetStateIdExpression)` helper method:

```
transition(on("next"), to("showConfirmPayment"))
transition(on("next"), to("${flowScope.nextStateId} "))
transition(on("cancel"), to("bean:cancelStateIdCalculator"))
```

Instead of using the `bean:id` form, Java flow builder can also directly instantiate and use a `TargetStateResolver` implementation.

---

**Tip** Remember that transition target state expressions are evaluated against the `RequestContext`.

---

Using OGNL for both transition matching criteria and the target state calculation gives you a lot of flexibility. Chapter 10, "Real-World Use Cases," shows an example that defines a global back transition that transitions the flow back to the previous view state.

## Decision States

Having the ability to use arbitrary OGNL expressions to specify transition matching criteria allows you to define a conditional branch in your flow, for instance:

```
<transition on="${#result=='next' and flowScope.person.minor} "
  to="showMinorWarning"/>
<transition on="${#result=='next' and !flowScope.person.minor} "
  to="processPerson"/>
```

This is obviously a very common requirement. Spring Web Flow defines a special state type, the *decision state*, to express this kind of conditional branching in a much more readable way:

```
<decision-state id="checkMinor">
  <if test="flowScope.person.minor" then="showMinorWarning"
    else="processPerson"/>
</decision-state>
```

Decision states make *routing decisions*, moving the flow to one of several possible target states. They often sit in between other state types, for instance, view states or action states. Here is a more complete example showing a decision state routing the flow to one of two possible paths:

```
<view-state ...>
  ...
  <transition on="next" to="checkMinor"/>
</view-state>

<decision-state id="checkMinor">
  <if test="flowScope.person.minor" then="showMinorWarning"
    else="processPerson"/>
</decision-state>

<view-state id="showMinorWarning" view="minorWarning">
  <transition on="confirm" to="processPerson"/>
</view-state>

<action-state id="processPerson">
  ...
</action-state>
```

A decision state is implemented by the `TransitionableState` subclass `org.springframework.webflow.engine.DecisionState`. A decision state can contain any number of `if` elements, defining an if-then-else structure that will be translated into transitions with corresponding matching criteria. The `test` attribute of the `if` element defines the transition criteria as an OGNL expression (so there is no need for `${. . .}`). The then and `else` attributes identify the target state and can use OGNL expressions to do so, just like normal transitions. A transition using a wildcard (*) matching criteria will be used to represent the `else` of the if-then-else structure. When the flow enters a decision state, the first matching transition is used to transition on to the next state. Consequently, it is only useful to have an `else` on the last `if`, for instance:

```
<decision-state id="switchOnPersonType">
  <if test="flowScope.person.minor" then="processMinor"/>
  <if test="flowScope.person.adult" then="processAdult"/>
  <if test="flowScope.person.elderly" then="processElderly"
    else="showProcessingError"/>
</decision-state>
```

---

**Note** If no matching transition can be found, an exception will be generated.

---

XML flow builders can use the `<decision-state>` element and nested `<if>` elements to define a decision state, as illustrated in the previous paragraphs. Java flow builders can use any of the `addDecisionState(. . .)` variants provided by the `AbstractFlowBuilder` to add a decision state to the flow, for instance:

```
addDecisionState("checkMinor",
    on("${flowScope.person.minor} "),
    "showMinorWarning", "processPerson");
```

Notice that this code uses the general purpose `on(transitionCriteriaExpression)` method, making use of the `${. . .}` expression delimiters required. Alternatively, a Java flow builder can directly configure a decision state with a number of transitions:

```
addDecisionState("switchOnPersonType",
    new Transition[] {
        transition(on("${flowScope.person.minor} "), to("processMinor")),
        transition(on("${flowScope.person.adult} "), to("processAdult")),
        transition(on("${flowScope.person.elderly} "), to("processElderly")),
        transition(on("*"), to("showProcessingError")) } );
```

Just as any other transitionable state in a web flow, decision states can have entry and exit actions.

---

**Note** The `test` expression of an `if` element in a decision state is evaluated against the `RequestContext`. This was to be expected, since `test` is really just a transition-matching criteria expression.

Similarly, OGNL expressions in the `then` and `else` attributes of an `if` element are also evaluated against the `RequestContext`. They are nothing more than expressions resolving a transition target state.

---

## Set Actions

The "OGNL" section introduced the set action. Spring Web Flow provides `SetAction` as a convenient way to set a value in a particular scope. `SetAction` leverages OGNL expressions for calculating the value to set and actually setting it:

```
<set attribute="${foo.bar} " scope="flow"
  value="${requestParameters.bar} "/>
```

The value expression is evaluated against the `RequestContext`, while the `attribute` expression will be evaluated against the identified scope map. If you do not explicitly specify one of the available scopes (request, flash, flow, or conversation), the request scope will be used by default. Recall that use of the ${. . .} delimiter around the expressions is optional, because the values of the attribute and value attributes are always expected to be expressions.

SetAction is an action like any other Spring Web Flow action. You can use it anywhere you can use a normal action, for instance, in action states or as part of a transition. SetAction always returns the success event, which you can ignore by turning the action into a *named action* as described in the "Action States" section of the previous chapter. Here is an example illustrating this:

```
<set attribute="showWarning" value="true" name="setShowWarning"/>
```

XML flow definitions can define set actions using the convenient <set> element, as shown previously. Java flow builders have no direct support for set actions and will have to instantiate the SetAction class directly before adding it to an action state or transition:

```
SetAction set = new SetAction(
    settableExpression("showWarning"),
    ScopeType.REQUEST,
    expression("true"));
addActionState("sampleActionState",
    name("setShowWarning", set),
    ...);
```

Notice how this code uses the settableExpression(expressionString) and expression(expressionString) helper methods.

### Bean Invoking Actions

Using actions to bridge the web tier and middle tier of your application was discussed in the "Implementing Actions" section of the previous chapter. That section showed a PaymentAction in the context of the "enter payment" use case of the Spring Bank sample application. This action obtains a Payment object from flow scope and passes it on to the PaymentProcessingEngine. As you can imagine, this kind of straightforward bridging code is very common. Spring Web Flow provides a bean invoking action, making this kind of bridging trivial. A *bean invoking action* can directly invoke any public method on any bean available in the application context defining the flow definition or in the flow local application context. This has two important benefits:

- It avoids a proliferation of lots of trivial Action implementations invoking methods on application (service) layer beans, like PaymentAction.

- The invoked bean can be a POJO (plain old Java object) and does not need to implement any Spring Web Flow interfaces. As a result, your code is less dependent on the framework, which is always a good thing.

Let's use such a bean invoking action to rework enterPayment-flow, dropping PaymentAction along the way. The following example shows a bean invoking action definition roughly equivalent to the PaymentAction developed in the previous chapter:

```
<bean-action bean="paymentProcessingEngine" method="submit">
  <method-arguments>
    <argument expression="${conversationScope.payment} "/>
  </method-arguments>
</bean-action>
```

This action will invoke the submit(payment) method directly on the paymentProcessingEngine bean in the application context, passing in the Payment object stored in conversation scope as a method argument.

Bean invoking actions are implemented using an AbstractBeanInvokingAction sub-class. Since they implement the Action interface, like any other action, they can be used anywhere a normal action can be used, for instance in action states, as state entry actions, or as part of transition execution. Just like all other actions, bean invoking actions can also be *named*, as explained in the previous chapter.

You can think of a bean invoking action as a decorator that adapts a public method on a POJO to the Action contract. To make this work, a bean invoking action needs three key pieces of information, as illustrated in Figure 5-1:

- An exact specification of the method to invoke, and the POJO (bean) to invoke it on. In Java, methods are described using a *method signature.*

- A specification of how result objects returned by the invoked method should be exposed to the flow execution.

- A strategy to create an action result event based on the outcome of the method invocation.

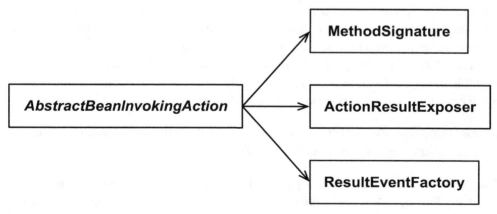

**Figure 5-1.** *Bean invoking action class diagram*

Let's investigate these three parts in more detail.

## POJO Method Signatures

XML flow definitions identify the bean to invoke methods on using the bean attribute of the <bean-action> element. The value of this attribute is the ID of a bean available from the Spring application context defining the flow definition. The name of the method to invoke is specified using the method attribute, while a nested <method-arguments> element specifies the arguments to be passed to the method. If the invoked method does not declare any parameters, the <method-arguments> can be omitted.

The expression attribute of <argument> elements, nested inside the <method-arguments> element, allows you to supply argument values to the method when it is invoked. The argument value is obtained by evaluating the provided OGNL expression against the RequestContext. The order of the <argument> elements should correspond with the order of the method parameters declared by the method. For instance, take the rename method defined by a fictitious PersonService interface, as shown in Listing 5-4.

**Listing 5-4.** *PersonService*

```
public interface PersonService {

  public void rename(Person person, String firstName, String lastName);
  public void notifyPersonsBornOn(Date date);
  public Person getPerson(Long id);
  public PersonStatus getPersonStatus(Long id);
}
```

This rename method can be invoked using the following bean invoking action declaration:

```
<bean-action bean="personService" method="rename">
  <method-arguments>
    <argument expression="${flowScope.person} "/>
    <argument expression="${'John'} "/>
    <argument expression="${'Doe'} "/>
  </method-arguments>
</bean-action>
```

This, of course, assumes that a PersonService bean with the ID personService is defined in the application context.

Java flow builders can use variants of the action(. . .) helper method to set up a bean invoking action. A method signature (modeled using the MethodSignature class) can be created using the method(signatureString) helper. Here is an example creating a bean invoking action invoking the `rename` method on the `personService` bean, as discussed before:

```
action("personService",
    method("rename(${flowScope.person} , ${'John'} , ${'Doe'} )"));
```

Notice how the argument expressions are embedded in the string-encoded method signature.

Spring Web Flow also supports automatic type conversion of method arguments. For instance, if a method declares a parameter of type `java.util.Date`, but the argument value is of type `java.lang.String`, Spring Web Flow can automatically convert the string into a `Date`. To enable this automatic type conversion, you need to explicitly specify the declared method parameter type using the `parameter-type` attribute, for instance:

```
<bean-action bean="personService" method="notifyPersonsBornOn">
  <argument expression="${requestParameters.date} "
    parameter-type="java.util.Date"/>
</bean-action>
```

Similarly, a Java flow builder can specify the parameter type by including it in the string-encoded method signature:

```
action("personService",
    method("notifyPersonsBornOn( \
        java.util.Date ${requestParameters.date} )"));
```

This type conversion functionality leverages the conversion service that will be discussed in "The Conversion Service" section.

---

**Tip** Remember that method argument value expressions are evaluated against the `RequestContext`.

---

### Action Result Exposers

Java methods can have return values. Bean invoking actions will expose the value returned by the invoked bean method to the flow execution using `ActionResultExposer`. If the method does not return any value (it is declared `void`), nothing needs to happen of course.

The `ActionResultExposer` strategy simply puts the method return value into a specified scope using a given name. XML flow definitions can configure the `ActionResultExposer` using the `<method-result>` element nested inside the `<bean-action>` element, like so:

```
<bean-action bean="personService" method="getPerson">
  <method-arguments>
```

```
    <argument expression="${flowScope.personId} "/>
  </method-arguments>
  <method-result name="person" scope="flow"/>
</bean-action>
```

If you do not explicitly specify the scope, request scope will be used as a default. Similarly, Java flow builders can use the action(beanId, methodSignature, resultExposer) method, passing in an ActionResultExposer object configured using the result(resultName, resultScope) helper method. Here is an example equivalent to the XML fragment shown previously:

```
action("personService",
    method("getPerson(${flowScope.personId} )"),
    result("person", ScopeType.FLOW));
```

If the invoked POJO method does not return a result object but instead throws an exception, that exception will be propagated by the bean invoking action. In the "Handling Exceptions" section, you will learn how to handle these exceptions.

### Result Event Factories

Recall that action execution methods return Event objects. The final aspect of adapting a normal POJO method to the Action interface is interpreting the method return value and returning an appropriate Event. This is the responsibility of a ResultEventFactory strategy.

Spring Web Flow will automatically decide which ResultEventFactory to use based on the declared return type of the invoked POJO method. The recognized return types and their corresponding event IDs are detailed in Table 5-3.

**Table 5-3.** *Mapping Method Return Types to Event IDs*

| Return Type | Event ID | Description |
| --- | --- | --- |
| Boolean or boolean | yes or no | A yes event indicates a true return value, while no means false. |
| LabeledEnum | The enum label | LabeledEnum instances, as defined by the Spring Framework, are recognized. An event will be generated having the *label* of the LabeledEnum as id. The actual LabeledEnum instance returned by the method will be included as payload in the event, keyed as result. Note that a Spring LabeledEnum is a JDK 1.3- and 1.4-compatible precursor to the Java 5 enum. |
| Enum | The enum name | A Java 5 enum (java.lang.Enum) return value will be mapped to an event having the *name* of the enum as its id. The Enum object itself will be included in the event as payload, indexed as result. |

**Table 5-3.** *Mapping Method Return Types to Event IDs (Continued)*

| Return Type | Event ID | Description |
|---|---|---|
| String | The string | When the invoked method returns a String, that string will be used as the event id. |
| Event | The event | In the odd case where the invoked method returns a Spring Web Flow Event, the event is used as-is. |
| Anything else | success | If the invoked method is declared void or has an unrecognized return type, the success event is generated. The returned object, if any, is included as payload in the generated event, keyed as result. |

If the declared method return type is recognized, but the actual return value of the method at runtime is null, a *null event* will be generated with event ID null.

There is no direct way to influence the ResultEventFactory logic from inside a flow definition. The mapping shown previously has proven to be sufficient in the majority of cases. The following example illustrates a simple action state calling the imaginary getPersonStatus(id) method of the PersonService:

```
<action-state id="queryPersonStatus">
  <bean-action bean="personService" method="getPersonStatus">
    <method-arguments>
      <argument expression="${flowScope.personId} "/>
    </method-arguments>
  </bean-action>
  <transition on="MINOR" to="processMinor" />
  <transition on="ADULT" to="processAdult" />
  <transition on="ELDERLY" to="processElderly" />
  <transition on="null" to="showProcessingError" />
</action-state>
```

The getPersonStatus(id) returns a PersonStatus enum:

```
public enum PersonStatus {

  MINOR, ADULT, ELDERLY;
}
```

**Note** Notice that this example shows that action states can fulfill a similar *routing* requirement like the decision states discussed in the "Decision States" section.

## Evaluate Actions

Bean actions can invoke any method on a bean defined in a Spring application context. *Evaluate actions* are similar but invoke a method on any object available via the RequestContext. While bean invoking actions invoke the identified method themselves, evaluate actions use OGNL's method invocation capability, as discussed in the "OGNL by Example" section. More generally, evaluate actions can evaluate any OGNL expression against the request context and expose the result to the flow execution.

Evaluate actions are implemented by the EvaluateAction class, a subclass of AbstractAction. Since evaluate actions are normal actions, you can use them anywhere you can use a normal action. Evaluate actions can also be given a name, turning them into *named actions*.

An XML flow definition can define an evaluate action using the <evaluate-action> element. The expression attribute of this element specifies the OGNL expression to evaluate:

```
<evaluate-action expression="flowScope.person.rename( \
  flowScope.person.friend.firstName, \
  flowScope.person.friend.lastName)"/>
```

Note that you don't need to use the ${. . .} delimiters since the value of the expression attribute is assumed to be an expression. Java flow builders can again use one of the overloaded variants of the action(. . .) helper method to add an evaluate action to the flow. The expression(expressionString) method can be used to parse the expression:

```
action(expression("flowScope.person.rename( \
  flowScope.person.friend.firstName, \
  flowScope.person.friend.lastName"));
```

Objects resulting from OGNL expression evaluation can be exposed to the flow using an ActionResultExposer, just like with bean invoking actions. XML flow definitions can configure the ActionResultExposer using the <evaluation-result> element, similar to the <method-result> element used for bean actions (consult the "Action Result Exposers" section for more details):

```
<evaluate-action expression="flowScope.person.sayHello()">
  <evaluation-result name="helloMessage" scope="flow"/>
</evaluate-action>
```

This will put the message returned by the sayHello() method into flow scope, keyed as helloMessage. If you do not explicitly specify the scope, request scope will be used. Java flow builders can use the result(resultName, resultScope) helper method to initialize an ActionResultExposer and pass that into the action(expression, resultExposer) method:

```
action(expression("flowScope.person.sayHello()"),
  result("helloMessage", ScopeType.FLOW));
```

The event returned by the `EvaluateAction` is determined using `ResultEventFactory`, just like in the case of bean invoking actions. Refer to the "Result Event Factories" section for exact details on how expression evaluation results will be mapped to action result events. The mapping detailed in Table 5-3 will be applied to the type of object resulting from expression evaluation.

---

**Tip** Remember that evaluate actions evaluate an expression against the `RequestContext`.

---

Evaluate actions are deceptively simple. Using them to invoke methods on stateful beans stored in one of the flow execution scopes provides an object-oriented, stateful programming model for web applications. Instead of storing only data in the flow execution scopes, and manipulating that data using actions, you can now put real *objects* into the flow execution scopes, combining data and behavior. A flow can trigger the behavior of such stateful objects using an evaluate action. This leads to a much more object-oriented style of programming web applications.

### Flow Variables

When using evaluate actions, objects that you invoke methods on need to be available through the `RequestContext`, typically in one of the flow execution scopes. You could use a normal `Action` to initialize such an object, but Spring Web Flow offers a more explicit approach: flow variables.

*Flow variables*, implemented as subclasses of the `FlowVariable` class, will be initialized when a flow session starts. They are essentially factories for the initial value of the variable, as returned by the `createVariableValue(context)` hook method. Two concrete `FlowVariable` implementations are provided, and they are shown in Figure 5-2.

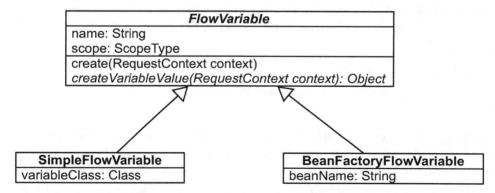

**Figure 5-2.** *Flow variable class diagram*

SimpleFlowVariable will instantiate a configured class using the default constructor each time createVariableValue(context) is called (for instance, when a new flow session is spawned). A BeanFactoryFlowVariable will look up a *prototype* bean using a configured ID in a Spring BeanFactory, typically the application context containing the flow definition. The identified bean must be configured as a prototype bean. This is enforced to avoid threading-related issues, as there might be multiple concurrent flow sessions for a flow definition defining a flow variable.

An XML flow definition can define a flow variable using the <var> element. The name attribute of this element is required and specifies the name used to index the variable value in the configured scope (if no scope is explicitly specified, flow scope is assumed by default):

```
<var name="person" scope="conversation"/>
```

This defines a BeanFactoryFlowVariable, where the bean ID defaults to the variable name. You can also explicitly specify the bean ID using the bean attribute:

```
<var name="person" bean="initialPerson" scope="conversation"/>
```

Defining SimpleFlowVariable is done using the class attribute instead of the bean attribute. The value of the class attribute is the fully qualified class name of the class to instantiate.

```
<var name="person" class="com.ervacon.sample.Person"
  scope="conversation"/>
```

---

**Caution**  Specifying both a bean and class attribute results in a BeanFactoryFlowVariable instance.

---

Since flow variables are an optional part of a flow definition, Java flow builders need to override the buildVariables() method. The AbstractFlowBuilder superclass of Java flow builders offers no direct support for flow variables. Instead, Java flow builders have to directly instantiate flow variables and add them to the flow under construction, available using getFlow():

```
public void buildVariables() throws FlowBuilderException {
  getFlow().addVariable(new BeanFactoryFlowVariable(
      "person", "initialPerson",
      getFlowServiceLocator().getBeanFactory(), ScopeType.CONVERSATION));
  getFlow().addVariable(new SimpleFlowVariable(
      "person", Person.class, ScopeType.CONVERSATION));
}
```

Notice how the bean factory containing the flow definition can be retrieved using `getFlowServiceLocator().getBeanFactory()`. Because Java flow builders directly instantiate the flow variable, they are not limited to using `SimpleFlowVariable` and `BeanFactoryFlowVariable`. You can also directly subclass `FlowVariable` and use your own implementation.

### Accessing Scoped Beans

Spring 2 introduced the concept of bean *scopes*. In previous versions of the Spring Framework, beans could only be singletons or prototypes. Spring 2 also supports web-application–related scopes like request, session, and global session. A bean declared to be in session scope will live in the HTTP session:

```
<bean id="person" class="com.ervacon.sample.Person" scope="session"/>
```

To be able to use Spring 2's web-related scopes, you need to add `ServletRequestListener` to your `web.xml` deployment descriptor (consult the Spring reference documentation for more details):

```
<web-app version="2.4" ...>

  ...

  <listener>
    <listener-class>
      org.springframework.web.context.request.RequestContextListener
    </listener-class>
  </listener>

  ...

</web-app>
```

Since web-scoped beans are normal beans as far as Spring Web Flow is concerned, you can use a bean invoking action to invoke methods on those beans, for instance:

```
<bean-action bean="person" method="sayHello">
  <method-result name="helloMessage" scope="flow"/>
</bean-action>
```

This is roughly equivalent to the following evaluate action:

```
<evaluate-action expression="externalContext.sessionMap.person.sayHello()">
  <evaluation-result name="helloMessage" scope="flow"/>
</evaluate-action>
```

The main difference between the two approaches is that a Spring 2 web-scoped bean will automatically be created the first time it is accessed, while an evaluate action does not do that.

---

**Tip** Using bean invoking actions to invoke methods on Spring 2 web-scoped beans provides an elegant way for a flow to share information with other parts of the application that do not live inside the flow execution, for instance, normal Spring Web MVC `Controller` implementations.

Furthermore, Spring Web Flow 2 enhances the scoping functionality in Spring 2 with support for the flow execution scopes defined by Spring Web Flow.

---

# The Conversion Service

Spring Web Flow type conversion support was already mentioned briefly in the "POJO Method Signatures" section, when talking about passing arguments to POJO methods. Internally, Spring Web Flow uses a powerful and flexible conversion service to do these kinds of type conversions. A *conversion service* is an implementation of the `org.springframework.binding.convert.ConversionService` interface.

By default, Spring Web Flow uses a conversion service containing converters that can convert from string representations to common Java types. Table 5-4 details the conversions that are supported out of the box.

**Table 5-4.** *Default Conversions from Text to Target Type*

| Target Type | Supported String Encodings |
| --- | --- |
| Class | A fully qualified class name (such as `java.lang.Integer`) and a recognized type alias (such as `integer`) are converted into the corresponding `Class` object. Using the `type:` prefix, you can explicitly indicate that the type is referenced by an alias, while the `class:` prefix indicates a fully qualified class name. |
| Number | This translates a number string recognized by the `java.text.NumberFormat` class or understood by the `decode(string)` method of the target type into the corresponding `Number` object. All `Number` subtypes are supported: `Integer`, `Short`, `Byte`, `Long`, `Float`, `Double`, `BigInteger`, and `BigDecimal`. |
| Boolean | Strings true, on, yes, and 1 will result in Boolean true, while false, off, no, and 0 are converted into Boolean false. |
| LabeledEnum | The string representation is assumed to be the label of a `LabeledEnum`, which will be looked up. `LabeledEnum` is compatible with JDK 1.3 and 1.4 and is a precursor to the Java 5 enum provided by the Spring Framework. |

In addition to these common Java types, the default conversion service also supports Spring Web Flow–specific types; for instance, there is a TextToTransitionCriteria converter that converts string representations of transition criteria into TransitionCriteria objects, as discussed in the "Transition Matching Criteria" section. Instead of specifying the target type of a conversion using a fully qualified class name, you can also use any of the recognized type aliases: string, short, integer, int, byte, long, float, double, bigInteger, bigDecimal, boolean, class, and labeledEnum. For instance, the following bean invoking action argument specifications are equivalent:

```
<argument expression="${requestParameters.id} "
  parameter-type="java.lang.Long"/>
<argument expression="${requestParameters.id} " parameter-type="long"/>
```

Implementing your own converters and using them in your flow definitions and executions is also possible. Converters are implementations of the org.springframework. binding.convert.Converter interface shown in Listing 5-5.

**Listing 5-5.** *The Converter Interface*

```
package org.springframework.binding.convert;

public interface Converter {

  public Class[] getSourceClasses();
  public Class[] getTargetClasses();
  public Object convert(Object source, Class targetClass,
    ConversionContext context) throws ConversionException;
}
```

The Converter class hierarchy is shown in Figure 5-3.

Instead of directly implementing the Converter interface, it is better to subclass AbstractConverter and implement the doConvert(source, targetClass, context) method. Converters that need to rely on other converters can subclass ConversionServiceAwareConverter to get access to the conversion service itself.

---

■**Caution**  When implementing converters, keep in mind that a converter needs to be *thread safe*!

---

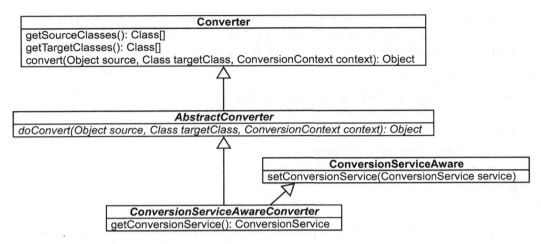

**Figure 5-3.** *Converter class diagram*

Once you have your converters implemented, you need to add them to a custom
ConversionService implementation. The GenericConversionService is a convenient
superclass you can extend. Initially, a GenericConversionService is empty, and you can
add converters to it using the addConverter(converter) method, for instance:

```
public class CustomConversionService extends GenericConversionService {

  public CustomConversionService() {
    addConverter(new TextToBoolean("ja", "nee"));
    addConverter(new PersonToEmployee());
    addDefaultAlias(Person.class); // alias will be "person"
    addAlias("employee", Employee.class);
  }
}
```

Converters are added in the constructor of the custom conversion service. The
example registers a custom configuration of the standard TextToBoolean converter that
recognizes the Dutch translations of "yes" and "no": ja and nee. A completely custom
converter that converts a Person object into an Employee object is also registered, together
with person and employee aliases for the Person and Employee classes.

To make your custom conversion service available for use by flow builders, you have to inject it into the `conversionService` property of the `XmlFlowRegistryFactoryBean` or `AbstractFlowBuilderFlowRegistryFactoryBean`, for instance:

```
<bean id="flowRegistry"
  class="org.springframework.webflow.engine.builder.xml. \
    XmlFlowRegistryFactoryBean">
  <property name="flowLocations" value="WEB-INF/*-flow.xml"/>
  <property name="conversionService">
    <bean class="com.ervacon.sample.CustomConversionService"/>
  </property>
</bean>
```

Configuring the `conversionService` property is only possible using classic Spring bean definitions, so you can't use the `<flow:registry>` convenience configuration element.

When using a custom conversion service, Spring Web Flow will ensure that all default converters are still available to the application, so there is no need to register common converters in your custom conversion service. However, converters registered with the custom conversion service take precedence over Spring Web Flow's default converters, giving you the ability to override the default converters.

---

**Note**   Java flow builders can get direct access to the configured `ConversionService` via the flow service locator: `getFlowServiceLocator().getConversionService()`.

---

# Annotating Flow Definition Artifacts

Another piece of flow definition syntax that needs to be introduced are *attributes* describing flow definition artifacts. Spring Web Flow allows all its core flow definition constructs— `Flow`, `State`, and `Transition` as well as `Action` and `FlowVariable` types, to be annotated with attributes. Attributes associate static metadata with flow definition artifacts, similar to the way Java 5 annotations describe Java syntax elements such as classes and methods. At run time, Java code (for instance, an `Action` implementation) can reason on the values of the attributes and take appropriate action.

---

**Note**   It is important to realize that flow artifact attributes are *static*, defined at flow definition time. Normally, you should not need to manipulate or change attributes at flow execution time. This is in line with the static nature of Java 5 annotations.

---

Without it being highlighted, you already encountered two attributes used to annotate an action: method and name. As explained in the "Implementing Actions" section of Chapter 4, "Spring Web Flow Basics," the method attribute indicates the action execution method to call on a MultiAction, while the name attribute turns an action into a named action. Because the method and name attributes are very commonly used, they have special syntax support in both the XML and Java flow builders.

XML flow definitions can annotate flow definition artifacts with nested <attribute> elements. Each attribute needs a name and a value. Just like in Spring, you can specify the value using either the value attribute or a nested <value> element:

```
<flow>
  <attribute name="requiredRole" value="ADMIN"/>

  ...

  <action-state id="sampleState">
    <action bean="sampleAction">
      <attribute name="props" type="java.util.Properties">
        <value>
          key1=foo
          key2=bar
        </value>
      </attribute>
    </action>
    <transition on="success" to="nextState"/>
  </action-state>

  ...

</flow>
```

Using the type attribute, you can specify a *from text* type conversion, similar to the type conversion supported by bean invoking action method arguments. Just like in the case of the bean invoking action, attribute value type conversion uses the configured ConversionService.

Java flow builders can programmatically annotate flow definition constructs subclassing the AnnotatedObject class, which exposes an attribute map (getAttributeMap()):

```
getFlow().getAttributeMap().put("requiredRole", "ADMIN");
```

Another way to annotate the flow is to override the flowAttributes() hook method:

```
protected AttributeMap flowAttributes() {
  return new LocalAttributeMap("requiredRole", "ADMIN");
}
```

Actions can be annotated using the `annotate(action)` convenience method:

```
Properties props = new Properties();
props.setProperty("key1", "foo");
props.setProperty("key2", "bar");
addActionState("sampleState",
    annotate(action("sampleAction")).putAttribute("props", props),
    transition(on(success()), to("nextState")));
```

For Java flow builders, attribute type conversion is, of course, not an issue.

It is interesting to notice that the `method` and `name` action attributes can also be specified using normal attributes:

```
<action bean="sampleAction" method="foo"/>
<action bean="sampleAction">
  <attribute name="method" value="foo"/>
</action>
```

The two preceding action definitions are equivalent.

## Handling Exceptions

The "Bean Invoking Actions" section explained that the following bean invoking action is *roughly* equivalent to the `PaymentAction` developed in the previous chapter:

```
<bean-action bean="paymentProcessingEngine" method="submit">
  <method-arguments>
    <argument expression="${flowScope.payment} "/>
  </method-arguments>
</bean-action>
```

Recall the code for the custom `PaymentAction`:

```
protected Event submitPayment(RequestContext context) throws Exception {
  try {
    Payment payment = (Payment)context.getConversationScope().get("payment");
    engine.submit(payment);
    return success();
  }
  catch (PaymentProcessingException ex) {
    return error(ex);
  }
}
```

The difference between the bean invoking action and the PaymentAction is the exception handling. The bean invoking action will let the PaymentProcessingException propagate, while the PaymentAction handles it and signals an error event. How can you handle the PaymentProcessingException and still use a bean invoking action? The answer is to use an exception handler.

Spring Web Flow provides *exception handlers* to handle exceptions that occur in a flow execution. An exception handler is an implementation of the FlowExecutionExceptionHandler interface shown in Listing 5-6.

**Listing 5-6.** *The FlowExecutionExceptionHandler Interface*

```
package org.springframework.webflow.engine;

public interface FlowExecutionExceptionHandler {

  public boolean handles(FlowExecutionException exception);
  public ViewSelection handle(FlowExecutionException exception,
    RequestControlContext context);
}
```

Using the handles(exception) method, an exception handler can indicate whether or not it handles a particular exception. The handle(exception, context) method selects a view used to communicate the exception to the user. If the handle(exception, context) method returns null, other exception handlers will still get a chance to handle the exception. Notice that the handle(exception, context) method receives RequestControlContext, and not a normal RequestContext as you have seen before. The RequestControlContext interface extends the RequestContext interface, adding methods that allow you to *control* the flow execution: executing transitions, spawning subflows, signaling events, and so on.

---

■**Note**  Spring Web Flow will wrap all exceptions that occur in a flow execution inside a FlowExecutionException. The original exception is returned by the getCause() method.

---

Implementing FlowExecutionExceptionHandler is a nontrivial matter. Luckily, you will not have to do that in most cases, since Spring Web Flow provides a TransitionExecutingStateExceptionHandler[1] out of the box. This exception handler will handle an exception by executing a transition, typically moving the flow to a view state that will display the error. The handled FlowExecutionException, and the

---

1. This class should really have been called TransitionExecutingFlowExceptionHandler, a small mistake in Spring Web Flow's API.

underlying root cause of that exception will be added to flash scope and indexed as stateException and rootCauseException, respectively.

---

**Note** Recall that all objects in flash scope need to be serializable. All Java exceptions are implicitly serializable, since the java.lang.Throwable class implements the Serializable interface.

---

Essentially, TransitionExecutingStateExceptionHandler is configured with a table mapping exception types to TargetStateResolvers. Handling an exception is a three-step process:

1. Look up the exception in the mapping table.

2. Create a transition for the mapped TargetStateResolver.

3. Execute that transition, moving the flow to another state.

When looking up exceptions, the TransitionExecutingStateExceptionHandler will not only consider the FlowExecutionException itself but also its cause chain. Furthermore, an exception will also match with a mapping for one of its superclasses, similar to Java catch blocks. For instance, a FlowExecutionException instance wrapping a FileNotFoundException will match with a mapping for IOException, since that is a superclass of FileNotFoundException.

Flow execution exception handlers can be attached to either a flow or a state. When an exception occurs in a flow execution, Spring Web Flow will first try the exception handlers attached to the current state of the flow. If none handles the exception, the exception handlers attached to the flow itself will be tried. If the exception is not handled by any of the available exception handlers, it will be rethrown, interrupting the flow execution.

XML flow builders can attach exception handlers to states or the flow itself by adding corresponding <exception-handler> elements. The bean attribute of this element identifies a FlowExecutionExceptionHandler bean available in the Spring application context defining the flow definition:

```
<flow>

  ...

  <view-state id="showView" view="view">
    <transition on="next" to="nextState" />
    <exception-handler bean="handleFoo"/>
  </view-state>
```

...

```
<exception-handler bean="handleBar"/>
```

...

```
</flow>
```

You can attach any number of exception handlers, to the flow or any of its states. Java flow builders have to override the optional buildExceptionHandlers() hook method to register exception handlers with the flow:

```
public void buildExceptionHandlers() throws FlowBuilderException {
  getFlow().getExceptionHandlerSet().add(
      getFlowServiceLocator().getExceptionHandler("handleBar"));
}
```

Notice how the FlowExecutionExceptionHandler is looked up using getFlowServiceLocator().getExceptionHandler(id). An exception handler can be attached to a state by directly passing it into one of the addStateType(. . .) convenience methods. Alternatively, you can attach exception handlers to a state after it has been added to the flow:

```
State showView = addViewState("showView", null,
    transition(on("next")), to("nextState")));
showView.getExceptionHandlerSet().add(
    getFlowServiceLocator().getExceptionHandler("handleFoo"));
```

Using the <exception-handler> element, you can add custom FlowExecutionExceptionHandler implementations to your flow definition. To make use of the TransitionExecutingStateExceptionHandler easy, Spring Web Flow provides special flow definition syntax. A transition using the on-exception attribute of the <transition> element, instead of the on attribute, will automatically be translated into a TransitionExecutingStateExceptionHandler object:

```
<transition
  on-exception="com.ervacon.springbank.domain.PaymentProcessingException"
  to="showConfirmPayment"/>
```

The value of the on-exception attribute should be either a fully qualified class name or a type alias recognized by the conversion service, as discussed in the section called "The Conversion Service." An on-exception transition defined in a state will attach an exception handler to that state. An on-exception transition defined as a global transition of the flow will be attached to the flow itself.

---

**Note** An on-exception transition can have execution criteria, defined by nested actions, just like any other transition (consult the "Transition Execution Criteria" section of the previous chapter for more details). However, since an on-exception transition is not a transition but an exception handler, the execution criteria will not *guard* the transition. Instead, TransitionExecutingStateExceptionHandler will just execute the actions defined for the transition, without interpreting the outcome of that execution.

---

Using on-exception transitions, we can complete the definition of the submitPayment action state of the "enter payment" flow, now using a bean invoking action:

```
<action-state id="submitPayment">
  <bean-action bean="paymentProcessingEngine" method="submit">
    <method-arguments>
      <argument expression="${flowScope.payment} "/>
    </method-arguments>
  </bean-action>
  <transition on="success" to="end"/>
  <transition
    on-exception="com.ervacon.springbank.domain.PaymentProcessingException"
    to="showConfirmPayment"/>
</action-state>
```

Java flow builders have no direct support for on-exception transitions. You can directly instantiate the TransitionExecutingStateExceptionHandler, however, and attach instances to your states or flow:

```
addActionState("submitPayment",
    action("paymentProcessingEngine",
      method("submit(${flowScope.payment} )")),
    transition(on(success()), to("end")),
    new TransitionExecutingStateExceptionHandler().add(
      PaymentProcessingException.class, "showConfirmPayment"));
```

# View Selections

Selecting a view to be rendered is an important responsibility of a controller in a web MVC framework. Let's revisit Spring Web Flow view selections and study them in more detail. In the last chapter, you saw how a FlowExecution makes (returns) a ViewSelection in response to start(input, context), signalEvent(eventId, context), and refresh (context) calls. View selections identify the view to be rendered and contain the model data needed to render it. Additionally, view selections also specify the *type* of response that should be generated.

View states pause a flow execution, selecting a view that needs to be rendered. Similarly, end states can select a confirmation view, rendered in case they end the entire flow execution. It is the view selection made by a view or end state that is returned to the client calling into the FlowExecution.

Recall the two phases of Spring Web Flow's request processing, as explained in the "Request Life Cycle" section of the previous chapter. The event processing phase processes an event signaled in a flow execution, while the render phase renders the selected view. For view states, these two phases can potentially occur in separate physical requests, particularly when applying the POST-REDIRECT-GET idiom using "always redirect on pause." As explained in the "End States" section, also in the previous chapter, end state confirmation views cannot be rendered after a redirect, forcing the event processing phase and render phase into the same physical request. This two-phase request life cycle has an impact on how view selections are made, as you will see next.

The org.springframework.webflow.execution.ViewSelection class represents a view selection performed by a view state or end state. Instead of making the view selection themselves, these state types delegate to a ViewSelector strategy shown in Listing 5-7.

**Listing 5-7.** *The ViewSelector Interface*

```
package org.springframework.webflow.engine;

public interface ViewSelector {

    public boolean isEntrySelectionRenderable(RequestContext context);
    public ViewSelection makeEntrySelection(RequestContext context);
    public ViewSelection makeRefreshSelection(RequestContext context);
}
```

The makeEntrySelection(context) method is used to make a view selection during the event processing phase, when the view or end state is entered (hence the name). Likewise, makeRefreshSelection(context) will select a view during the render phase, when performing a flow execution refresh. Using isEntrySelectionRenderable(context), you can determine whether or not the view selection made during the event processing phase will actually be rendered; this can, for instance, be the case when always redirect on pause is disabled or in an end state, which cannot be refreshed.

Spring Web Flow recognizes several different types of view selectors out of the box, and you can plug in your own custom implementation. The view selector used by a view or end state is determined by the value of the `view` attribute (or the equivalent in a Java flow builder). Let's look at the possible encodings.

## Empty String

An empty string results in a null view. No view is selected, and the flow is expected to have generated a response directly, for instance, using an action. Null views are useful when you want to programmatically generate the response, for example, streaming HTML from a database. They are also common in subflow end states, when the parent flow will select a view.

Here are a couple of examples:

```
<view-state id="showPdf">
<end-state id="endCancel"/>
```

## viewName

The `viewName` encoding selects the identified application view. The hosting framework will typically resolve this logical view name into a physical view template such as a JSP. All parts of the view name delimited using `${. . .}`, potentially the entire view name, are interpreted as OGNL expressions, evaluated against the `RequestContext`.

The model exposed to the selected view contains all information available in the flow execution scopes, as returned by `RequestContext.getModel()`.

Here are some examples:

```
<view-state id="showEnterPaymentInfo" view="enterPaymentInfo">
<view-state id="showStep" view="step${flowScope.stepNr} ">
<end-state id="end" view="goodbye"/>
<end-state id="end" view="${flowScope.endViewName} "/>
```

## redirect:viewName

This encoding requests that the identified application view is rendered after a client-side redirect, as prescribed by the POST-REDIRECT-GET idiom. In Spring Web Flow terminology, this kind of view selection is called a *flow execution redirect*. Just as with a normal application view, the view name can be expressed as or contain OGNL expressions that are evaluated against the `RequestContext`. Use ${. . .} delimiters to delimit the OGNL expressions.

The `redirect:` prefix is particularly useful when "always redirect on pause" is disabled. It allows you to selectively apply POST-REDIRECT-GET to some of the views rendered by your flow. When using "always redirect on pause," the `redirect:` prefix has no effect, since all views will already be rendered after a redirect. The `redirect:` prefix will also be ignored for a confirmation view rendered by an end state, because end states cannot be refreshed.

Some examples follow:

```
<view-state id="showEnterPaymentInfo"
  view="redirect:enterPaymentInfo">
<view-state id="showStep" view="redirect:step${flowScope.stepNr} ">
```

---

**Tip**  A flow execution redirect issues a client side redirect to a stable URL that refreshes the flow execution. Such a flow execution refresh URL is targeted at the Spring Web Flow flow controller and contains a single request parameter: the unique flow execution key, for instance, `/helloworld/flows.html?_flowExecutionKey=ABCXYZ`.

In some situations, it can be useful to manually generate such a URL to refresh an active flow execution, such as when using AJAX techniques.

---

## externalRedirect:url

This encoding redirects to the specified external URL, outside of the control of Spring Web Flow. The external URL can be specified using an OGNL expression, or it can contain OGNL expressions, delimited using ${. . .}.

Relative URLs, those starting with a backslash (/), are expected to be context relative and will be prepended with the context root of the application. For instance, `externalRedirect:/controller` will cause a redirect to `/context/controller`, assuming `/context` is the context path of the web application.

External redirects are particularly useful to trigger a redirect to a stable external URL after flow completion. In this case, they are used from an end state. An external redirect used in a view state will cause the unique flow execution key to be embedded in the URL as a request parameter named `_flowExecutionKey`. This allows the external system to jump back into the flow execution by constructing an appropriate URL and redirecting to it.

Here are some examples:

```
<view-state id="authenticate"
  view="externalRedirect: \
    http://auth.server.com?credentials=${flowScope.credentials} ">
<end-state id="endAndSearch"
  view="externalRedirect: \
    http://www.google.be/search?q=${flowScope.queryString} "/>
<end-state id="endCancel" view="externalRedirect:/balances/show.html"/>
```

## flowRedirect:flowId?input1=value1&. . .&inputN=valueN

The `flowRedirect:flowId?input1=value1&. . .&inputN=valueN` encoding launches the identified flow after a redirect, in a new request. OGNL expressions can be used to specify the flow ID or any input provided to the launched flow. The input will be delivered to the new flow as URL embedded request parameters.

Not specifying the `flowId` will launch a new flow execution for the flow definition containing the flow redirect (a restart basically).

Flow definition redirects are useful when you want to launch a flow from another flow, for instance to restart a flow on completion. They are mostly used from end states.

Examples follow:

```
<end-state id="endRestart" view="flowRedirect:"/>
<end-state id="endRestartWithOtherPerson"
  view="flowRedirect:?personId=${flowScope.personId} "/>
<end-state id="end" view="flowRedirect:search-flow"/>
<end-state id="end" view="flowRedirect: \
  person-flow?personId=${flowScope.personId} "/>
```

## bean:id

Use `bean:id` to load a custom `ViewSelector` bean from the application context containing the flow definition. The bean is looked up using the specified ID, for example:

```
<end-state id="endCancel" view="bean:cancelViewSelector"/>
```

All of the encodings illustrated in the preceding examples are also supported by the `addViewState(. . .)`, `addEndState(. . .)`, and `viewSelector(viewName)` methods available to Java flow builders.

> **Tip** Confirmation views shown by end states cannot directly benefit from the POST-REDIRECT-GET idiom. The reason is that the flow execution has ended because of the end state and can no longer be refreshed. Using an external redirect or a flow definition redirect in an end state of the flow provides an elegant way to still issue a redirect after flow completion. Redirecting to a stable external URL, or a newly launched flow execution, will make the confirmation view refreshable.

We can now finish up the end state definitions of the `enterPayment-flow`, developed for the "enter payment" use case of the Spring Bank sample application. When the flow finishes successfully in the `end` end state, the flow triggers a redirect to the external `/balances/show.html` URL, passing along a `confirmationMessage` request parameter. As will become clear in Chapter 9, "The Sample Application," this URL maps to a simple Spring MVC controller that presents the balances for all the accounts of the user. The balances overview will give direct feedback on the submitted payment by showing the specified confirmation message and can be safely refreshed:

```
<end-state id="end" view="externalRedirect:/balances/show.html? \
  confirmationMessage=paymentSubmitted">
<end-state id="endCancel" view="externalRedirect:/balances/show.html"/>
```

The same `/balances/show.html` URL is used in the `endCancel` end state, but without the `confirmationMessage` request parameter. The balances overview is a reference point for all payment related functions in the Spring Bank sample application, so jumping back to this page also makes sense when canceling the payment.

## Custom View Selectors

Plugging in a custom `ViewSelector` can be useful if you want to have fine-grained control over the model exposed to the selected view. Notice how a `ViewSelector` implementation has access to the `RequestContext`, allowing it to retrieve required model data and add it to the `ViewSelection`.

There is one important rule to keep in mind when implementing custom `ViewSelector` implementations: view selectors should always select one of the provided `ViewSelection` classes, or subclasses thereof. The reason for this is that Spring Web Flow recognizes these core view selection types and will make sure the hosting framework takes appropriate action. Figure 5-4 details the five core view selection types supported by Spring Web Flow.

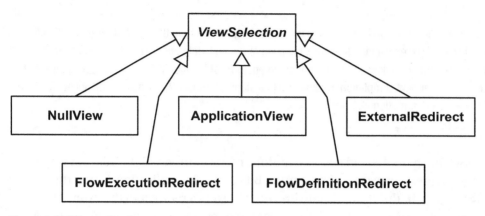

**Figure 5-4.** *View selection types*

# Data Binding and Validation

Among the important functionalities provided by most web application frameworks are data binding and validation. Data binding is the process of mapping incoming request parameters to the model, potentially converting the String request parameters into richly typed objects, such as AccountNumber objects. Validation is the process of verifying the model information after it has been updated by the data binding process, ensuring it is valid and consistent. Data binding and validation are typically the responsibility of the controller in the MVC triad.

As an MVC controller, Spring Web Flow provides advanced data binding and validation support, leveraging the DataBinder machinery provided by the Spring Framework. The Spring DataBinder uses the JavaBean conventions to perform data binding. For instance, an HTML form input field named debitAccount

```
<input type="text" name="debitAccount"/>
```

will bind onto a debitAccount property of the form-backing object, a Payment object in the case of the "enter payment" web flow:

```
public class Payment implements Serializable {

  private Account debitAccount = new Beneficiary();
```

```java
public Account getDebitAccount() {
    return debitAccount;
}

public void setDebitAccount(Account debitAccount) {
    this.debitAccount = debitAccount;
}
}
```

To convert the `String`-valued `debitAccount` request parameter into an `Account` object, the `DataBinder` will use a `java.beans.PropertyEditor`. Property editors typically implement `setAsText(text)` and `getAsText()` methods to do to-string and from-string conversions:

```java
public class AccountNumberEditor extends PropertyEditorSupport {

    public void setAsText(String text) throws IllegalArgumentException {
        setValue(StringUtils.hasText(text) ? new AccountNumber(text) : null);
    }

    public String getAsText() {
        return getValue() == null ? "" : getValue().toString();
    }
}
```

The `DataBinder` will automatically detect property editors located in the same package as the subject class, with a class name having the `Editor` suffix, for instance, `AccountNumberEditor` for `AccountNumber` objects. You can also manually register property editors with a `DataBinder` (which is a `PropertyEditorRegistry`) by implementing a `PropertyEditorRegistrar`:

```java
public class PaymentPropertyEditorRegistrar
    implements PropertyEditorRegistrar {

    private AccountRepository accountRepository;

    public void setAccountRepository(AccountRepository accountRepository) {
        this.accountRepository = accountRepository;
    }
```

```
public void registerCustomEditors(PropertyEditorRegistry registry) {
  registry.registerCustomEditor(Account.class, "debitAccount",
    new PropertyEditorSupport() {
      public void setAsText(String text)
          throws IllegalArgumentException {
        setValue(accountRepository.getAccount(new AccountNumber(text)));
      }
    } );
  }
}
```

The preceding registrar registers a property editor for the debitAccount property of the form-backing object, loading the identified Account object from the repository (database). Out of the box, Spring provides several reusable property editor implementations, such as a CustomDateEditor, which can be configured with a java.text.DateFormat to define the string representation of the dates.

---

■**Note** In Spring Web Flow 1, the DataBinder is not aware of the Spring Web Flow conversion service. As a result, it will not use the converters registered with the conversion service during data binding.

---

Once data binding has completed, the form-backing object can be validated using an org.springframework.validation.Validator implementation:

```
public class PaymentValidator implements Validator {

  public boolean supports(Class clazz) {
    return Payment.class.isAssignableFrom(clazz);
  }

  public void validate(Object obj, Errors errors) {
    Payment payment = (Payment)obj;
    if (payment.getAmount() == null ||
        payment.getAmount().compareTo(new BigDecimal(0)) < 0) {
      errors.rejectValue("amount", "error.invalidPaymentAmount",
        "The payment amount is invalid");
    }
```

```
    ValidationUtils.rejectIfEmpty(errors, "debitAccount.number",
        "error.debitAccountRequired", "The debit account is required");
    ValidationUtils.rejectIfEmpty(errors, "creditAccount.number",
        "error.creditAccountRequired", "The credit account is required");
  }
}
```

The following screen shot below shows the Enter Payment Information page, displaying a validation error generated by the preceding validator:

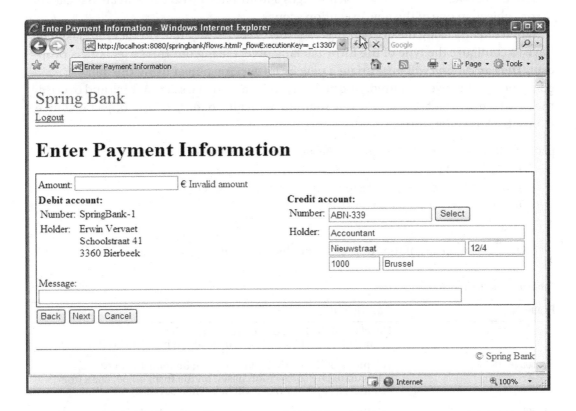

Notice that a Spring Validator is not web specific and can be reused in other parts of the system. During the data binding and validation process, all errors that occur are recorded in an Errors object. This object can be exposed to a view for rendering, for instance, using the Spring form tag library (introduced in Spring 2.x) or the Spring binding tag library.

The Spring DataBinder has support for binding indexed properties on collection types such as arrays, lists, or maps. For instance, a request parameter named map['key'].prop maps to the prop property of the object indexed as key in a map. The map itself is the map property of the form-backing object. Similar logic applies to a parameter named list[3].prop.

## The FormAction

A web flow can easily use the Spring DataBinder machinery with the help of a specialized action: the FormAction. A FormAction manages a form-backing object, and an associated Errors object, in one of the flow execution scopes.

When directly using the org.springframework.webflow.action.FormAction class, you have to configure the type of the form-backing object using the formObjectClass property. The FormAction will instantiate a new form-backing object using the default constructor whenever required. Alternatively, you can subclass FormAction and override the createFormObject(context) hook method, typically loading a form object instance from a backing data store:

```
protected Object createFormObject(RequestContext context)
    throws Exception {
  Long objectId = context.getFlowScope().getLong("objectId");
  return serviceLayer.loadObject(objectId);
}
```

All useful properties of the FormAction are listed in Table 5-5.

**Table 5-5.** *FormAction Properties*

| Property | Description |
|---|---|
| formObjectClass | The class of the form object; required unless createFormObject(context) is overridden in a subclass |
| formObjectName | The name of the form-backing object; defaults to formObject, or is calculated by convention based on the form object class (for instance, a Payment object will be named payment) |
| formObjectScope | The flow execution scope to store the form-backing object in; defaults to flow scope |
| formErrorsScope | The flow execution scope to store the Errors object in; defaults to flash scope |
| propertyEditorRegistrar | PropertyEditorRegistrar used to register custom property editors with the DataBinder |
| validator | Validator implementation to use |

Configuring `FormAction` for use in the `enterPayment-flow` is simple; just set up an appropriate bean definition:

```
<bean id="formAction"
  class="org.springframework.webflow.action.FormAction">
  <property name="formObjectClass"
    value="com.ervacon.springbank.domain.Payment"/>
  <property name="formObjectName" value="payment"/>
  <property name="formObjectScope" value="CONVERSATION"/>
  <property name="formErrorsScope" value="CONVERSATION"/>
  <property name="propertyEditorRegistrar">
    <bean class="com.ervacon.springbank.web.PaymentPropertyEditorRegistrar"
      autowire="byName"/>
  </property>
  <property name="validator">
    <bean class="com.ervacon.springbank.domain.PaymentValidator"/>
  </property>
</bean>
```

A `Payment` object is used as a form-backing object and stored in conversation scope. The associated `Errors` instance is also stored in conversation scope.

---

**Tip** `FormAction` beans are typically specific to a web flow and are preferably defined in the flow local application context. Refer to the "Flow Local Bean Definitions" section in Chapter 4 for more information.

---

When defining the scope of the form-backing object and `Errors` object, you typically want to stick to one of two combinations:

- *The form object in flow scope and the* `Errors` *object in flash scope*: This is the default. Using these settings you will get undo behavior when pressing the Back button; the previous page is redisplayed and all future edits have been undone.

- *Both the form object and* `Errors` *object in conversation scope*: In this case, all the edits to the form-backing object will be maintained, even when pressing the browser's Back button.

Other combinations are, of course, also possible. Unless you have a real requirement for special behavior however, use one of the two combinations mentioned in the preceding list.

---

■**Tip** Give this a try! Configure the FormAction bean used by the "enter payment" flow to use one of the combinations listed in this section, and see how the flow reacts when you click the browser's Back button on the Confirm Payment page.

Recall that you can obtain the completed Spring Bank sample application from the Ervacon Subversion repository available at https://svn.ervacon.com/public/spring/samples/trunk/springbank.

---

## Form-Handling Methods

FormAction is a MultiAction subclass hat defines five action execution methods for handling HTML input forms. Let's take a look at each of these methods:

### setupForm(context)

Before a form can be properly displayed, the DataBinder needs to be initialized, possibly registering custom property editors, and the form-backing object needs to be created or loaded. These tasks are the responsibility of the setupForm(context) action execution method, which always signals the success event.

---

■**Tip** Normally, you should always make the setupForm(context) action a render action of your view state. This ensures that the form handling machinery and form-backing object are properly initialized before the form view is rendered.

---

### bindAndValidate(context)

Bind incoming request parameters to the form-backing object and then validate the form object. Validation is only done when a Validator has been registered with the FormAction using the validator property.

The success event is signaled when binding and validation were successful; otherwise, error is signaled.

### bind(context)

This is similar to bindAndValidate(context), but it performs only data binding, not validation.

It will signal the success event when data binding succeeded or error otherwise (for instance, when there are type conversion problems).

**validate(context)**

Validate the form-backing object using the configured Validator, signaling success or error, depending on the outcome of validation.

---

■**Tip** The bindAndValidate(context), bind(context), and validate(context) actions are best used when linked to a transition of a view state, as *transition execution criteria*, for instance, a submit transition that does bindAndValidate(context). This way, the transition will roll back if the data binding or validation fails, reentering the view state to display the errors. If data binding and validation succeed, the flow moves on to the next state.

---

**resetForm(context)**

Use this to reset the form-backing object, recreating or reloading it. The associated Errors object will also be reinitialized. Always signals the success event.

Using the action methods provided by the FormAction, you can define a view state that does powerful and flexible form handling, typically called a *form state*. The following example shows the complete definition of the showEnterPaymentInfo form state of the enterPayment-flow:

```
<view-state id="showEnterPaymentInfo" view="enterPaymentInfo">
  <render-actions>
    <action bean="formAction" method="setupForm"/>
  </render-actions>
  <transition on="next" to="showConfirmPayment">
    <action bean="formAction" method="bindAndValidate"/>
  </transition>
</view-state>
```

Before the enterPaymentInfo view is rendered, the form-handling machinery will be set up with a call to setupForm(context). Every time the form is submitted along with the next event, data binding and validation will take place with the help of bindAndValidate(context). Notice that the global cancel transition that was added to the flow definition before does not do any data binding or validation. This is exactly what you typically want: canceling the flow shouldn't fail because of validation errors!

Besides the DataBinder initialization and setup of the form-backing object, as done by the setupForm(context) action, there is typically an additional task to execute before a form can be displayed: loading reference data. For instance, consider a form that includes a drop-down with predefined values, loaded from the database. The FormAction has no support for loading reference data. Instead, you can just add an additional render action to your flow to load the reference data, for instance:

```
<render-actions>
  <action bean="formAction" method="setupForm"/>
  <bean-action bean="accountRepository" method="getAccounts">
    <method-arguments>
      <argument expression="externalContext.sessionMap.user.clientId"/>
    </method-arguments>
    <method-result name="accounts"/>
  </bean-action>
</render-actions>
```

This example uses a bean invoking action to load an accounts list from the account repository. Keep in mind that the FormAction is a multiaction, making it possible to add additional action execution methods in a subclass. Such an extra action method could also be used to load reference data.

---

**Note** A flow can potentially deal with multiple different form-backing objects. In this case, just define multiple FormAction implementations and configure them with a different form object name.

---

## Piecemeal Validation

By default, the Validator implementation registered with the FormObject will be used to validate the entire form object. In a flow, you typically want piecemeal validation on intermediate steps and complete validation at the end of the flow.

Spring Web Flow allows piecemeal validation by specifying the validatorMethod attribute of the bindAndValidate(context) or validate(context) actions:

```
<action bean="formAction" method="bindAndValidate">
  <attribute name="validatorMethod" value="validateFirstStep"/>
</action>
```

This will invoke the validateFirstStep(formObject, errors) method on the registered Validator. You can add any number of piecemeal validation methods to the validator, as long as they adhere to the following signature:

```
public void methodName(FormObjectClass formObject, Errors errors);
```

---

■**Note** Notice that the signature of a piecemeal validation method defines a parameter of the class of the form object, not just Object like in the case of the Validator interface. This saves you from doing an extra type cast in each piecemeal validation method.

---

## Subclassing FormAction

If you need to customize input form handling beyond what is possible using the properties of the FormAction, you can subclass FormAction and override one of the defined hook methods—a form of the Template Method design pattern (Gamma et al 1995).

Four hook methods are available; they are explained in the following sections.

### createFormObject(context)

This method was already mentioned previously. The default implementation instantiates the form object class using the default constructor. If you want to load an existing form-backing object, override this method and add the necessary code.

### initBinder(context, binder)

This hook allows advanced configuration of the DataBinder. For instance, using the initDirectFieldAccess() method of the DataBinder, you can have the DataBinder bind directly onto public fields of the form object, instead of requiring property getters and setters.

Another typical example of DataBinder configuration is setting the allowed fields for automatic data binding. This prevents a malicious user from injecting values into your form-backing object by adding request parameters to a request.

### registerPropertyEditors(context, registry)

Overriding this method is an alternative to configuring FormAction with a PropertyEditorRegistrar. You can register any required custom property editors with the DataBinder. The default implementation just delegates to the registered PropertyEditorRegistrar, if any. In general, it is preferred to use a PropertyEditorRegistrar.

---

■**Caution** Do not use the initBinder(context, binder) method to register custom property editors with the data binder. The initBinder(context, binder) method will only be called when a new data binder is created. As a result, property editors registered in this method will not be available in all situations. Instead, override registerPropertyEditors(context, registry), or configure the propertyEditorRegistrar property of the FormAction.

---

**validationEnabled(context)**

Use this hook to determine, based on information available in the RequestContext, whether or not validation should occur in the current request. The default implementation always returns true.

This concludes the discussion of the data binding and validation support available in Spring Web Flow. Keep in mind that data binding and validation are not a core part of Spring Web Flow. In some situations, particularly when integrating with JSF, it is better to have the JSF components do basic data binding and validation. FormAction validation support can still prove useful for *cross validation*: ensuring that the combination of selected field values is valid.

Let's now move on to another important topic: reusing flows as subflows.

# Subflows

An important topic still left to cover is modularity. How does Spring Web Flow tackle the modularity concern identified in Chapter 1, "Introducing Spring Web Flow"? Ideally, the framework would make it possible to capture use cases as coarse-grained application modules, having a well-defined input-output contract to allow black box reuse. Spring Web Flow allows exactly this. In Spring Web Flow, a flow definition *is* a reusable module. The enterPayment-flow we have been developing is a coarse-grained representation of the "enter payment" use case in the Spring Bank sample application. You have already seen flows used as top-level modules, launched directly in response to a request targeted at the flow controller and containing a _flowId request parameter. This section will explain how flows can be reused as subflows, from inside other flows.

Here is a useful analogy to keep in mind when discussing subflows: a subflow is similar to a method call in Java, where one method invokes another method, for instance:

```
public void foo() {
  bar();
}
```

As you can see, method foo() calls into method bar(). Similarly, a foo-flow can call into another flow, bar-flow, using a subflow state:

```
<subflow-state id="launchBar" flow="bar-flow">
  <transition on="end" to="someState"/>
</subflow-state>
```

A subflow state is an instantiation of the org.springframework.webflow.engine. SubflowState class, a subclass of TransitionableState. Since a subflow state is transitionable, it can contain any number of transition definitions. These transitions will fire when they match an event signaled on subflow completion. Just like any other flow, a subflow will end when it enters an end state, for instance:

```
<end-state id="end"/>
```

The ID of the end state, end in this case, will be signaled as an event in the subflow state of the parent flow that launched the subflow. In the example, the on="end" transition will fire when the bar-flow terminates by entering an end state with the ID end. Recall that a flow can have any number of end states. By defining appropriate transitions, a parent flow can react differently to each possible subflow outcome.

---

**Note** In the "End States" section of the previous chapter, you learned about end states and the fact that they can have a view attribute to identify a confirmation view. I explained that the confirmation view will only be rendered when the flow is running as a top-level flow, terminating the entire flow execution when entering the end state. If the flow is running as a subflow of another flow, the flow execution will continue in the parent flow, making that parent flow responsible for view selection. You can now see how the parent flow can fulfill this responsibility, by transitioning to an appropriate view state.

---

XML flow definitions use the <subflow-state> element to define a subflow state, identifying the subflow to spawn using the flow attribute. This was already illustrated previously. Java flow builders can use any of the available addSubflowState(. . .) helper methods, loading the subflow using the flow(id) method:

```
addSubflowState("launchBar", flow("bar-flow"), null,
    transition(on("end"), to("someState")));
```

The null argument passed into the method is the attribute mapper to use (none in this case), which will be discussed shortly.

---

**Note** Just like any other transitionable state type, subflow states can have entry and exit actions, as well as exception handlers.

---

## Inline Flows

The flow definition for a subflow launched by a parent flow needs to reside in the same flow definition registry as the parent flow, or in a parent registry of that registry. Refer to the "Flow Definition Registries" section of the previous chapter for more details. Using inline flows, you can limit the visibility of a flow definition to a single parent flow, similar to a private inner class in Java. This can be useful if you want to break up a large flow definition but don't want to make the pieces available as normal flow definitions. Recall that the flow definition registry associates an ID with a flow. For inline flows, this is the responsibility of the parent flow defining the inline flows. A flow can have any number of inline flows, but those inline flows are only available to the parent flow defining them. XML flow definitions can use the `<inline-flow>` element to define an inline flow and give it an `id`:

```
<flow>

  ...

  <inline-flow id="bar-flow">
    <flow>
      ...
    </flow>
  </inline-flow>
</flow>
```

Java flow builders have to override the optional `buildInlineFlows()` method, programmatically adding inline `Flows` to the parent flow:

```
public void buildInlineFlows() throws FlowBuilderException {
  BarFlowBuilder barFlowBuilder = new BarFlowBuilder();
  barFlowBuilder.setFlowServiceLocator(getFlowServiceLocator());
  Flow flow = new FlowAssembler("bar-flow", barFlowBuilder).assembleFlow();
  getFlow().addInlineFlow(flow);
}
```

There are no direct provisions to build inline flows from a Java flow builder. You'll have to manually assemble the flow using a separate flow builder (refer to the "Flow Builders" section of Chapter 4 for more details). Notice how the preceding code makes the flow service locator of the parent flow builder available to the inline subflow builder.

## Flow Sessions Revisited

Before continuing with the discussion of subflow states, let's revisit the concept of a flow session. The previous chapter, in the "Flow Sessions" section, talked about the relationship between a flow execution and a flow session. A flow execution maintains a stack of flow sessions. When the flow execution starts, a flow session for the root flow definition of the flow execution will be pushed onto the stack. A subflow state will create a new flow

session for the subflow and push it onto the stack. The subflow session will become
ACTIVE, while the parent flow session is SUSPENDED. End states end the active flow session,
popping it off the stack and resuming the parent flow session. If the root session of the
flow execution ends, the entire flow execution terminates. This is illustrated in Figure 5-5.

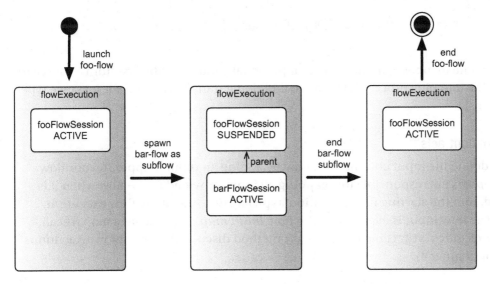

**Figure 5-5.** *The flow session stack*

## Declaring an Input-Output Contract

The bar() method called by the foo() method in the preceding example did not declare
any method parameters, nor did it return a value. Invoking one method from another
becomes much more useful if the caller can pass argument values to the callee and receive
back a return value. The same is true for a parent flow spawning a subflow. In Java, you
can declare the parameters of a method and its return value in the method signature, for
instance:

```
public Object bar(String str, Date date)
```

This signature captures the input-output contract of the method. Along the same lines,
Spring Web Flow allows you to define an input-output contract for a flow.

A flow input-output contract can be defined using *attribute mappers*, implementations
of the org.springframework.binding.mapping.AttributeMapper interface, as shown in
Listing 5-8.

**Listing 5-8.** *The AttributeMapper Interface*

```
package org.springframework.binding.mapping;

public interface AttributeMapper {

  public void map(Object source, Object target, MappingContext context);
}
```

An attribute mapper maps an object (or potentially multiple objects) from a source to a target. The mapping process is free to do additional transformations, for instance type conversions.

### Flow Input Contracts

You can define the input contract of a flow by adding an input mapper to your flow. *Input mappers* are responsible for mapping all input provided to the flow when it is launched, into the starting flow execution, typically into one of the flow execution scopes. The flow input is available in the *flow input map*, a simple Java map (recall the FlowExecution.start(input, context) method discussed in the "Flow Executions" section of Chapter 4).

---

**Tip** When Spring Web Flow launches a new flow execution, all request parameters will automatically be made available as input to the starting flow session. For instance, launching a flow with a request to the /helloworld/flows.html?_flowId=hello-flow&param=value URL, will automatically put the param=value into the hello-flow input map when it launches.

The flow input map and flow output map (discussed shortly) provide a uniform and simple way to exchange data with a flow. This allows the flow to be used unchanged, both as a stand-alone top-level flow and as a subflow nested in another flow.

---

For instance, the equivalent of the str and date parameters declared by the previous example foo(. . .) method would be as follows:

```
<input-mapper>
  <input-attribute name="str" scope="flow" required="true"/>
  <mapping source="date" target="flowScope.date" required="true"/>
</input-mapper>
```

All mappings done by the input mapper are nested inside the <input-mapper> element, a child element of the <flow> element. You have two ways of defining input mappings: <input-attribute> and <mapping>.

### <input-attribute>

The `<input-attribute>` element provides a convenient way to map an object from the flow input map into one of the flow execution scopes. The same key is used to look up the object in the flow input map and index it in the identified flow execution scope (the default is flow scope).

The example maps the `str` object from the flow input map into flow scope. By specifying that the mapping is `required`, an exception will be generated when the `str` object is not available in the flow input map (the default is *not* `required`).

### <mapping>

If you need more flexibility than available with the `<input-attribute>` element, use the general purpose `<mapping>` element. The `source` attribute specifies an OGNL expression to obtain the value to map. This expression will be evaluated against the flow input map. The `target` attribute specifies a settable OGNL expression used to put the value into the flow execution. It is evaluated against the `RequestContext`. The `required` attribute behaves in the same way as for an `<input-attribute>`.

You can specify an arbitrary type conversion using the `from` and `to` attributes:

```
<mapping source="date" target="flowScope.date" required="true"
  from="java.lang.String" to="java.util.Date"/>
```

The type conversion leverages the conversion service, as discussed in the "The Conversion Service" section. The values of the `from` and `to` attributes can be fully qualified class names or type aliases recognized by the conversion service.

A final functionality offered by a generic `<mapping>` is mapping to a collection. This will add the source object to the identified target collection. Use the `target-collection` attribute, instead of the `target` attribute, to accomplish this:

```
<mapping source="id" target-collection="flowScope.idList"/>
```

The value of the `target-collection` attribute is an OGNL expression that will be evaluated against the `RequestContext`.

---

**Note** Remember that flow input mappings map from the flow input map (a normal Java map) to the `RequestContext`.

---

## Flow Output Contracts

Similarly, the output contract for a flow can be defined using an output mapper. *Output mappers* map information available in the flow execution into a *flow output map*, a simple

Java map. All mappings done by an output mapper are nested inside the `<output-mapper>` child element of the `<flow>` element, for instance:

```
<output-mapper>
  <output-attribute name="result"/>
  <mapping source="flowScope.result" target="result"/>
</output-mapper>
```

These two mappings are actually equivalent: they both map the `result` object from flow scope into the flow output map.

The `<output-attribute>` is similar to the `<input-attribute>` discussed previously. It maps an object from one of the flow execution scopes (flow scope by default) to the flow output map. The `scope` and `required` attributes are also supported. The `<mapping>` element is identical to that discussed for input mappings. The only difference is that in this case the `source` expression will be evaluated against the `RequestContext`, while the `target` expression is evaluated against the flow output map.

There is an additional way to specify the output contract for a flow: end states can also have an output mapper, for instance:

```
<end-state id="end" view="endView">
  <output-mapper>
    <output-attribute name="result"/>
  </output-mapper>
</end-state>
```

If a flow has multiple end states, you can provide different output in each case, using end state output mappers. End state output mappings are executed before the global flow output mappings.

---

**Note**   Remember that flow output mappings map from the `RequestContext` to the flow output map (a normal Java map).

---

## What About Java Flow Builders?

The preceding examples detail how you can define a flow input or output mapper in an XML flow definition. Java flow builders have to override the `buildInputMapper()` and `buildOutputMapper()` hooks. Start by creating a `DefaultAttributeMapper` and adding mappings to it. Mappings can be created using the `MappingBuilder` returned by the `mapping()`

helper. A `MappingBuilder` allows you to conveniently construct a `Mapping` object, returned by the `value()` method of the builder. `Mapping` objects implement the `AttributeMapper` interface. Here are a few examples corresponding with the XML examples shown previously:

```
public void buildInputMapper() throws FlowBuilderException {
  DefaultAttributeMapper mapper = new DefaultAttributeMapper();
  mapper.addMapping(
    mapping().source("str").target("flowScope.str").required().value());
  mapper.addMapping(
    mapping().source("date").target("flowScope.date").required().
    from(String.class).to(Date.class).value());
  mapper.addMapping(
    mapping().source("id").targetCollection("flowScope.idList").value());
  getFlow().setInputMapper(mapper);
}

public void buildOutputMapper() throws FlowBuilderException {
  DefaultAttributeMapper mapper = new DefaultAttributeMapper();
  mapper.addMapping(
    mapping().source("flowScope.result").target("result").value());
  getFlow().setOutputMapper(mapper);
}
```

There are no Java equivalents for the `<input-attribute>` and `<output-attribute>` XML elements.

You can define the output mapper for an end state by directly passing it into the `addEndState(. . .)` method:

```
addEndState("end", "endView",
  mapping().source("flowScope.result").target("result").value());
```

Alternatively, you can set the output mapper of `EndState` after it has been added to the flow.

## Mapping Input and Output Arguments

With the input-output contract of the flow defined, how do you pass input values into a flow, or retrieve output values? This is the responsibility of another mapper, a `FlowAttributeMapper` interface associated with a subflow state (see Listing 5-9).

**Listing 5-9.** *The FlowAttributeMapper Interface*

```
package org.springframework.webflow.engine;

public interface FlowAttributeMapper {

  public MutableAttributeMap createFlowInput(RequestContext context);
  public void mapFlowOutput(AttributeMap flowOutput, RequestContext context);
}
```

The createFlowInput(context) method creates the subflow input map, mapping information from the RequestContext into a newly created attribute map. The mapFlowOutput (flowOutput, context) method exposes the subflow output to the resuming parent flow, by mapping information from the subflow output map back into the RequestContext. The default FlowAttributeMapper implementations internally use AttributeMapper implementations (as discussed in the previous section) to do the mapping.

---

**Note**   Remember that a subflow input mapper maps from the RequestContext to the subflow input map. A subflow output mapper maps from the subflow output map back into the RequestContext.

---

XML flow builders can define the FlowAttributeMapper used by a subflow state using the <attribute-mapper> element. Nested <input-mapper> and <output-mapper> elements define the mappings to execute during createFlowInput(context) and mapFlowOutput (flowOutput, context) respectively. As was explained in the previous section, you can use the <input-attribute> or <output-attribute> convenience elements or the general purpose <mapping> element to define mappings:

```
<subflow-state id="launchBar" flow="bar-flow">
  <attribute-mapper>
    <input-mapper>
      <input-attribute name="str"/>
    </input-mapper>
    <output-mapper>
      <mapping source="result" target="flowScope.str"/>
    </output-mapper>
```

```
</attribute-mapper>
<transition on="end" to="someState"/>
</subflow-state>
```

In the example, the str object available in the parent flow scope will be mapped to the subflow input map, before the subflow launches. On subflow completion, the result object in the subflow output map is mapped back into parent flow scope as str, over-writing the previous value. All of the elements are optional. If you leave out the <attribute-mapper> element, no mapping will be done by the subflow state. Omitting <input-attribute> or <output-attribute> is also allowed. Alternatively, you can refer-ence a custom FlowAttributeMapper bean deployed in the Spring application context containing the flow definition, using the bean attribute:

```
<attribute-mapper bean="customMapper"/>
```

Java flow builders can pass the flow attribute mapper to use directly into the addSubflowState(. . .) helper methods. A custom flow attribute mapper can be obtained using the attributeMapper(id) utility:

```
addSubflowState("launchBar", flow("bar-flow"),
    attributeMapper("customMapper"),
    transition(on("end"), to("someState")));
```

Using the ConfigurableFlowAttributeMapper, Java flow builders can set up a subflow state attribute mapper using Mapping objects created with the help of a MappingBuilder, as discussed in the previous section:

```
ConfigurableFlowAttributeMapper mapper =
  new ConfigurableFlowAttributeMapper();
mapper.addInputMapping(
  mapping().source("flowScope.str").target("str").value());
mapper.addOutputMapping(
  mapping().source("result").target("flowScope.str").value());
addSubflowState("launchBar", flow("bar-flow"), mapper,
    transition(on("end"), to("someState")));
```

---

**■Note**  Keep in mind that the parent flow and subflow have a different flow session in the flow execution. Since flow scope and flash scope are tied to the flow session, the parent flow will have a different flow scope than the subflow. That is why it makes sense to map from parent flow scope to subflow flow scope (passing through the subflow input map along the way), or vice versa.

---

Figure 5-6 summarizes the whole subflow input and output mapping system. The process is as follows:

1. The input mapper of the subflow state launching the subflow maps information available using the `RequestContext` into the subflow input map.

2. The input mapper defined by the subflow maps the data available in the flow input map into the `RequestContext`, typically the subflow session.

3. When the subflow completes, the output mapper of the end state that was entered, and the output mapper defined by the flow itself will get a chance to map all information available using the `RequestContext` into the flow output map.

4. The output mapper of the subflow state that launched the subflow maps data available in the subflow output map back into the `RequestContext`, typically the parent flow session.

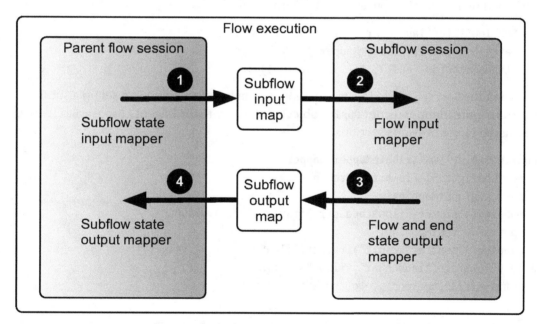

**Figure 5-6.** *Subflow input and output mapping*

■**Note**   Since a parent flow and subflow share the same request scope and conversation scope, mapping from and to the request or conversation scope when launching a subflow or resuming a parent flow is useless. Refer to the "Flow Execution Scopes" section of the previous chapter for more information.

## Enhancing the "Enter Payment" Flow

To make all of this a little bit more tangible, let's enhance enterPayment-flow with a subflow that allows the user to select the beneficiary of the payment. Adding a Select button that signals the selectBeneficiary event to the enterPaymentInfo page will do the trick. A corresponding transition in the showEnterPaymentInfo view state is, of course, also necessary:

```
<view-state id="showEnterPaymentInfo" view="enterPaymentInfo">
  <render-actions>
    <action bean="formAction" method="setupForm"/>
  </render-actions>
  <transition on="next" to="showConfirmPayment">
    <action bean="formAction" method="bindAndValidate"/>
  </transition>
  <transition on="selectBeneficiary" to="launchBeneficiariesFlow">
    <action bean="formAction" method="bind"/>
  </transition>
</view-state>
```

Note how the transition calls the bind(context) action method defined by the FormAction. Doing that will ensure that all data entered by the user is captured before launching the subflow to select a beneficiary. A new launchBeneficiariesFlow subflow state will spawn the beneficiaries-flow:

```
<subflow-state id="launchBeneficiariesFlow" flow="beneficiaries-flow">
  <attribute-mapper>
    <output-mapper>
      <mapping source="beneficiary"
        target="conversationScope.payment.creditAccount"/>
    </output-mapper>
  </attribute-mapper>
  <transition on="endSelected" to="showEnterPaymentInfo"/>
  <transition on="endCancel" to="showEnterPaymentInfo"/>
</subflow-state>
```

The beneficiaries-flow does not declare any input attributes and has only a single output attribute: the selected beneficiary. Using the method calling analogy, spawning the beneficiaries-flow as a subflow is equivalent to invoking the following method:

```
public Account selectBeneficiary()
```

The launchBeneficiariesFlow subflow state adheres to this input-output contract. It does not provide any data as input to the subflow but maps the resulting beneficiary (an Account object) back into the creditAccount property of the payment form-backing object (which is managed by the FormAction, as discussed in the "Data Binding and Validation" section). The beneficiary output attribute is put into the subflow output map using an output mapper in the endSelected end state of the beneficiaries-flow:

```
<end-state id="endSelected">
  <output-mapper>
    <output-attribute name="beneficiary"/>
  </output-mapper>
</end-state>
```

By defining appropriate transitions for the endSelected and endCancel outcomes of the beneficiaries-flow, the parent flow can resume, showing the updated payment information.

---

**Note**  Spring Web Flow 1 does not allow a subflow state output mapper to be linked to a particular transition. For instance, the output mapping defined for the launchBeneficiariesFlow will also be executed when the subflow ended in the endCancel end state. In that case, no beneficiary object will be available in the subflow output map. This does not cause problems, however, because a mapping for which no source object can be found will automatically be skipped, unless the mapping is marked as required.

---

Chapter 9 will discuss the Spring Bank sample application in more detail. This chapter will also elaborate the beneficiaries-flow, showing the complete flow definition of the web flow.

## Flow Start and End Actions

The final pieces of flow definition syntax left to be covered are the flow start and end actions. You have already seen actions used in numerous different places: in action states, associated with a transition, as a view state render action, or as general state entry or exit actions. Actions can also be associated directly with a flow.

Flow *start actions* are executed every time a new flow session for the flow definition starts. Start actions execute after flow variables have been initialized and input mapping has been done. You can use flow start actions to properly initialize the flow execution or execute processing that needs to be done at the start of every flow session.

■**Caution** When implementing flow start actions, keep in mind that the flow session is still STARTING (see Figure 4-8 for details). As a result, some things, such as the current state of the flow session, have not yet been initialized.

Similarly, flow *end actions* execute every time a flow session for the flow definition ends. Flow end actions execute before flow output mapping is done. They can do all types of flow shutdown logic, potentially preparing data for output mapping.

XML flow builders can define flow start and end actions inside the <start-actions> and <end-actions> elements respectively. As always, any type of action can be used:

```
<flow>

  ...

  <start-actions>
    <evaluate-action expression="flowScope.person.initialize()"/>
  </start-actions>

  ...

  <end-actions>
    <action bean="shutdownFlowAction"/>
  </end-actions>

  ...

</flow>
```

A Java flow builder will have to override the optional buildStartActions() and buildEndActions() hooks to define flow start and end actions:

```
public void buildStartActions() throws FlowBuilderException {
  getFlow().getStartActionList().add(
      action(expression("flowScope.person.initialize()")));
}

public void buildEndActions() throws FlowBuilderException {
  getFlow().getEndActionList().add(action("shutdownFlowAction"));
}
```

# The Complete "Enter Payment" Flow Definition

Using many of these flow definition constructs, the complete enterPayment-flow definition now looks like this:

```
<flow>
  <start-state idref="showSelectDebitAccount"/>

  <view-state id="showSelectDebitAccount" view="selectDebitAccount">
    <render-actions>
      <action bean="formAction" method="setupForm"/>
      <bean-action bean="accountRepository" method="getAccounts">
        <method-arguments>
          <argument expression="externalContext.sessionMap.user.clientId"/>
        </method-arguments>
        <method-result name="accounts"/>
      </bean-action>
    </render-actions>
    <transition on="next" to="showEnterPaymentInfo">
      <action bean="formAction" method="bind"/>
    </transition>
  </view-state>

  <view-state id="showEnterPaymentInfo" view="enterPaymentInfo">
    <render-actions>
      <action bean="formAction" method="setupForm"/>
    </render-actions>
    <transition on="next" to="showConfirmPayment">
      <action bean="formAction" method="bindAndValidate"/>
    </transition>
    <transition on="selectBeneficiary" to="launchBeneficiariesFlow">
      <action bean="formAction" method="bind"/>
    </transition>
  </view-state>

  <subflow-state id="launchBeneficiariesFlow" flow="beneficiaries-flow">
    <attribute-mapper>
```

```xml
      <output-mapper>
        <mapping source="beneficiary"
          target="conversationScope.payment.creditAccount"/>
      </output-mapper>
    </attribute-mapper>
    <transition on="endSelected" to="showEnterPaymentInfo"/>
    <transition on="endCancel" to="showEnterPaymentInfo"/>
  </subflow-state>

  <view-state id="showConfirmPayment" view="confirmPayment">
    <transition on="submit" to="submitPayment"/>
  </view-state>

  <action-state id="submitPayment">
    <bean-action bean="paymentProcessingEngine" method="submit">
      <method-arguments>
        <argument expression="${conversationScope.payment} "/>
      </method-arguments>
    </bean-action>
    <transition on="success" to="end"/>
    <transition
      on-exception="com.ervacon.springbank.domain.PaymentProcessingException"
      to="showConfirmPayment"/>
  </action-state>

  <end-state id="end" view="externalRedirect:/balances/show.html? \
    confirmationMessage=paymentSubmitted"/>

  <end-state id="endCancel" view="externalRedirect:/balances/show.html"/>

  <global-transitions>
    <transition on="cancel" to="endCancel"/>
  </global-transitions>

  <import resource="enterPayment-context.xml"/>
</flow>
```

We can incorporate the additional details of the flow definition into the UML state diagram, as illustrated in Figure 5-7.

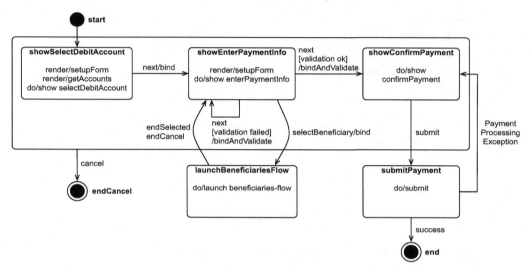

**Figure 5-7.** *Detailed "enter payment" state diagram*

By completing the original UML state diagram from Figure 4-1, we've come full circle.

The enterPayment-flow definition follows the general flow definition template for XML flow definitions, shown in Listing 5-10.

**Listing 5-10.** *XML Flow Definition Template*

```
<flow>
  <attribute>
  <var>
  <input-mapper>
  <start-actions>
  <start-state idref="startStateId"/>

  <!--
    your view, action, end, decision and subflow state definitions
    go here
  -->

  <global-transitions>
  <end-actions>
  <output-mapper>
  <exception-handler>
```

```
<import resource="flowLocalApplicationContext.xml">
<inline-flow>
</flow>
```

A similar template can be defined for Java flow definitions (see Listing 5-11).

**Listing 5-11.** *Java Flow Definition Template*

```java
public class JavaFlowBuilder extends AbstractFlowBuilder {

  protected AttributeMap flowAttributes() { ... }
  public void buildVariables() throws FlowBuilderException { }
  public void buildInputMapper() throws FlowBuilderException { }
  public void buildStartActions() throws FlowBuilderException { }

  public void buildStates() throws FlowBuilderException {
    /*
      add view, action, end, decision and subflow state definitions
      to the flow (available as getFlow())
    */
  }

  public void buildGlobalTransitions() throws FlowBuilderException { }
  public void buildEndActions() throws FlowBuilderException { }
  public void buildOutputMapper() throws FlowBuilderException { }
  public void buildExceptionHandlers() throws FlowBuilderException { }
  public void buildInlineFlows() throws FlowBuilderException { }
}
```

# Summary

In this chapter, we completed the enterPayment-flow, a web flow for the "enter payment" use case of the Spring Bank sample application. Along the way, a number of advanced flow definition constructs were introduced, completing the basic elements explained in the previous chapter.

Spring Web Flow flow definitions can leverage the powerful OGNL expression language in a number of different places: to define transition matching criteria or resolve transition target states, to set attributes in a flow execution scope, and to directly invoke arbitrary methods on a POJO bean. A fourth state type, the decision state, builds on the ability to express conditions using OGNL expressions. Closely linked with Spring Web Flow's OGNL integration is the conversion service, capable of converting an object of one type into an object of another type.

By integrating with the data binder machinery provided by the Spring Framework, Spring Web Flow allows powerful and flexible POJO-based data binding and validation. FormAction, a reusable action implementation, allows you to incorporate data binding and validation into your flow definitions.

A fifth and final state type, the subflow state, makes it possible to reuse a flow definition from inside another flow, as a *subflow*. This essentially turns a flow definition into a reusable, coarse-grained application module. Using input and output mappers, flows can define an input-output contract and pass information to or retrieve information from a spawned subflow.

Finally, this chapter covered a number of other useful flow definition constructs. Using flow execution exception handlers, flows can handle exceptions that occur in a flow execution, typically by firing a transition. Spring Web Flow view selectors give you control over the type of response generated by a flow, while flow start and end actions allow startup and shutdown hooks.

All flow definition constructs offered by Spring Web Flow have now been covered. The next chapter focuses in on flow execution management, detailing the runtime state management options provided by Spring Web Flow.

# CHAPTER 6

■ ■ ■

# Flow Execution Management

**Y**ou now know about all the details of Spring Web Flow's flow definition language, as covered in the previous two chapters. This chapter discusses another important topic—how Spring Web Flow manages all data associated with an ongoing flow execution (conversation).

The Flow Execution Repository subsystem, the Conversation Management subsystem and the Executor layer (as introduced in Chapter 3), will be the subject of this chapter focusing on flow executions and related topics. Recall that the relationship between a flow definition and a flow execution is similar to the relationship between a Java class and an object. A flow definition captures the structure and behavior of a flow execution, and a single flow definition can be many flow executions, each one tracking the execution of the flow definition on behalf of a particular client. This was explained in some detail in the "Flow Executions" section of Chapter 4.

Let's get started by looking at flow execution repositories, the Spring Web Flow component tasked with the management of flow executions.

## Introducing Flow Execution Repositories

Typically, a web flow will define a process spanning multiple requests into the web application. While completing the process, the user interacts with the application through several different pages, accumulating data along the way. The "enter payment" web flow developed in the previous chapters is an excellent example. It is the responsibility of a *flow execution repository* to maintain all data associated with a flow execution in between separate requests participating in that flow execution.

---

**Note** "Flow execution repository," "execution repository," and just "repository," are used interchangeably in the context of Spring Web Flow. The same is true for "flow execution" and "conversation."

---

The flow-execution–related data that needs to be maintained consists of two types of information, both contained in a FlowExecution object:

- *Application data*: Application data can be in any of the flow execution scopes: flash, flow, and conversation. Note that the request scope is not stored, because it is tied to a single request into the flow execution and does not need to be maintained across individual requests.

- *Housekeeping data*: Mostly technical in nature, this data might include the currently active flow session in the flow execution and the current state.

To properly maintain this information throughout the flow execution and across request boundaries, Spring Web Flow will store a flow execution in a repository when one request ends, restoring it on the next request that comes in for that flow execution. Spring Web Flow will identify the flow execution in which a particular request participates by looking at the _flowExecutionKey request parameter.

The FlowExecutionRepository interface captures these core responsibilities, as shown in Listing 6-1.

**Listing 6-1.** *The FlowExecutionRepository Interface*

```
1   package org.springframework.webflow.execution.repository;
2
3   public interface FlowExecutionRepository {
4
5     public FlowExecutionKey generateKey(FlowExecution flowExecution)
6        throws FlowExecutionRepositoryException;
7     public FlowExecutionKey getNextKey(FlowExecution flowExecution,
8        FlowExecutionKey previousKey) throws FlowExecutionRepositoryException;
9     public FlowExecutionKey parseFlowExecutionKey(String encodedKey)
10       throws FlowExecutionRepositoryException;
11
12    public FlowExecutionLock getLock(FlowExecutionKey key)
13       throws FlowExecutionRepositoryException;
14
15    public FlowExecution getFlowExecution(FlowExecutionKey key)
16       throws FlowExecutionRepositoryException;
17    public void putFlowExecution(FlowExecutionKey key,
18       FlowExecution flowExecution) throws FlowExecutionRepositoryException;
19    public void removeFlowExecution(FlowExecutionKey key)
20       throws FlowExecutionRepositoryException;
21  }
```

Here are the important details about Listing 6-1:

- *Line 5*: To adequately manage flow executions, a flow execution repository needs to assign a unique key to each flow execution. Using generateKey(flowExecution), a new FlowExecutionKey will be generated for a freshly launched flow execution. When an existing flow execution, with a key already assigned, needs to be persisted again, getNextKey(flowExecution, previousKey) generates the next key to use. This implies that a new key can be obtained every time a flow execution needs to be stored in a repository, allowing the repository to potentially change the key every time.

  FlowExecutionKey objects can be marshaled into a string form using their toString() method. This string form will be embedded in HTML pages and later travels back to the server using the _flowExecutionKey request parameter. Using parseFlowExecutionKey(encodedKey), you can unmarshal a string form of a flow execution key back into its object form.

- *Line 12*: To make sure all access to a flow execution object occurs in an orderly fashion, a flow execution repository provides a FlowExecutionLock. A flow execution needs to be locked before it is manipulated and unlocked afterward to ensure that all processing done by a flow execution is serialized: the next request is only processed when the previous one completed processing.

- *Line 15*: Finally, the FlowExecutionRepository interface provides methods to store FlowExecution objects in the repository (putFlowExecution(key, flowExecution)), obtain them from the repository (getFlowExecution(key)), or remove them from the repository (removeFlowExecution(key)). Before using any of these methods, the flow execution needs to be locked in the repository.

### MORE ABOUT FLOW EXECUTION KEYS

Notice that a FlowExecutionRepository has complete control over the FlowExecutionKey implementation class that it uses: it is responsible for creating new keys (using generateKey(flowExecution) and getNextKey(flowExecution, previousKey)) as well as parsing existing keys (using parseFlowExecutionKey(encodedKey)).

Also note that the flow execution key of a flow execution is managed *outside* of that flow execution. In theory, a flow execution does not know that it has been assigned a key. As a consequence, Spring Web Flow does not allow you to directly obtain the flow execution key from *inside* the flow execution. It is still possible to obtain the key from the request parameters, however, which are available from the RequestContext:

```
RequestContext context = ...;
String key =
  context.getRequestParameters().get("_flowExecutionKey");
```

As mentioned previously, a request containing a _flowExecutionKey request parameter is assumed to participate in the identified flow execution. If a request comes in that contains a _flowId instead of a _flowExecutionKey request parameter, Spring Web Flow will launch a new flow execution for the identified flow definition. In that case a new FlowExecution needs to be created, instead of loading an existing one from the repository. As was discussed in Chapter 4, creating new FlowExecution objects is the responsibility of a FlowExecutionFactory (see Listing 4-5).

Normally, you will never directly interact with a FlowExecutionFactory or FlowExecutionRepository when working with Spring Web Flow. Instead, a flow executor makes sure flow executions are created and managed properly. Let's take a more detailed look at flow executors.

# Flow Executors

Chapter 3 explained how flow executors act as a high-level facade for Spring Web Flow, shielding users from the details of driving flow executions. To be able to manage a flow execution on behalf of a particular client, a flow executor needs to leverage three key components:

- A FlowDefinitionRegistry instance containing the flow definitions for which flow executions can be started. Flow definition registries were discussed in the "Flow Definition Registries" section of Chapter 4.

- A FlowExecutionFactory instance to create new FlowExecution objects when launching new flow executions. This was discussed in the "Flow Executions" section of Chapter 4.

- A FlowExecutionRepository instance to persist flow executions that outlive a single request and restore them on a subsequent request, as explained previously.

The previous section already mentioned a few rules about how a new flow execution will be launched or resumed. A FlowExecutor implementation formalizes these processes, determining how to *launch* a new flow execution, how to *resume* it, and how to handle a *refresh*. The FlowExecutor interface is shown in Listing 6-2. Spring Web Flow provides a single implementation of this interface: org.springframework.webflow.executor.FlowExecutorImpl.

**Listing 6-2.** *The FlowExecutor Interface*

```
package org.springframework.webflow.executor;

public interface FlowExecutor {
```

```
    public ResponseInstruction launch(String flowDefinitionId,
        ExternalContext context) throws FlowException;
    public ResponseInstruction resume(String flowExecutionKey, String eventId,
        ExternalContext context) throws FlowException;
    public ResponseInstruction refresh(String flowExecutionKey,
        ExternalContext context) throws FlowException;
}
```

Notice that the FlowExecutor interface directly relates to the FlowExecution interface (see Listing 4-6). This makes sense since a flow executor manages and drives a flow execution on behalf of a client. A call to launch(flowDefinitionId, context) will create a new FlowExecution object using a FlowExecutionFactory and invoke the start(input, context) method on that FlowExecution. Resuming a flow execution using resume(flowExecutionKey, eventId, context) will load the identified FlowExecution from the FlowExecutionRepository, and signal an event in it using signalEvent(eventId, context). Finally, refreshing a flow execution simply loads the identified FlowExecution using the repository and triggers refresh(context).

All of the operations defined by the FlowExecutor interface return a ResponseInstruction object instructing the hosting framework how to issue a response. The ResponseInstruction wraps the ViewSelection made by the FlowExecution, adding the flow execution key and a reference to the FlowExecutionContext.

The processing used by the default FlowExecutor implementation (FlowExecutorImpl) in response to a launch, resume, or refresh request is explained in the following sections. Each operation is detailed using an actual FlowExecutorImpl code fragment.

---

■**Note**  The default FlowExecutor implementation, FlowExecutorImpl, is not used when Spring Web Flow is integrated with JSF. In that case, a special JSF flow executor is used that takes equivalent actions. This will be further detailed in Chapter 7.

---

## Launching a Flow Execution

Launching a new flow execution is a straightforward process involving delegating to the flow definition registry, flow execution factory, and repository as appropriate (see Listing 6-3).

**Listing 6-3.** *Flow Executor launch Processing*

```
1   public ResponseInstruction launch(String flowDefinitionId,
2       ExternalContext context) throws FlowException {
3
```

```
4    FlowDefinition flowDefinition =
5      registry.getFlowDefinition(flowDefinitionId);
6    FlowExecution flowExecution =
7      executionFactory.createFlowExecution(flowDefinition);
8    MutableAttributeMap input = createInput(context);
9    ViewSelection selectedView = flowExecution.start(input, context);
10   if (flowExecution.isActive()) {
11     FlowExecutionKey key = executionRepository.generateKey(flowExecution);
12     FlowExecutionLock lock = executionRepository.getLock(key);
13     lock.lock();
14     try {
15       executionRepository.putFlowExecution(key, flowExecution);
16     }
17     finally {
18       lock.unlock();
19     }
20     return new ResponseInstruction(
21       key.toString(), flowExecution, selectedView);
22   }
23   else {
24     return new ResponseInstruction(flowExecution, selectedView);
25   }
26 }
```

The key items to note in Listing 6-3 follow:

- *Line 4*: First of all, the flow executor loads the identified flow definition from the flow definition registry.

- *Line 6*: Next, a new flow execution is created for the loaded flow definition using the flow execution factory.

- *Line 8*: A map containing input for the new flow execution is set up. By default, the FlowExecutorImpl will put all request parameters into the input map. You can change this by configuring the FlowExecutorImpl with an appropriate AttributeMapper using the inputMapper property.

- *Line 9*: Start the flow execution, passing in the input.

- *Line 10*: If the flow execution is still active after having been started, it needs to be stored in the flow execution repository. To do that, the flow executor obtains a flow execution key, locks the flow execution, and puts it in the repository.

  If the flow execution is no longer active, nothing has to be done. This can happen when the flow reached an end state as a result of launching.

- *Line 20*: Generate a response instruction for the selected view. If the flow execution is still active, the flow execution key will be embedded in the response instruction, making sure a next request can use it.

## Resuming a Flow Execution

Similar to launching a flow execution, resuming a flow execution is a straightforward process (see Listing 6-4).

**Listing 6-4.** *Flow Executor resume Processing*

```
1   public ResponseInstruction resume(String flowExecutionKey,
2     String eventId, ExternalContext context) throws FlowException {
3
4     FlowExecutionKey key =
5       executionRepository.parseFlowExecutionKey(flowExecutionKey);
6     FlowExecutionLock lock = executionRepository.getLock(key);
7     lock.lock();
8     try {
9       FlowExecution flowExecution =
10        executionRepository.getFlowExecution(key);
11      ViewSelection selectedView =
12        flowExecution.signalEvent(eventId, context);
13      if (flowExecution.isActive()) {
14        key = executionRepository.getNextKey(flowExecution, key);
15        executionRepository.putFlowExecution(key, flowExecution);
16        return new ResponseInstruction(
17          key.toString(), flowExecution, selectedView);
18      }
```

```
19      else {
20         executionRepository.removeFlowExecution(key);
21         return new ResponseInstruction(flowExecution, selectedView);
22      }
23    }
24    finally {
25      lock.unlock();
26    }
27  }
```

The salient points about resume processing follow:

- *Line 4*: Using the flow execution repository, the flow executor parses the incoming flow execution key string into its object form.

- *Line 6*: The flow executor then locks the flow execution in the repository to make sure no other threads are manipulating it.

- *Line 9*: Next, the flow execution is loaded from the repository.

- *Line 11*: The event is now signaled in the flow execution. As a result, the flow execution makes a view selection.

- *Line 13*: If the flow execution is still active, it's stored in the flow execution repository again. Before doing that, the *next* key will be generated.

- *Line 16*: If the flow execution is no longer active (it has reached an end state), it's removed from the repository. This cleans up all associated resources.

- *Line 20*: Finally, a response instruction is issued for the selected view.

## Refreshing a Flow Execution

Refreshing a flow execution is the simplest process supported by the flow executor (see Listing 6-5).

**Listing 6-5.** *Flow Executor refresh Processing*

```
1  public ResponseInstruction refresh(String flowExecutionKey,
2    ExternalContext context) throws FlowException {
3
4    FlowExecutionKey key =
5       executionRepository.parseFlowExecutionKey(flowExecutionKey);
```

```
 6     FlowExecutionLock lock = executionRepository.getLock(key);
 7     lock.lock();
 8     try {
 9       FlowExecution flowExecution =
10         executionRepository.getFlowExecution(key);
11       ViewSelection selectedView = flowExecution.refresh(context);
12       executionRepository.putFlowExecution(key, flowExecution);
13       return new ResponseInstruction(
14         key.toString(), flowExecution, selectedView);
15     }
16     finally {
17       lock.unlock();
18     }
19 }
```

Key details from Listing 6-5 follow:

- *Line 4*: Just like in the case of a resume request, the flow executor starts by parsing the flow execution key string into its object form.

- *Line 6*: The flow executor then locks the flow execution in the repository.

- *Line 9*: The flow execution is loaded from the repository.

- *Line 11*: A refresh call is done on the flow execution, reconstituting the last view selection.

- *Line 12*: Although a refresh request should be idempotent, not causing any side effects, the flow executor still stores the flow execution in the repository. This ensures that any possible changes made to the flow execution, for instance, by a view state render action, are properly maintained. Notice that, in contrast with a resume request, the next flow execution key is *not* obtained. Instead, the current flow execution key is reused to update the flow execution in the repository.

- *Line 13*: A response instruction is returned for the reissued view selection.

---

**Tip**  In general, try to keep view state render actions free of side effects to application state. It's OK, however, to manipulate data purely intended to support view rendering. For instance, the setupForm(context) operation supported by the FormAction discussed in the previous chapter, sets up a form-backing object and form-handling infrastructure, which are, technically speaking, side effects. However, these side effects do not cause problems when the user tries to refresh the view.

---

## Request Handling

You now understand how a flow executor launches a new flow execution, how it resumes an ongoing flow execution, and the way it handles a flow execution refresh. A question still left unanswered is how Spring Web Flow decides whether a particular request is a launch, resume, or refresh request.

Spring Web Flow's detection and interpretation of the _flowId and _flowExecutionKey request parameters has already been mentioned a few times now. Let's formalize the exact rules in a step-by-step process, detailing how incoming requests are processed:

1. If no _flowExecutionKey request parameter is found, the _flowId request parameter is extracted from the request, and the identified flow is *launched*. If no flow definition ID can be determined, an error will be generated.

2. If the _flowExecutionKey request parameter is available, along with an _eventId request parameter, the identified flow execution is *resumed* by signaling the specified event.

3. If the _flowExecutionKey request parameter is found but the _eventId request parameter is not, the identified flow execution is *refreshed*.

This algorithm is also shown in Figure 6-1.

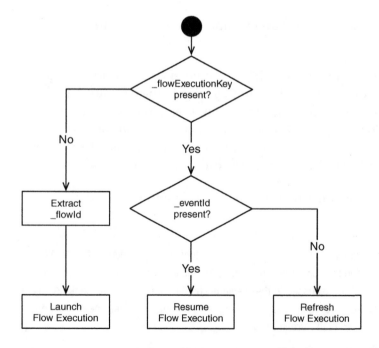

**Figure 6-1.** *Spring Web Flow request-handling flow chart*

The process shown in Figure 6-1 is implemented by the FlowRequestHandler helper class, part of the org.springframework.webflow.executor.support package. The FlowController flow executor front-end that integrates Spring Web Flow into the Spring Web MVC framework uses this helper class. Some of the other hosting framework integrations discussed in the next chapter also delegate to this helper class or implement equivalent processing.

## Configuring a Flow Executor

You have already seen the basic flow executor configuration in previous chapters. Using the Spring Web Flow convenience configuration namespace, a flow executor bean can be defined using the <flow:executor> tag. For instance, the following configuration was used in the "Hello World" example of Chapter 2:

```
1   <?xml version="1.0" encoding="UTF-8"?>
2   <beans xmlns="http://www.springframework.org/schema/beans"
3     xmlns:xsi="http://www.w3.org/2001/XMLSchema-instance"
4     xmlns:flow="http://www.springframework.org/schema/webflow-config"
5     xsi:schemaLocation="
6       http://www.springframework.org/schema/beans
7       http://www.springframework.org/schema/beans/spring-beans-2.5.xsd
8       http://www.springframework.org/schema/webflow-config
9       http://www.springframework.org/schema/webflow-config/ \
10        spring-webflow-config-1.0.xsd">
11
12  <bean name="/flows.html"
13      class="org.springframework.webflow.executor.mvc.FlowController">
14      <property name="flowExecutor" ref="flowExecutor"/>
15  </bean>
16
17  <flow:executor id="flowExecutor"
18    registry-ref="flowRegistry"/>
19
20  <flow:registry id="flowRegistry">
21      <flow:location path="/WEB-INF/hello-flow.xml"/>
22  </flow:registry>
23  </beans>
```

Here are the key things you'll need to know about the preceding listing:

- *Line 4*: The Spring Web Flow configuration schema, `spring-webflow-config-1.0.xsd`, is referenced in the schema declaration and associated with the `flow:` namespace.

- *Line 12*: The `FlowController`, a Spring Web MVC controller implementation that integrates Spring Web Flow into the Spring Web MVC framework, references the flow executor using the `flowExecutor` property. The `FlowController` serves as a *flow executor front-end*. Other front-ends are used when integrating Spring Web Flow into other hosting frameworks. One thing remains constant however: they all delegate to a flow executor to take care of the real work.

- *Line 17*: The flow executor is defined using the `<flow:executor>` tag. This will define a bean of type `FlowExecutor`. Using the `registry-ref` attribute, you can identify the flow definition registry the flow executor should use to load flow definitions. This is the only required configuration attribute.

Of course, you can also define a `FlowExecutor` bean using classic Spring bean definitions. Spring Web Flow provides a special `FlowExecutorFactoryBean` to make this easy. Here is a definition equivalent to the preceding one, but now using nothing but classic Spring bean definitions:

```xml
<?xml version="1.0" encoding="UTF-8"?>
<beans xmlns="http://www.springframework.org/schema/beans"
  xmlns:xsi="http://www.w3.org/2001/XMLSchema-instance"
  xsi:schemaLocation="
    http://www.springframework.org/schema/beans
    http://www.springframework.org/schema/beans/spring-beans-2.5.xsd">

  <bean name="/flows.html"
    class="org.springframework.webflow.executor.mvc.FlowController">
    <property name="flowExecutor" ref="flowExecutor"/>
  </bean>

  <bean id="flowExecutor"
    class="org.springframework.webflow.config.FlowExecutorFactoryBean">
    <property name="definitionLocator" ref="flowRegistry"/>
  </bean>
```

```
<bean id="flowRegistry"
  class="org.springframework.webflow.engine.builder.xml. \
    XmlFlowRegistryFactoryBean">
  <property name="flowLocations" value="/WEB-INF/hello-flow.xml"/>
</bean>
</beans>
```

As in the case of flow definition registries, using direct Spring bean definitions to define a FlowExecutor is a little bit more verbose but also offers more flexibility and power. For instance, you can change the input mapper used by the flow executor to prepare the input map passed to a launching flow execution, as mentioned in the "Launching a Flow Execution" section, by setting the inputMapper property of the FlowExecutorFactoryBean.

### Flow Execution Attributes

A flow executor can assign *execution attributes* to a flow execution when it is launched. These execution attributes are similar to the attributes you can associate with flow definition constructs, such as states or transitions, and can potentially influence the flow execution. They provide static metadata the flow execution can take into account.

One important example of such a flow execution attribute is a flag indicating whether or not to apply "always redirect on pause," as discussed in the "Request Life Cycle" section of Chapter 4. Using the Spring Web Flow configuration schema, you can configure this attribute using the <flow:alwaysRedirectOnPause> element:

```
<flow:executor id="flowExecutor" registry-ref="flowRegistry">
  <flow:execution-attributes>
    <flow:alwaysRedirectOnPause value="false"/>
  </flow:execution-attributes>
</flow:executor>
```

---

**Tip** Remember that "always redirect on pause" is enabled by default. Unless you have clear requirements that force you to disable it, leave it turned on.

Also recall that even if "always redirect on pause" is disabled, you can still trigger a POST-REDIRECT-GET for a particular view state using the redirect: prefix. This was discussed in the "View Selections" section of Chapter 5.

---

Other arbitrary execution attributes for a flow execution can be specified using the `<flow:attribute>` element:

```
<flow:execution-attributes>
  <flow:attribute name="foo" value="bar"/>
</flow:execution-attributes>
```

Of course, you can also specify execution attributes when using the `FlowExecutorFactoryBean` and classic Spring bean definitions:

```
<bean id="flowExecutor"
  class="org.springframework.webflow.config.FlowExecutorFactoryBean">
  <property name="definitionLocator" ref="flowRegistry"/>
  <property name="executionAttributes">
    <map>
      <entry key="alwaysRedirectOnPause" value="false"/>
      <entry key="foo" value="bar"/>
    </map>
  </property>
</bean>
```

The `alwaysRedirectOnPause` flag is the only flow execution attribute Spring Web Flow recognizes out of the box. Specifying custom execution attributes can be useful if you want the flow execution to behave differently depending on the deployment context: just specify different values for the attributes in each flow executor bean definition. The attribute values can then be taken into account by flow artifacts. Here is an example showing an action checking the value of a `foo` attribute:

```
String foo =
  context.getFlowExecutionContext().getAttributes().getString("foo");
if (foo.equals("bar")) {
  // do something
}
```

Notice how flow execution attributes are available from the `FlowExecutionContext`, which can be accessed via the `RequestContext`.

Let's now focus our attention back on flow execution repositories and study the different repository implementations Spring Web Flow provides.

---

■**Note**  Do not confuse the attributes associated with the request context, as returned by the getAttributes() method of the RequestContext, with the flow execution attributes returned by the getAttributes() method of the FlowExecutionContext.

The request context attributes are local to the current request and can be changed using the RequestContext.setAttributes(attributes) method. The flow execution attributes, on the other hand, are statically defined and remain the same throughout the flow execution.

---

# Flow Execution Repositories

The previous sections explained the core responsibilities of a flow execution repository:

- It assigns unique keys to flow executions and manages the relationship between a flow execution and its key, making it possible to look up a flow execution by key.

- It manages the long-term persistence of FlowExecution objects, allowing such objects to be put into storage, obtained from storage, or removed altogether. This is in line with the notion of a repository as defined by the Repository pattern (Evans 2004).

Both responsibilities are, of course, closely related. Spring Web Flow provides three distinct strategies for fulfilling these tasks, translating into three separate FlowExecutionRepository implementations: SimpleFlowExecutionRepository, ContinuationFlowExecutionRepository, and ClientContinuationFlowExecutionRepository. The FlowExecutionRepository class hierarchy is detailed in Figure 6-2.

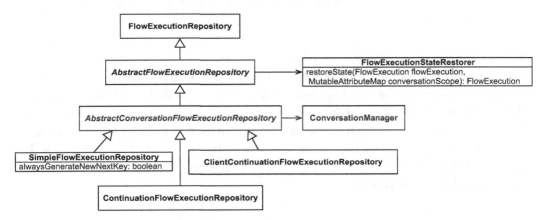

**Figure 6-2.** *Flow execution repository class diagram*

There are several interesting things to note here. First of all, AbstractFlowExecutionRepository implementations use a FlowExecutionStateRestorer to restore a FlowExecution object to its original state when retrieving it from storage. Some of the flow execution repository implementations shipped with Spring Web Flow will serialize a FlowExecution when storing it in the repository. To optimize the serialized size of a FlowExecution object, some parts of it are not serialized, for instance, the referenced flow definitions. Leaving parts out, of course, implies that those parts need to be restored again when the FlowExecution object is reconstructed by the repository. The FlowExecutionStateRestorer interface shown in Listing 6-6 has exactly this responsibility.

**Listing 6-6.** *The FlowExecutionStateRestorer Interface*

```
package org.springframework.webflow.execution.repository.support;

public interface FlowExecutionStateRestorer {

  public FlowExecution restoreState(FlowExecution flowExecution,
    MutableAttributeMap conversationScope);
}
```

---

**Note**  Because some flow execution repository implementations, notably ContinuationFlowExecutionRepository and ClientContinuationFlowExecutionRepository, serialize FlowExecution objects when storing them in the repository, all objects in the flash and flow scopes need to be serializable. Objects in the request scope are not persisted in the repository, so they do not have this constraint. Similarly, objects in the conversation scope do not need to be serializable, because they will be stored outside of the flow execution repository, as reflected in the signature of the restoreState method of the FlowExecutionStateRestorer interface that receives the conversation scope map as an argument.

---

A second interesting thing to notice is the ConversationManager shown in Figure 6-2. All repository implementations shipped with Spring Web Flow subclass AbstractConversationFlowExecutionRepository, so they will all delegate actual storage of the (serialized) FlowExecution data to a ConversationManager service. In other words, the repository implementation provides the algorithm used to put in flow executions, or get executions from the repository, while actually storing the flow execution data is the responsibility of a conversation manager. Let's take a more detailed look at the Conversation Management subsystem.

# Conversation Management

When the Conversation Management subsystem was introduced in Chapter 3, I compared it to the ServletContext, HttpSession, and HttpServletRequest concepts provided by the Servlet (or Portlet) API. The ServletContext provides a way to share objects throughout the entire application. The HttpSession scopes objects at the level of an HTTP session, and the HttpServletRequest is limited to single requests into the application.

Clearly, Spring Web Flow cannot use the HttpServletRequest to store flow execution data: a flow execution typically outlives a single request. However, the ServletContext and HttpSession are too coarse grained. You could have multiple flow executions (conversations) over the course of a single HTTP session for instance. The Conversation Management subsystem provides a system that can manage data attributes at the level of a *conversation*. As mentioned before, all flow execution repository implementations provided by Spring Web Flow use such a conversation manager to persist *conversation-related data*: FlowExecution objects and the contents of conversation scope.

The ConversationManager interface (shown in Listing 6-7) is the central facade of the Conversation Management subsystem. A ConversationManager manages Conversation objects, which are identified by a unique ConversationId.

**Listing 6-7.** *The ConversationManager Interface*

```
package org.springframework.webflow.conversation;

public interface ConversationManager {

  public Conversation beginConversation(ConversationParameters params)
    throws ConversationException;
  public Conversation getConversation(ConversationId id)
    throws ConversationException;
  public ConversationId parseConversationId(String encodedId)
    throws ConversationException;
}
```

Conversations are simple data attribute collections. To ensure orderly manipulation of those attributes, a conversation can be locked and unlocked. At the end of its life, a conversation will end. These key functionalities are captured in the Conversation interface, shown in Listing 6-8.

**Listing 6-8.** *The Conversation Interface*

```
package org.springframework.webflow.conversation;

public interface Conversation {

  public ConversationId getId();
  public void lock();
  public Object getAttribute(Object name);
  public void putAttribute(Object name, Object value);
  public void removeAttribute(Object name);
  public void end();
  public void unlock();
}
```

## The Session-Binding Conversation Manager

Spring Web Flow provides a default ConversationManager implementation out of the box: the SessionBindingConversationManager, which simply manages conversational state in the HttpSession.

Naturally, the SessionBindingConversationManager requires the use of HTTP sessions in the web application. It will automatically create a new HttpSession if it is asked to begin a new conversation and no existing session is available. If the application has already set up an HTTP session, for instance, during a login procedure, the SessionBindingConversationManager will just use the existing session.

By piggy-backing flow execution state on the HTTP session, Spring Web Flow can leverage the advanced HTTP session management options provided by application servers and Servlet engines. For instance, session replication in a cluster will automatically replicate Spring Web Flow flow executions throughout the cluster. Another implication of storing conversational state in the HTTP session is that this state expires when the session expires. Spring Web Flow 1 does not provide flow execution expiry and, instead, just relies on the HTTP session timeout and cleanup facilities provided by the application server.

By default, the SessionBindingConversationManager will allow five concurrent conversations (flow executions) in a single session. Using a first-in-first-out algorithm, it will automatically terminate the oldest conversation when the sixth conversation starts. Putting a limit on the number of concurrent conversations allowed in a single session is important to avoid denial of service attacks, where an attacker tries to launch a large amount of flow executions to exhaust server memory resources. Using the Spring Web

Flow configuration schema, you can easily configure the maximum number of allowed conversations using the maxConversations property:

```
<flow:executor id="flowExecutor" registry-ref="flowRegistry">
  <flow:repository type="continuation" max-conversations="1"/>
</flow:executor>
```

The `<flow:repository>` element gives you fine-grained control over the flow execution repository used by the flow executor and the conversation manager used by that flow execution repository.

---

**Tip** Setting the maximum allowed number of concurrent conversations to one ensures that you can only have a single active conversation per HTTP session. If you launch a new conversation, for instance, from a centralized menu, without terminating the active one, Spring Web Flow will automatically terminate it for you, cleaning up any associated data.

---

### Custom Conversation Managers

The ConversationManager interface is a primary extension point offered by Spring Web Flow. Chapter 11 will describe how you can implement your own conversation manager, storing flow executions in a relational database using JDBC. It is easy to plug in such a custom conversation manager using the conversation-manager-ref attribute of the `<flow:repository>` element:

```
<flow:executor id="flowExecutor" registry-ref="flowRegistry">
  <flow:repository type="continuation" max-conversations="1"
    conversation-manager-ref="conversationManager"/>
</flow:executor>

<bean id="conversationManager" class="my.CustomConversationManager"/>
```

When using the FlowExecutorFactoryBean and classic Spring bean definitions, you can use the maxConversations and conversationManager properties to set up equivalent configurations.

Let's now look at the different repository implementations Spring Web Flow provides. Keep in mind that each of these repository implementations delegates flow execution storage to a ConversationManager. The only difference among them is the algorithm used to manage flow executions.

## The Simple Repository

The simplest `FlowExecutionRepository` implementation shipped with Spring Web Flow is, not surprisingly, called `SimpleFlowExecutionRepository`. It manages a single snapshot of an ongoing flow execution, guarding access to the `FlowExecution` object using the flow execution key. Figure 6-3 illustrates this algorithm.

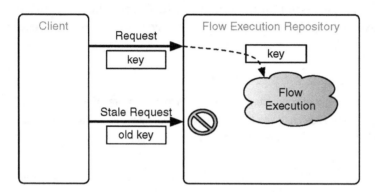

**Figure 6-3.** *The simple repository*

As you can see, this results in a situation very similar to the use of a synchronizer token, as described in Chapter 1 and illustrated in Figure 1-3.

The simple repository guards access to the flow execution by changing the flow execution key for every request. In other words, the `getNextKey(flowExecution, previousKey)` method always returns a new key, different from the previous key. This ensures that a stale request, resulting from the user using the browser navigational aides (for instance, the Back button), can no longer access the flow execution. The end result is that use of the Back button or the browser history is completely disallowed. A user who tries to go back will receive an error stating that doing so is not allowed. The same is true, of course, when the conversation ends (because the flow reached an end state). At that point, Spring Web Flow will clean up all conversational state, preventing a user from resuming the terminated conversation or causing a double submit.

You can configure the flow executor to use the simple repository by specifying `simple` as the repository type on the `<flow:executor>` element:

```
<flow:executor id="flowExecutor" registry-ref="flowRegistry"
  repository-type="simple"/>
```

Alternatively, you can specify the repository type on the `<flow:repository>` element:

```
<flow:executor id="flowExecutor" registry-ref="flowRegistry">
  <flow:repository type="simple"/>
</flow:executor>
```

When using classic Spring bean definitions instead of the Spring Web Flow configuration schema, set the `repositoryType` property to value `SIMPLE`:

```
<bean id="flowExecutor"
  class="org.springframework.webflow.config.FlowExecutorFactoryBean">
  <property name="definitionLocator" ref="flowRegistry"/>
  <property name="repositoryType" value="SIMPLE"/>
</bean>
```

---

**■Tip** It's a good idea to try the different repository implementations for yourself. Change the configuration of the flow executor used in the Spring Bank sample application and experiment to see how the application behaves when using the Back button with any of the repositories Spring Web Flow provides.

---

### Simple Repository Pros and Cons

The most important benefit of using the simple repository is that it only maintains a single copy of the `FlowExecution` data. This results in very low memory requirements, making this repository type ideal for environments where memory resources are scarce or load requirements are very high.

As a downside, the simple repository does not support use of the browser Back button or navigation history and generates an exception if Back button usage is detected. This kind of strict no-Back-button policy enforcement is typically not suited for Internet-facing applications. It can be ideal, however, in intranet settings, where you might be able to deploy a custom browser that can completely disable the browser navigational aides.

---

**■Note** An interesting thing to note about the simple flow execution repository is that it does not serialize the `FlowExecution` object. Instead of really taking a *snapshot*, it just maintains a reference to the actual `FlowExecution` object.

This also implies that flash and flow scope attributes are no longer required to be serializable. I advise sticking to that constraint, however, to make sure you can easily switch from the simple repository to another repository type if requirements change.

---

## The Single Key Repository

The single key repository is a variation on the simple repository. Essentially, the `SimpleFlowExecutionRepository` will be configured to keep the flow execution key constant for the entire flow execution. Instead of changing the flow execution key on every request, as done by the simple repository, the single key repository maintains a single key for every flow execution.

As a result, the single key repository allows use of the Back button. It does not really *support* use of the Back button, however, since it maintains only a single snapshot of the flow execution (just like the simple repository). For instance, in the "enter payment" web flow of the Spring Bank sample application, if you click the Back button on the Confirm Payment page to move back to the Enter Payment Information page and then try to signal the selectBeneficiary event, you will receive an error like the following screenshot shows:

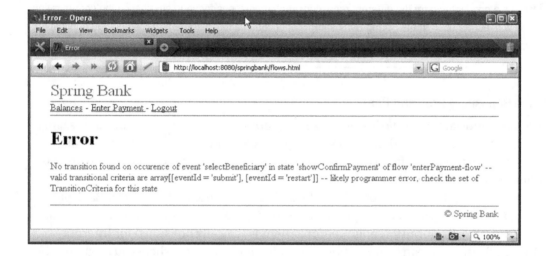

The cause is already hinted at in the error message Spring Web Flow generated. Although you moved back to the Enter Payment Information page by clicking the Back button, the flow execution still thinks you are in the showConfirmPayment state, which does not have a transition matching the selectBeneficiary event.

The single key repository has a trick up its sleeve to work around this problem. When used in combination with "always redirect on pause", all pages of the flow will appear to have been served from exactly the same URL. The reason for this is the redirect Spring Web Flow issues before rendering a view. This redirect causes a flow execution refresh (that is, a *flow execution redirect*). As explained in the "Request Handling" section, a request triggering a flow execution refresh contains a single request parameter: the flow execution key. Since the flow execution key remains constant for the entire flow execution when using the single key repository, all pages of the flow will appear to have been served from a URL like this:

```
http://server/springbank/flows.html?_flowExecutionKey=ABCXYZ
```

The cool thing here is that the browser will not notice that you are actually navigating from one page to another, because every page of the flow has exactly the same URL. The end result is that the browser does not build up a navigation history, making the Back button useless. If you click the Back button, you end up on the last page before the flow execution started!

---

**Caution** Keep in mind that the way the single key repository tricks the browser into thinking all requests are served from the same URL only works when "always redirect on pause" is enabled (which is the default)!

---

Just like all other repository implementations, the single key repository will also remove a flow execution when it ends. This prevents a user from jumping back into a terminated conversation or causing a double submit.

To configure the flow executor to use the single key repository, just specify `singlekey` as repository type (or `SINGLEKEY` when directly using the `FlowExecutorFactoryBean`).

### Single Key Repository Pros and Cons

Just like the simple repository, the single key repository has the important benefit of using very little memory (since it only stores a single flow execution snapshot). This makes it ideal for high-load or low-memory environments.

While the simple repository completely disallows use of the Back button, the single key repository tricks the browser into not accumulating any browsing history *inside* the flow execution. This makes going back in the flow using the Back button impossible. This compromise, unlike the strict rules enforced by the simple repository, is typically acceptable for Internet applications.

# The Continuation Repository

The most powerful flow execution repository provided by Spring Web Flow is the continuation repository, implemented by the ContinuationFlowExecutionRepository class. As the name suggests, the continuation repository manages flow executions using a *web continuations* algorithm. Web continuations are an elegant way to deal with complex navigation in web applications. They allow web applications to respond correctly if the user uses the browser Back button or navigation history or even if the user opens multiple windows on a single conversation. The "Understanding Continuations" sidebar explains continuations in more detail.

### UNDERSTANDING CONTINUATIONS

*Continuations* have their origins in functional programming. Using continuations, functional programming languages can express the control flow of a sequential, imperative program. Functional programs using this technique follow the continuation-passing style. A continuation can be defined as follows (Belapurkar 2004):

> *A continuation is a saved snapshot of the executable state of a program at any given point in time. It is possible to restore this state and restart the execution of the program from that point onward.*

An interesting analogy to help you understand continuations is to think of a save feature in a computer game. Most modern computer games allow you to save the game at any point in time, allowing you to load the saved game again later and continue where you left off. Once you have defeated that horde of monsters, you want to save the game to make sure you don't get killed trying to defeat them again. Instead, you just load up your saved game and continue from a point where they have already been slaughtered.

Although continuations and the continuation-passing style are general programming constructs, one type of continuation usage has proven to be particularly useful in web application development, hence the name "web continuations." Spring Web Flow's continuation repository will use such web continuations to allow the application to behave correctly when the user opens multiple windows on a single flow execution or uses the browser's Back button.

Essentially, the continuation repository will take a snapshot of the FlowExecution object at the end of every request that comes into the flow execution. In other words, the "game" is saved at the end of every request. Each continuation snapshot has a unique ID, which is part of the flow execution key. When a request comes in, Spring Web Flow restores the flow execution from the identified continuation snapshot and continues processing. Figure 6-4 shows this graphically.

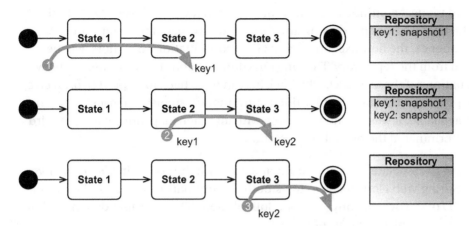

**Figure 6-4.** *Web continuations*

Figure 6-4 illustrates the following scenario:

1. The first request that comes into the flow executor does not contain a flow execution key. As a result, the flow executor launches a new flow execution for this simple three-state flow. The flow progresses from the first state to the second state, a view state, and pauses. Before control is returned to the browser, the flow execution repository takes a snapshot of the FlowExecution and assigns it a unique key. This key is embedded in the rendered view to make sure a next request can submit it again.

   At the end of the first request, the continuation repository contains a flow execution continuation snapshot, snapshot1, indexed by key1.

2. The second request coming into the flow contains key1 as a flow execution key. In response to this request, the flow executor restores the flow execution from the identified continuation, snapshot1. The flow resumes processing, moves to the third state, and pauses. At this point, the flow execution repository takes another snapshot of the FlowExecution and assigns it a new unique key, which is embedded in the rendered view.

   The second request caused a second continuation snapshot, snapshot2, to be stored in the repository, indexed using key2. Notice that the first snapshot is still there. This allows the user to click the Back button, jumping back to the previous request (request two), and continue from that point onward. Opening a new browser window on the same conversation would allow the user to continue from the current snapshot (snapshot2) independently in each window.

3. The third request continues from the continuation identified using key2. In this case, the flow resumes processing and terminates by reaching an end state. As a consequence, the flow execution, and all its continuation snapshots, will be removed from the repository. This prevents double submits, even when using web continuations: if the user clicks the Back button to go back to request two, an error will be produced because the identified continuation snapshot (snapshot2) is no longer available. It was cleaned up along with all other snapshots when the third request terminated the overall conversation.

To be able to associate continuation snapshots with the governing *logical* conversation, Spring Web Flow needs to track both a continuation snapshot ID and the unique ID of the overall conversation. Both of these IDs are embedded in the flow execution key, which consists of two parts:

```
flows.htm?_flowExecutionKey=_c<conversation id>_k<continuation id>
```

4. The conversation ID is prefixed using _c, followed by the continuation ID prefixed with _k. The conversation ID always remains constant throughout a conversation, while the continuation ID changes on every request.

---

■**Note**  No *new* continuation snapshot will be generated for a flow execution refresh. Instead, the snapshot used by the request will be updated. Recall that the flow executor does not generate a new flow execution key and updates the flow execution in the repository when it processes a flow execution refresh (see the "Refreshing a Flow Execution" section for details).

---

The continuation repository is the default repository in Spring Web Flow. You can explicitly configure a flow executor to use the continuation repository by specifying continuation as repository type (or CONTINUATION when using the FlowExecutorFactoryBean). The continuation repository has one additional property that can be configured: the maximum number of continuation snapshots allowed per conversation. Using a first-in-first-out algorithm, the oldest snapshot will be thrown away when a new one needs to be taken and the maximum has been reached. Here is a configuration example:

```
<flow:executor id="flowExecutor" registry-ref="flowRegistry">
 <flow:repository type="continuation" max-continuations="5"/>
</flow:executor>
```

The same configuration using classic Spring bean definitions follows:

```
<bean id="flowExecutor"
  class="org.springframework.webflow.config.FlowExecutorFactoryBean">
  <property name="repositoryType" value="CONTINUATION"/>
  <property name="maxContinuations" value="5"/>
</bean>
```

By default, a maximum of 30 continuation snapshots per conversation are maintained. In practice, this is equivalent with an unlimited number of snapshots, since it allows a user to backtrack 30 steps in the browsing history—more than any normal user would ever do. Constraining the number of continuation snapshots is important to prevent an attacker from doing a denial of service attack by generating a large amount of snapshots.

### Conversation Scope Revisited

The continuation repository takes continuation snapshots of the flow execution by serializing the FlowExecution object and storing the resulting bytes. As explained before, this is the reason why all objects in the flash and flow scopes need to be serializable. Unlike the flash and flow scopes, the conversation scope is not stored *inside* the FlowExecution object (recall the restoreState method of Listing 6-6). As a result, objects in the conversation scope do not need to be serializable, because they will not be part of any snapshot.

---

■ **Caution**  Because the continuation repository takes a snapshot of the flow execution, including all objects in the flash or flow scope, make sure you don't put large objects into these scopes! If you need to store a large object in one of the flow execution scopes, consider the conversation scope as an alternative.

---

The fact that objects in the conversation scope are not part of the continuation snapshots causes them to behave differently from objects in the flash or flow scope when the Back button is used. If an object is stored in the flow scope, for instance, clicking Back will jump back to the version of the object in the previous continuation snapshot, *undoing* any edits since. Modifications done to an object in conversation scope will be *preserved*, since that object is not part of the continuation snapshots. Of course, this also ties in with the form object scope and Errors scope combinations suggested in the "The FormAction" section of Chapter 5.

---

■ **Tip**  Try this with the "enter payment" web flow of the Spring Bank sample application: Change the configuration of the FormAction to store the form backing object and Errors instance in various scopes.

---

### Continuation Repository Pros and Cons

The continuation repository allows you to have completely controlled navigation, while still allowing the user to use all of the browser navigational aides. This promise is a very compelling indeed and is the reason why this is the default repository used by Spring Web Flow.

The most important downside of the continuation repository is the increased memory usage caused by the multiple continuation snapshots that are potentially maintained for each flow execution. By appropriately configuring the maxContinuations property, you can control this, however, making the continuation repository ideal for most web applications.

## The Client Continuation Repository

The last type of flow execution repository provided by Spring Web Flow is the client continuation repository, implemented by the ClientContinuationFlowExecutionRepository class. As the name suggests, the client continuation repository also uses a web-continuations–based approach to flow execution management, similar to the default continuation repository. The difference between the two is in where they store the continuation snapshots. The default continuation repository stores continuation snapshots on the server side, in the HTTP session (using the SessionBindingConversationManager). The client continuation repository stores the continuation snapshots on the client side, avoiding use of any server-side state. To make this possible, the client continuation repository encodes the entire continuation snapshot inside the flow execution key. Here is an example of a hidden field in an HTML form, containing a flow execution key generated by the client continuation repository:

```
<input type="hidden" name="_flowExecutionKey"
  value="_cNoOpConversation id_krOOABXNyAGFvcmcuc3ByaW5nZnJhbWV3b3JrL \
  ndlYmZsb3cuZXhlY3V0aW9uLnJlcG9zaXRvcnkuY29udGludWF0aW9uLlNlcmlhbGl6 \
  lvbi5GbG93RXhlY3V0aW9uQ29udGludWF0aW9ujvgpwtO1430CAAB4cHoAAAQAAAAM- \
  ...
  L3VDqmZZMURBDF7-I73_3g1IND_5AqBLBJQ14z4tUZQRPZFvz_gzBNwW37Z9uff3bRv \
  V1SH-1h7xERqN7--uOTd_Y_VVNH6uJkmYYGLgpLzRWn1XHSxuS5tbgYniCt6hNPkGG3 \
  OxFhQME1Wdb1BOjLVgMeee364-3eNtM_MW9xgp9c3n8v4NL2FNyjEbHcNZxcvqBbj8i \
  7lZtyOSeXy_OXxBYpbwUkAAABeA.."/>
```

The continuation ID is a base-64–encoded, GZIP-compressed form of the serialized FlowExecution object.

To avoid all use of server-side state, the client continuation repository, by default, does not use the SessionBindingConversationManager. Instead it uses a no-op conversation manager that effectively does nothing (note the NoOpConversation id in the example flow execution key shown previously). This has the benefit of not requiring the use of HTTP sessions but also has two important drawbacks:

1. Recall that conversation scope is not contained inside the FlowExecution. Instead, it is stored directly in the conversation managed by the ConversationManager. Since the client continuation repository does not use a real conversation manager, the conversation scope is not maintained across requests.

2. Without the use of a conversation manager, Spring Web Flow has no way of tracking the continuation snapshots associated with a particular conversation. As a consequence, all snapshots cannot be invalidated (or cleaned up) when one of the continuation snapshots causes the flow execution to end. In other words, the client continuation repository does not prevent double submits with its default configuration.

Both of these drawbacks can be alleviated by configuring the client continuation repository with a real conversation manager. For instance, you could configure it with the SessionBindingConversationManager, but that would, of course, mean you again need server-side state and an HTTP session—although much less state needs to be maintained as compared with the default continuation repository, since the continuation snapshots are still stored on the client side.

There is another consequence of using the client continuation repository. The HTTP GET method embeds request parameters inside the query string, which is part of the URL. The maximum overall length of a URL is limited, making it impossible to embed a very long flow execution key inside it. Applications using the client continuation repository are constrained to using only POST requests. POST requests have no limitation on the amount of data they can send to the server.

---

**Caution** When using "always redirect on pause", Spring Web Flow automatically applies the POST-REDIRECT-GET idiom. The redirect causes a GET request that refreshes the flow execution. This GET request contains a single request parameter: the flow execution key. As explained in the "Client Continuation Repository" section, GET requests cannot be used in applications using the client continuation repository, ruling out the use of "always redirect on pause".

---

Configuring a flow executor to use the client continuation repository is again simple. Just specify client as the repository type (or CLIENT in the case of the FlowExecutorFactoryBean). Configuring the client continuation repository with a real conversation manager can be done using the conversation-manager-ref attribute or the conversationManager property, as described earlier in the "Custom Conversation Managers" section.

### Client Continuation Repository Pros and Cons

The client continuation repository is a remarkable specimen. It has the major advantage of not requiring any server-side state. This has important benefits in terms of scalability, failover, and application and server management. Additionally, since this repository uses web continuations, it has complete support for use of the browser's Back button.

There is a high cost to pay however:

- By default, the client continuation repository does not use a real conversation manager. As a consequence, it cannot properly prevent double submits and does not support the conversation scope. These issues can be resolved, however, by plugging in a real ConversationManager.

- Because of the long flow execution key, applications are limited to using POST requests. This also rules out applying the POST-REDIRECT-GET idiom using "always redirect on pause".

- Exchanging a relatively large flow execution key between the client and server on every request consumes quite a bit of bandwidth, potentially making the application slower for users on slow connections.

- Storing state on the client has security implications. An attacker could try to reverse engineer the continuation snapshot, extracting sensitive data or manipulating certain data structures. The ClientContinuationFlowExecutionRepository was designed for extensibility, however, allowing you to plug in continuation snapshot encryption.

The client continuation repository provided by Spring Web Flow is an interesting experiment. Future versions of Spring Web Flow will certainly investigate this idea in more depth, for instance, in trying to manage conversations using state stored in client-side cookies. For now, make sure you understand the consequences of using the client continuation repository before deciding to use it.

## Selecting a Repository

I will complete my explanation of Spring Web Flow's flow execution repositories by giving you a quick overview of the available options. The matrix shown in Figure 6-5 makes it easy to pick the correct repository depending on whether or not you need to support browser Back button usage and on the memory constraints of the deployment environment.

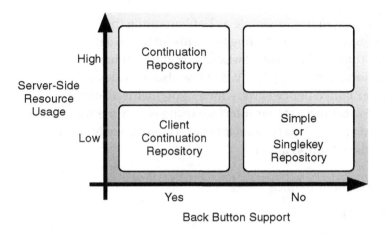

**Figure 6-5.** *Repository selection matrix*

In general, though, most applications are best served using the continuation repository. Since this is the default repository in Spring Web Flow, you don't need to configure anything. Only select a different repository type if you have real requirements or constraints that force you away from the default repository.

# Flow Execution Listeners

As a last flow-execution–related subject, let's look at flow execution listeners. Spring Web Flow allows you to observe the life cycle of a flow execution from application code. You can do this by implementing a FlowExecutionListener and attaching it to a FlowExecution. Flow execution listeners are an example of the classic Observer pattern (Gamma et al 1995). A *flow execution listener* will be notified whenever something interesting happens in the flow execution (or executions) to which it is attached.

Flow execution listeners are useful in many situations. They allow you to modularize behavior separate from the flows to which it will be applied, similar to the way aspect-oriented programming addresses cross-cutting concerns using aspects. For instance, you could use a flow execution listener to apply security constraints to your flows or do audit logging. Chapter 8 will also show how flow execution listeners can help you test your flow executions. A listener that builds a breadcrumb trail will be shown in Chapter 10.

Developing a flow execution listener is as simple as implementing the FlowExecutionListener interface, detailed in Listing 6-9. This interface defines quite a few callback methods that will be invoked when certain things happen in the course of a flow execution life cycle. Spring Web Flow also provides a FlowExecutionListenerAdapter convenience class, which implements all of the methods defined by the FlowExecutionListener interface using empty method bodies. You can subclass FlowExecutionListenerAdapter and override only those methods that are relevant to the situation at hand.

**Listing 6-9.** *The FlowExecutionListener Interface*

```
1   package org.springframework.webflow.execution;
2
3   public interface FlowExecutionListener {
4
5     public void requestSubmitted(RequestContext context);
6     public void requestProcessed(RequestContext context);
7
8     public void sessionStarting(RequestContext context,
9       FlowDefinition definition, MutableAttributeMap input);
10    public void sessionCreated(RequestContext context, FlowSession session);
11    public void sessionStarted(RequestContext context, FlowSession session);
12
13    public void eventSignaled(RequestContext context, Event event);
14
15    public void stateEntering(RequestContext context,
16      StateDefinition state) throws EnterStateVetoException;
17    public void stateEntered(RequestContext context,
18      StateDefinition previousState, StateDefinition state);
19
20    public void paused(RequestContext context,
21      ViewSelection selectedView);
22    public void resumed(RequestContext context);
23
24    public void sessionEnding(RequestContext context,
25      FlowSession session, MutableAttributeMap output);
26    public void sessionEnded(RequestContext context,
27      FlowSession session, AttributeMap output);
28
29    public void exceptionThrown(RequestContext context,
30      FlowExecutionException exception);
31  }
```

Key details about Listing 6-9 follow:

- *Line 5*: The `requestSubmitted(context)` and `requestProcessed(context)` methods mark the beginning and end of a request coming into a flow execution. They are, respectively, the first and last callback called.

  Plugging code into these methods is useful if you want the effects of that code to be applied to all of the processing Spring Web Flow does for a request. This is similar to how a servlet `Filter` can intercept an entire request in the Servlet API.

  Keep in mind that the flow execution might not yet be, or no longer be, active when `requestSubmitted(context)` or `requestProcessed(context)` is called. The `requestSubmitted(context)` call for a request launching a flow execution will find that the flow execution is not yet active. The same is true when `requestProcessed(context)` is called for a request that caused a flow execution to end. You can test whether or not the flow execution is active using `context.getFlowExecutionContext().isActive()`.

- *Line 8*: Three callbacks are defined that are related to the start of a flow session in a flow execution:

  - Using `sessionStarting(context, definition, input)`, Spring Web Flow informs you that the flow execution is going to start a new flow session for the specified flow definition. When this callback is invoked, that flow session has not yet been spawned, so the parent flow session is still active. A listener could veto the start of the new session by throwing a relevant runtime exception. The input map that will be passed to the spawning flow, as prepared by subflow state output mappers or provided externally, is also available as an argument to the callback. This allows a listener to manipulate that input.

  - The `sessionCreated(context, session)` method is called as soon as the new flow session has been created but before it enters the flow start state or executes any other flow startup behavior (for example, start actions). A listener can use this callback to manipulate the flow session before it becomes active and starts processing, for instance, putting objects into flow scope. Using `session.isRoot()`, a listener can find out whether it is the root flow session or a subflow session of the flow execution that is starting.

  - Finally, `sessionStarted(context, session)` is called *after* the new flow session has started processing and entered the start state of the flow. This callback is useful if you want to do something every time a flow session has been spawned successfully.

- *Line 13*: The eventSignaled(context, event) callback is simple. It is invoked every time an event is signaled in the flow execution. The event could be an event signaled by the user or an event signaled internally, for instance, by an action.

- *Line 15*: Two callbacks are provided to observe the flow entering states:

  - The first callback, stateEntering(context, state), indicates that the flow execution is about to enter the given state. Since the state has not yet been entered at this point, the listener can veto that by throwing an EnterStateVetoException.

  - The second callback, stateEntered(context, previousState, state), informs the listener that the flow has successfully transitioned from one state to the next.

---

**Note**  Exceptions thrown by flow execution listeners, for instance, EnterStateVetoException, can be handled by flow execution exception handlers registered at the state or flow level, as explained in the "Handling Exceptions" section of Chapter 5.

---

- *Line 20*: The pause(context, viewSelection) callback will be invoked when a flow execution pauses to render a view in a view state. The listener will be called after the active flow session was effectively paused. The view selection that was made by the view state is also available to the listener. Note that pause(context, viewSelection) will *not* be called if the flow execution terminates in an end state, because the flow session does not pause, but ends at that time.

  Using the resumed(context) callback, Spring Web Flow informs the listener that a paused flow session has been resumed and is now active again.

- *Line 24*: As counterparts to the callbacks for observing the start of a flow session, Spring Web Flow also defines two callbacks that inform a flow execution listener that a flow session will end (or has ended).

  The sessionEnding(context, session, output) method is called when a flow session is going to end because the associated flow reached an end state. When the callback is called, the flow session is still active but has completed all processing. The flow output map, prepared by the flow and end state output mappers, is also available to the listener. This allows the listener to manipulate the output returned to the parent flow (if any).

Once a flow session has completely ended, sessionEnded(context, session, output) is invoked. At this point, the session is no longer active and the flow output map has been finalized (can no longer be manipulated). If there is a parent flow session, it has already been reactivated by this time but has not yet resumed processing.

Using session.isRoot(), a listener can find out whether the entire flow execution, or just a subflow session, has ended.

- *Line 29*: The last callback method defined by the FlowExecutionListener interface is exceptionThrown(context, exception). It will be called whenever an exception occurs during flow execution processing, before the exception is handled using any registered flow exception handlers. Every Exception type will pass through exceptionThrown(context, exception) before being handled and possibly wrapped in a FlowExecutionException.

## Listener Invocation Examples

To better illustrate when the different listener callbacks are invoked, it's useful to look at some examples. The traces in the following examples were produced by a LoggingListener attached to executions of the "enter payment" web flow in the Spring Bank sample application. They show you when the listener callbacks are invoked and what the status of the flow execution and active flow session are at that point in time.

The listener source code is included in the Spring Bank sample application source code.

### Launching the "Enter Payment" Flow

Simply launching the "enter payment" flow in the Spring Bank sample application produces the following output. The first column indicates whether or not the flow execution is active. The second column shows you whether or not the root flow session is active, and the third column displays the status of the active flow session.

```
requestSubmitted [ active = false | root = false | status =          ]
 sessionStarting [ active = false | root = false | status =          ]
  sessionCreated [ active = true  | root = true  | status = Starting ]
   stateEntering [ active = true  | root = true  | status = Starting ]
    stateEntered [ active = true  | root = true  | status = Active   ]
  sessionStarted [ active = true  | root = true  | status = Active   ]
          paused [ active = true  | root = true  | status = Paused   ]
requestProcessed [ active = true  | root = true  | status = Paused   ]
```

```
requestSubmitted [ active = true  | root = true  | status = Paused  ]
        resumed [ active = true  | root = true  | status = Active  ]
         paused [ active = true  | root = true  | status = Paused  ]
requestProcessed [ active = true  | root = true  | status = Paused  ]
```

When the request launching the flow comes in, you see Spring Web Flow starting a new flow session and entering the start state of the enterPayment-flow. Notice that sessionStarted(context, session) is only called *after* the flow start state has been entered. The flow then pauses in the showSelectDebitAccount view state, and request processing finishes.

Because "always redirect on pause" is enabled, a redirect was issued, causing an additional flow execution refresh request. The flow execution refresh simply resumes the flow execution, renders the view, and pauses the flow execution again. This flow execution refresh request is omitted from the traces shown in the following sections.

### Signaling an Event

When you signal the next event by selecting a debit account on the Select Debit Account screen, you see the following trace:

```
requestSubmitted [ active = true  | root = true  | status = Paused  ]
        resumed [ active = true  | root = true  | status = Active  ]
   eventSignaled [ active = true  | root = true  | status = Active  ]
   stateEntering [ active = true  | root = true  | status = Active  ]
    stateEntered [ active = true  | root = true  | status = Active  ]
         paused [ active = true  | root = true  | status = Paused  ]
requestProcessed [ active = true  | root = true  | status = Paused  ]
```

The flow execution resumes and the next event is signaled. This causes the flow to enter the showEnterPaymentInfo view state and pause again.

### Spawning and Ending a Subflow

Clicking the Select button on the Enter Payment Information screen spawns the beneficiaries-flow as a subflow:

```
requestSubmitted [ active = true  | root = true  | status = Paused   ]
        resumed [ active = true  | root = true  | status = Active   ]
   eventSignaled [ active = true  | root = true  | status = Active   ]
   stateEntering [ active = true  | root = true  | status = Active   ]
    stateEntered [ active = true  | root = true  | status = Active   ]
 sessionStarting [ active = true  | root = true  | status = Active   ]
  sessionCreated [ active = true  | root = false | status = Starting ]
   stateEntering [ active = true  | root = false | status = Starting ]
    stateEntered [ active = true  | root = false | status = Active   ]
```

```
      sessionStarted [ active = true  | root = false | status = Active  ]
             paused [ active = true  | root = false | status = Paused  ]
   requestProcessed [ active = true  | root = false | status = Paused  ]
```

You can see the selectBeneficiary event being signaled, causing the enterPayment-flow to enter the launchBeneficiariesFlow subflow state. As a result, a new flow session is created, and the subflow enters its start state: showBeneficiaries. This is a view state, causing the flow execution to pause and render the selected view.

If you now select one of the beneficiaries, the following trace is produced:

```
 requestSubmitted [ active = true  | root = false | status = Paused  ]
          resumed [ active = true  | root = false | status = Active  ]
     eventSignaled [ active = true  | root = false | status = Active  ]
     stateEntering [ active = true  | root = false | status = Active  ]
      stateEntered [ active = true  | root = false | status = Active  ]
     eventSignaled [ active = true  | root = false | status = Active  ]
     stateEntering [ active = true  | root = false | status = Active  ]
      stateEntered [ active = true  | root = false | status = Active  ]
     sessionEnding [ active = true  | root = false | status = Active  ]
      sessionEnded [ active = true  | root = true  | status = Active  ]
     eventSignaled [ active = true  | root = true  | status = Active  ]
     stateEntering [ active = true  | root = true  | status = Active  ]
      stateEntered [ active = true  | root = true  | status = Active  ]
           paused [ active = true  | root = true  | status = Paused  ]
  requestProcessed [ active = true  | root = true  | status = Paused  ]
```

Signaling the select event causes the beneficiaries-flow to enter the loadBeneficiary action state. The bean action executed by that action state automatically signals the success event, moving the flow into the endSelected end state and causing the subflow session to end. The parent flow resumes in the subflow state, where the endSelected event (the ID of the subflow end state) is signaled, transitioning the enterPayment-flow back to the showEnterPaymentInfo view state. The flow execution then pauses again to render the selected view.

## Handling an Exception

If you complete the Enter Payment Information form by filling in a very large amount (for example, 50.000,00 ) and try to submit the payment, you see the following output:

```
 requestSubmitted [ active = true  | root = true  | status = Paused  ]
          resumed [ active = true  | root = true  | status = Active  ]
     eventSignaled [ active = true  | root = true  | status = Active  ]
     stateEntering [ active = true  | root = true  | status = Active  ]
      stateEntered [ active = true  | root = true  | status = Active  ]
```

```
    exceptionThrown [ active = true  | root = true  | status = Active  ]
    stateEntering [ active = true  | root = true  | status = Active  ]
     stateEntered [ active = true  | root = true  | status = Active  ]
           paused [ active = true  | root = true  | status = Paused  ]
 requestProcessed [ active = true  | root = true  | status = Paused  ]
```

The flow execution resumes to process the submit event, moving to the submitPayment action state. In this case, the triggered action does not submit an event, and instead throws a PaymentProcessingException, because the payment amount exceeds the balance of the debit account. As a result, the flow reenters the showConfirmPayment view state and pauses.

## Ending the Flow Execution

Finally, if you change the payment amount to something more realistic and submit the payment, you get the following output:

```
 requestSubmitted [ active = true  | root = true  | status = Paused  ]
          resumed [ active = true  | root = true  | status = Active  ]
     eventSignaled [ active = true  | root = true  | status = Active  ]
    stateEntering [ active = true  | root = true  | status = Active  ]
     stateEntered [ active = true  | root = true  | status = Active  ]
     eventSignaled [ active = true  | root = true  | status = Active  ]
    stateEntering [ active = true  | root = true  | status = Active  ]
     stateEntered [ active = true  | root = true  | status = Active  ]
    sessionEnding [ active = true  | root = true  | status = Active  ]
      sessionEnded [ active = false | root = false | status =        ]
 requestProcessed [ active = false | root = false | status =        ]
```

Signaling the submit event moves the flow the submitPayment action state, which submits the payment and signals the success event. This event causes the flow to transition to the end end state, terminating the entire flow execution (since the root flow session was active).

One thing to notice in this case is that there is no additional request to process a flow execution refresh. This is normal, since end state confirmation views cannot be rendered after a redirect.

## Listener Configuration

How do you attach a flow execution listener to a flow execution? To do that, you need to configure the flow executor to have it attach the listener when a new flow execution is launched. Here is an example taken from the Spring Bank sample application:

```
<flow:executor id="flowExecutor" registry-ref="flowRegistry">
  <flow:execution-listeners>
    <flow:listener ref="loggingListener"/>
  </flow:execution-listeners>
</flow:executor>

<bean id="loggingListener"
  class="com.ervacon.springbank.web.LoggingListener"/>
```

As usual, the listener is configured using a simple Spring bean. The listener bean is then referenced using the `<flow:listener>` element. The preceding configuration will attach the loggingListener to *all* flow executions launched by the flow executor, regardless of the flow definition used. You can use the criteria attribute to specify that the listener should only be attached to flow executions of particular flow definitions:

```
<flow:listener ref="loggingListener" criteria="foo-flow"/>
```

By default, the criteria will be *, meaning that the listener will be attached to all flow executions. You can also specify a comma-separated list of flow IDs:

```
<flow:listener ref="loggingListener"
  criteria="foo-flow,bar-flow"/>
```

---

■**Caution** Keep in mind that a flow execution listener observes a flow execution and not a particular flow session in an execution. In other words, the criteria you specify in the flow executor configuration will only be used to decide whether or not to attach the listener when a new flow execution is launched. For instance, using `criteria="enterPayment-flow"` will attach the listener to all flow executions that have the `enterPayment-flow` as root flow. Once attached, however, the listener will also receive events from the `beneficiaries-flow`, which executes as a subflow of the `enterPayment-flow`, in the same flow execution.

---

If you are using classic Spring bean definitions instead of the Spring Web Flow configuration schema, you need to configure the executionListenerLoader property of the FlowExecutorFactoryBean with a FlowExecutionListenerLoader. FlowExecutionListenerLoader implementations are simple objects that "load" the listeners that need to be attached to executions of a particular flow definition. This is reflected in the FlowExecutionListenerLoader interface in Listing 6-10.

**Listing 6-10.** *The FlowExecutionListenerLoader Interface*

```
package org.springframework.webflow.execution.factory;

public interface FlowExecutionListenerLoader {

  public FlowExecutionListener[] getListeners(FlowDefinition flow);
}
```

You can implement your own FlowExecutionListenerLoader, but Spring Web Flow also provides a ConditionalFlowExecutionListenerLoader out of the box:

```
<bean id="flowExecutor"
  class="org.springframework.webflow.config.FlowExecutorFactoryBean">
  <property name="definitionLocator" ref="flowRegistry"/>
  <property name="executionListenerLoader">
    <bean class="org.springframework.webflow.execution.factory. \
      ConditionalFlowExecutionListenerLoader">
      <property name="listeners">
        <map>
          <entry key-ref="loggingListener" value="foo-flow,bar-flow"/>
        </map>
      </property>
    </bean>
  </property>
</bean>
```

The listeners property of the ConditionalFlowExecutionListenerLoader is set to be a map with FlowExecutionListener objects as keys and loader criteria as values. The loader criteria can be specified using either a string (* for all flow IDs or a comma-separated list of IDs) or a FlowExecutionListenerCriteria object. This last option gives you the possibility to plug in custom criteria, implementing the FlowExecutionListenerCriteria interface shown in Listing 6-11.

**Listing 6-11.** *The FlowExecutionListenerCriteria Interface*

```
package org.springframework.webflow.execution.factory;

public interface FlowExecutionListenerCriteria {

  public boolean appliesTo(FlowDefinition definition);
}
```

If you only want to configure a listener that should apply to all flow executions launched by a flow executor, you can also use the executionListener or executionListeners convenience properties of the FlowExecutorFactoryBean:

```
<bean id="flowExecutor"
  class="org.springframework.webflow.config.FlowExecutorFactoryBean">
  <property name="definitionLocator" ref="flowRegistry"/>
  <property name="executionListener" ref="loggingListener"/>
</bean>
```

This avoids the verbose configuration of the ConditionalFlowExecutionListenerLoader for simple cases.

# Summary

This concludes our considerably detailed discussion of Spring Web Flow's flow execution management.

This chapter started with an introduction to flow execution repositories. These components are tasked with identifying and persisting flow executions in between requests. Flow executors use the services of a flow execution repository, together with a flow execution factory, to drive flow executions for flow definitions loaded from a flow definition registry. I explained the exact processing done by Spring Web Flow's default flow executor implementation when it launches, resumes, or refreshes a flow execution, along with Spring Web Flow's overall request handling.

Spring Web Flow provides four different flow execution repository flavors out of the box. The simple and single key repositories store a single snapshot of an ongoing flow execution, making them resource efficient but unable to properly handle the browser Back button. The continuation repository (Spring Web Flow's default repository) and the client continuation repository use web continuations to deal with Back button issues. They do consume more memory, however, because they need to take a snapshot of the flow execution for every request.

All four flow execution repository implementations shipped with Spring Web Flow delegate the actual storage of conversational state to a conversation manager. By default, Spring Web Flow uses `SessionBindingConversationManager` and stores state in the HTTP session.

This chapter finished off with a discussion of flow execution listeners. Such listeners allow you to observe a flow execution from application code, providing an elegant and flexible extension point.

In the next chapter, you'll learn about integrating Spring Web Flow with several hosting frameworks and driving flow executions from those environments.

# CHAPTER 7

■ ■ ■

# Driving Flow Executions

The previous chapters explained the basic building blocks that make up Spring Web Flow. You learned about flow definitions and how you can use them to define the navigational rules of a use case. Using its advanced execution management system, Spring Web Flow automatically enforces those navigational rules and controls state management and cleanup. A flow executor ties all the building blocks together:

- It loads flow definitions eligible for execution from a flow definition registry.

- It creates executions for those definitions using a flow execution factory, abstracting away the underlying execution engine.

- It persists ongoing flow executions in between individual requests with the help of a flow execution repository.

In essence, a flow executor is a high-level facade for Spring Web Flow. Since Spring Web Flow is not a complete web MVC framework, but instead just a controller component for such a framework, it needs to be integrated into a hosting framework. In practice, this integration makes a flow executor available to the hosting framework. Spring Web Flow 1 integrates with several well-known web MVC frameworks, namely:

- Spring Web MVC

- Spring Portlet MVC

- Struts

- JavaServer Faces (JSF)

---

### INTEGRATION WITH OTHER FRAMEWORKS

This chapter discusses only the host framework integrations that ship with Spring Web Flow. Spring Web Flow has also been integrated with other frameworks, notably Struts 2 and Grails. For more details, consult the documentation of those frameworks.

The Spring Web Flow plug-in that integrates Spring Web Flow into the Apache Struts 2 framework can be found at `http://cwiki.apache.org/S2PLUGINS/spring-webflow-plugin.html`.

Grails, a rapid web application development framework heavily based on the convention-over-configuration concept and the Groovy language, completely encapsulates Spring Web Flow as a flow engine. For instance, Grails provides its own Groovy-based flow definition syntax. By doing that, Grails can offer users a very integrated and consistent development experience, while still leveraging Spring Web Flow's navigational control and state management. For more information about Grails, visit `http://www.grails.org`.

Chapter 11 will illustrate how to build your own integration code, using a `FlowServlet` as an example.

---

Before diving into actual integration details, let's first look at some general topics related to this subject.

# Flow Executor Integration

Code that integrates Spring Web Flow into a particular hosting framework acts as a *front-end* to a flow executor. As such, it needs to fulfill two responsibilities:

- *Extracting flow executor method arguments from the request*: Key arguments here are the flow ID, the flow execution key, and the event to signal.

- *Exposing values such as the flow execution key to the view that will be rendered*: These values are contained in the `ResponseInstruction` returned by the `FlowExecutor`. Making them available to the view ensures that the view can embed those values into later requests.

**Note** Recall that Spring Web Flow will encapsulate a framework-specific request, such as an `HttpServletRequest` in a typical Java web application, inside an `ExternalContext` object. This decouples Spring Web Flow from details specific to the hosting framework or protocols used. Refer to the "Flow Executions" section in Chapter 4 for more details.

Clearly, both responsibilities need to be in sync: values need to be exposed in such a way that they can be extracted again on a subsequent request. To enforce this, Spring Web Flow defines the concept of a `FlowExecutorArgumentHandler`, which combines the responsibilities of a `FlowExecutorArgumentExtractor` and a `FlowExecutorArgumentExposer`, as shown in Figure 7-1. As the name suggests, a `FlowExecutorArgumentHandler` will handle extracting flow executor arguments from the external context and exposing those arguments again later on.

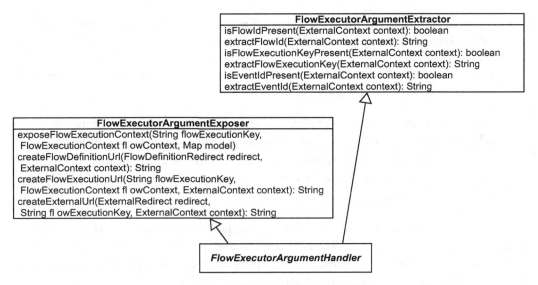

**Figure 7-1.** *FlowExecutorArgumentHandler class diagram*

Spring Web Flow provides three FlowExecutorArgumentHandler implementations out of the box. The default argument handler is the RequestParameterFlowExecutorArgumentHandler, which extracts and exposes flow executor argument values as HTTP request parameters. There is also a RequestPathFlowExecutorArgumentHandler, capable of extracting and exposing flow executor arguments in the request path, giving REST-style URLs. Finally, the FlowIdMappingArgumentHandlerWrapper simply wraps another FlowExecutorArgumentHandler, applying a flow ID mapping along the way (for example, enterPayment is mapped to enterPayment-flow). This mapping allows you to control the flow IDs that are visible in the URLs and pages of your web application. You can, of course, also implement your own FlowExecutorArgumentHandler.

All host framework integrations discussed in the "Host Framework Integrations" section are essentially flow executor front-ends performing the following simple steps:

1. They wrap the incoming request in an ExternalContext implementation, abstracting away framework and protocol details.

2. Using an argument handler, they extract flow executor arguments from the request (which has been wrapped in an ExternalContext).

3. They call into the flow executor, passing in all extracted arguments as well as the ExternalContext object itself.

4. They convert the ResponseInstruction returned by the flow executor into an appropriate response (for example, rendering a view or issuing a redirect) using hosting framework specific techniques. Flow executor arguments for a subsequent request are exposed to the view using the same argument handler used to extract values from the request.

It clearly follows that a flow executor front-end needs three components to function properly: a FlowExecutor, a FlowExecutorArgumentHandler, and an appropriate ExternalContext implementation. You will see this pattern appear again and again in the "Host Framework Integrations" section, which discusses actual integration details.

Before coming to that, let's first take a deeper look at developing views that participate in a web flow. What model data will Spring Web Flow expose to views, and how do you build requests from which Spring Web Flow can extract the necessary values?

# Spring Web Flow View Development

Since Spring Web Flow is essentially a controller component in an MVC framework, it does not dictate the view technology used. Any view technology supported by the hosting framework can be used, for instance, JavaServer Pages (JSP), Velocity (http://velocity.apache.org), or FreeMarker (http://freemarker.sourceforge.net) templates, XSLT style sheets, and so on. However, there are a few common Spring Web Flow–specific things to point out.

## Model Data

As an MVC controller, Spring Web Flow prepares model data that will be rendered by the view it selects. Making the model data available for view rendering is the responsibility of the hosting framework. When using JSP, for instance, the model is typically made available to the view as request attributes. This might be different for other view technologies though. For instance, in the case of XSLT style sheets, the model will need to be turned into an XML document before being transformed.

The model data prepared by Spring Web Flow consists largely of application-specific information supplemented with some extra attributes exposed using the FlowExecutorArgumentHandler, this time in its role of FlowExecutorArgumentExposer. Overall, Spring Web Flow will make the following information available in the model:

- *The union of all flow execution scopes (request, flash, flow, and conversation scopes)*: This essentially exposes all application data managed by the flow to the view for rendering. As a developer, you just need to put objects into one of the flow execution scopes, and Spring Web Flow will make sure the view has access to them.

  If there are name clashes between objects in the different scopes, the request scope takes precedence over the flash scope, which takes precedence over the flow scope, which, in turn, takes precedence over the conversation scope. For instance, if there is an object indexed as foo in both the flash and conversation scopes, the foo object from the flash scope will end up in the model.

- *The unique key of the flow execution rendering the view*: This key is assigned by the flow execution repository and placed in the model as flowExecutionKey. View developers can use this value to submit the flow execution key back to the server on a next request.

- *The flow execution context*: This object implementing the FlowExecutionContext interface is available in the model as flowExecutionContext. View developers can use the flow execution context to learn about the flow execution that is rendering the view. For instance, using FlowExecutionContext.getActiveSession().isRoot(), the view can decide not to display a Back button if the flow is running as a top-level flow, instead of a subflow.

To make this a bit more tangible, let's look at a few examples of how you would access this model data in JSP. Most of these examples are taken from the Spring Bank sample application. Similar techniques can be used when using other view technologies.

At a very basic level, a JSP page can use Java scriptlets to access model information as request attributes:

```
<%@ page import="com.ervacon.springbank.domain.Payment" %>
<td valign="top">
  <%=((Payment)request.getAttribute("payment")).getCreditAccount(). \
    getNumber() %>
</td>

<input type="hidden" name="_flowExecutionKey"
  value="<%=request.getAttribute("flowExecutionKey") %>"/>

<%@ page
  import="org.springframework.webflow.execution.FlowExecutionContext" %>
<%
  FlowExecutionContext flowExecutionContext =
    (FlowExecutionContext)request.getAttribute("flowExecutionContext");
  if (!flowExecutionContext.getActiveSession().isRoot()) {
%>
  <input type="submit" name="_eventId_back" value="Back"/>
<%
  }
%>
```

A servlet can, of course, do something similar. With the advent of the JSP Standard Tag Library (JSTL), it is no longer necessary to pollute your JSP pages with bloated Java scriptlets like those shown in the preceding example. Instead, you can simply use the JSTL and its expression language:

```
<%@ taglib uri="http://java.sun.com/jsp/jstl/core" prefix="c" %>

<td valign="top">
  <c:out value="${payment.creditAccount.number} "/>
</td>

<input type="hidden" name="_flowExecutionKey"
  value="<c:out value="${flowExecutionKey} "/>"/>

<c:if test="${!flowExecutionContext.activeSession.root} ">
  <input type="submit" name="_eventId_back" value="Back"/>
</c:if>
```

This avoids the need for type casts and null checks, which are necessary in the Java scriptlets, making the overall page much cleaner and more readable. JSP 2.0 directly supports the JSTL expression language, making it possible to leave out the <c:out> tags:

```
<td valign="top">
  ${payment.creditAccount.number}
</td>

<input type="hidden" name="_flowExecutionKey"
  value="${flowExecutionKey} "/>

<c:if test="${!flowExecutionContext.activeSession.root} ">
  <input type="submit" name="_eventId_back" value="Back"/>
</c:if>
```

You still need the JSTL in some cases, for instance, to do "if" tests or to properly escape text (and avoid cross-site scripting attacks).

---

**Note**  Notice that all flow execution scopes are merged together to form the model. As a result, you do not need to specify flashScope, flowScope, or any of the other scopes like you would in an OGNL expression inside a flow definition. Instead, you directly access the object using its key in the model, for instance, payment in this example: ${payment.creditAccount.number}. This avoids unnecessary coupling between the view implementations and Spring Web Flow.

---

Next to rendering model data, views also have the important responsibility of constructing requests that lead back into the flow execution.

## Building Requests

Previous chapters already identified the three types of requests recognized by Spring Web Flow, and Figure 6-1 clarified the algorithm Spring Web Flow uses to classify a request. Let's look at each request type in a bit more detail, illustrating how to build such a request in JSP.

The FlowExecutorArgumentHandler, this time in its capacity of FlowExecutorArgumentExtractor, of course influences the way you need to build up request URLs. When using the RequestParameterFlowExecutorArgumentHandler, values will need to be included in the request as request parameters, while they are part of the request path when using the RequestPathFlowExecutorArgumentHandler.

I'll start by looking at Spring Web Flow's default configuration, using request parameters and the `RequestParameterFlowExecutorArgumentHandler`.

---

**Note** Unless noted otherwise, it is assumed that the `/flows.html` URI maps to a Spring Web Flow controller.

---

## Launching Flows

A request coming into Spring Web Flow that does not contain a `_flowExecutionKey` request parameter will be seen as a request launching a new flow execution. The ID of the flow to launch is specified using the `_flowId` request parameter. If no `_flowId` request parameter is found, the configured default flow ID is used or, if the default ID is lacking, an error is generated.

---

**Tip** The `FlowExecutorArgumentHandler` class has a `defaultFlowId` property that you can use to specify the ID of the flow to launch if no other flow ID can be extracted from the request. More specific configuration details will follow in the "Host Framework Integrations" section.

---

For instance, the HTML anchor rendered by the following JSP fragment launches the `enterPayment-flow`:

```
<a href="<c:url value="/flows.html?_flowId=enterPayment-flow"/>">
  <fmt:message key="enterPayment"/>
</a>
```

This produces the following HTML:

```
<a href="/springbank/flows.html?_flowId=enterPayment-flow">
  Enter Payment
</a>
```

Similarly, you can launch a flow using an HTML form:

```
<form action="<c:url value="/flows.html"/>">
  <input type="hidden" name="_flowId" value="enterPayment-flow"/>
  <input type="submit" value="<fmt:message key="enterPayment"/>"/>
</form>
```

---

**Tip** All request parameters contained in the request will also be provided as input to the launching flow, making it easy to launch a flow and pass some input to it.

---

### Signaling Events

A request that resumes a flow execution and signals an event needs to contain both a _flowExecutionKey and an _eventId request parameter.

The following example shows an HTML anchor that submits the next event, along with a selected debit account number:

```
<c:url value="/flows.html" var="nextUrl">
  <c:param name="_flowExecutionKey">${flowExecutionKey} </c:param>
  <c:param name="_eventId">next</c:param>
  <c:param name="debitAccount">${account.number} </c:param>
</c:url>
<a href="${nextUrl} ">${account.number} </a>
```

Notice how the flowExecutionKey is accessed in the model using a simple JSP 2.0 expression. The resulting HTML looks like this:

```
<a href="/springbank/flows.html?_flowExecutionKey=_c6F..._kD8... \
  &_eventId=next&debitAccount=SpringBank-0">SpringBank-0</a>
```

Of course, you can also submit events using HTML forms:

```
<form action="<c:url value="/flows.html"/>">
  <input type="hidden" name="_flowExecutionKey" value="${flowExecutionKey} "/>
  <input type="hidden" name="_eventId" value="next"/>
  <input type="hidden" name="debitAccount" value="${account.number} "/>
  <input type="submit" value="${account.number} "/>
</form>
```

The preceding form uses a separate hidden field to explicitly submit the _eventId request parameter. Spring Web Flow also allows you to embed the event ID in the name of a *submit* field, like so:

```
<form action="<c:url value="/flows.html"/>">
  <input type="hidden" name="_flowExecutionKey" value="${flowExecutionKey} "/>
  <input type="hidden" name="debitAccount" value="${account.number} "/>
  <input type="submit" name="_eventId_next"
    value="${account.number} "/>
</form>
```

This technique is particularly useful if you have a single HTML form with multiple buttons that each signal a different event. Finally, Spring Web Flow will also recognize events submitted by image buttons:

```
<form action="<c:url value="/flows.html"/>">
  <input type="hidden" name="_flowExecutionKey" value="${flowExecutionKey} "/>
  <input type="hidden" name="debitAccount" value="${account.number} "/>
  <input type="image" src="images/account.png"
    name="_eventId_next" value="${account.number} "/>
</form>
```

### Refreshing Flow Executions

A request that contains only a _flowExecutionKey request parameter, but no _eventId, will trigger a flow execution refresh. This was explained in detail in the "Request Life Cycle" section of Chapter 4.

---

**Note**  Recall that when using "always redirect on pause," Spring Web Flow will automatically generate a redirect causing a flow execution refresh.

---

Although this is not generally useful, the following HTML anchor will trigger a flow execution refresh:

```
<a href="<c:url
  value="/flows.html?_flowExecutionKey=${flowExecutionKey} "/>">
  Refresh
</a>
```

The resulting HTML is simply this:

```
<a href="/springbank/flows.html?_flowExecutionKey=_c6F..._kD8...">
  Refresh
</a>
```

It goes without saying that you can also use an HTML form to trigger a refresh:

```
<form action="<c:url value="/flows.html"/>">
  <input type="hidden" name="_flowExecutionKey"
    value="${flowExecutionKey} "/>
  <input type="submit" value="Refresh"/>
</form>
```

■**Tip** Although you can submit extra request parameters with a flow execution refresh request, Spring Web Flow will not automatically process them. However, you can still use them from inside a view state render action for instance.

## REST-style Requests

The examples shown in the previous sections use HTTP request parameters to submit the _flowId, _flowExecutionKey, and _eventId values. Using the RequestPathFlowExecutorArgumentHandler, Spring Web Flow also allows you to use URLs that follow the REST style by embedding the _flowId and _flowExecutionKey values inside the path of the resource identified by the URL.

■**Tip** The RequestPathFlowExecutorArgumentHandler always falls back to request parameters if it cannot find the necessary values (for example, a flow execution key) in the request path. In other words, you can also use the request parameters discussed in the previous section with this argument handler.

For instance, the following anchor is equivalent to the one shown in the "Launching Flows" section; it launches the enterPayment-flow:

```
<a href="<c:url value="/flows/enterPayment-flow.html"/>">
  <fmt:message key="enterPayment"/>
</a>
```

To make this work, a slightly modified request mapping is required. The front controller of the web MVC framework (for example, the DispatcherServlet in the case of Spring Web MVC) is still mapped to all *.html requests. The Spring Web Flow controller, on the other hand, is now mapped to all requests matching with /flows/*, instead of just /flows.html, which would obviously not work. Here is the REST-style URL generated by the preceding code:

```
/springbank/flows/enterPayment-flow.html
```

To participate in an ongoing flow execution, the flow execution key can be appended to the end of the resource path, using /k/ as a delimiter:

```
/springbank/flows/k/_c50..._kE3...html
```

The preceding URL would trigger a flow execution refresh because it contains a flow execution key but no event ID. The _eventId value still has to be submitted as a normal request parameter, for instance:

```
/springbank/flows/k/_c50..._kE3...html?_eventId=next
```

You can, of course, also use HTML forms in combination with REST-style URLs. In that case, there is no need for hidden form fields that submit the flow ID or flow execution key, since those values will already be embedded in the action of the form:

```
<form action="<c:url value="/flows/k/${flowExecutionKey} "/>">
  <input type="hidden" name="_eventId" value="next"/>
  <input type="hidden" name="debitAccount" value="${account.number} "/>
  <input type="submit" value="${account.number} "/>
</form>
```

---

■**Note** Only the flow ID and flow execution key are embedded in the path of the resource when using REST-style URLs. The event ID, along with all application-specific values, still needs to be submitted using normal request parameters.

---

# Host Framework Integrations

The general pattern followed when integrating Spring Web Flow into a hosting framework was discussed in the "Flow Executor Integration" section. Integrations with request-based frameworks such as Spring Web MVC or Struts follow this pattern very closely. Integrating with a component-based framework such as JSF is more complex, because component-based frameworks typically enforce a strict request life cycle and provide multiple extension points.

Keep in mind that the following sections explain how to integrate Spring Web Flow into a number of web MVC frameworks. They do not try to cover web application development using those frameworks in any detail. For more information, refer to the relevant documentation of each framework.

## INTEGRATE OR CONVERT?

One question that is frequently asked on the Spring Web Flow forums is this: should you integrate Spring Web Flow into an application or convert the entire application to use Spring Web Flow? Unfortunately, there is no easy answer.

In essence, Spring Web Flow was designed as a controller component for web MVC frameworks that targets *controlled navigation* use cases. It complements simple controllers handling *free browsing* requirements. In this line of thinking, it is natural to combine both simple controller implementations, as offered by the hosting framework, and Spring Web Flow in a single application. The Spring Bank sample application illustrates this approach. It uses Spring Web Flow for those parts of the application that have a real flow, like entering a new payment. Simple Spring Web MVC controllers are used for other parts of the application, however, such as logging out or displaying the account balances of a user. The advantage is this approach is that it allows you to use the right tool for the job in each situation, taking maximum advantage of each tool's strengths. Using multiple development techniques in a single application does introduce extra complexity however. Developers have to learn how to work with each technique and think about what option to use in each case.

On the other hand, you can decide to use Spring Web Flow for all use cases in your application. Of course, you will still need a hosting framework, but application developers will mostly use Spring Web Flow to develop controller functionality. This approach has the advantage of allowing you to set up a single, consistent development style for the entire application. The fact that Spring Web Flow's development model scales well from simple uses cases to very complex requirements makes this possible. The downside here is that, for the simple use cases, you will have to deal with some extra complexity, for instance, the configuration and runtime overhead imposed by Spring Web Flow's state management.

In the end, whether to integrate or convert is subjective, determined by your own preferences and the culture and preferences of the application's development team.

## Spring Web MVC

The example applications developed in previous chapters all used the Spring Web MVC framework as the hosting framework. Integrating Spring Web Flow with Spring Web MVC is as simple as defining a Spring Web Flow `FlowController`:

```
<bean id="flowController"
  class="org.springframework.webflow.executor.mvc.FlowController">
  <property name="flowExecutor" ref="flowExecutor"/>
</bean>
```

The FlowController is a Spring Web MVC Controller implementation (it subclasses AbstractController) that wraps incoming requests in a ServletExternalContext, extracts the relevant flow executor arguments, and delegates to the configured FlowExecutor.

The ServletExternalContext class is an ExternalContext implementation that wraps a ServletContext, an HttpServletRequest, and an HttpServletResponse.

In addition to the mandatory flowExecutor property, the FlowController also allows you to configure the FlowExecutorArgumentHandler it uses. By default, this will be the RequestParameterFlowExecutorArgumentHandler, but you can also plug in the RequestPathFlowExecutorArgumentHandler or a custom argument handler:

```
<bean id="flowController"
  class="org.springframework.webflow.executor.mvc.FlowController">
  <property name="flowExecutor" ref="flowExecutor"/>
  <property name="argumentHandler">
    <bean class="org.springframework.webflow.executor.support. \
      RequestPathFlowExecutorArgumentHandler"/>
  </property>
</bean>
```

**Tip** A single flow controller can manage the execution of all flows in your application. This minimizes configuration overhead. Having multiple flow controllers in a single application is also possible, and can be useful in a number of situations such as when you want to spread your flow definitions over multiple flow definition registries, when you do not want to expose all flows of your application under the same URL (for instance, to be able to do URL-based security checks), and when you want to use a differently configured flow executor for particular flows. Using the default continuation repository for some flows, but the single key repository for others, could be an example.

The names of the views selected by Spring Web Flow (determined by the view attribute of a view or end state), will be mapped to actual view templates using Spring Web MVC's ViewResolver mechanism.

Developing views for a web flow in the context of a Spring Web MVC application was explained in the "Spring Web Flow View Development" section. You can use any view technology supported by Spring Web MVC. When using JSP pages, you can use Spring's binding tag library, as well as the form tag library, for instance:

```
<form:form action="flows.html" commandName="payment">

    ...
```

```
<td colspan="2">
  <fmt:message key="amount"/>:
  <form:input path="amount" /> &euro;
  <form:errors cssClass="error" path="amount"/>
</td>

...

<input type="hidden" name="_flowExecutionKey"
  value="${flowExecutionKey} "/>
<input type="submit" name="_eventId_next"
  value="<fmt:message key="next"/>"/>
<input type="submit" name="_eventId_cancel"
  value="<fmt:message key="cancel"/>"/>
</form:form>
```

## Spring Portlet MVC

The Spring Portlet MVC framework closely follows the design of the Spring Web MVC framework but applies it to a Portlet environment (Java Community Process 2003). Integrating Spring Web Flow with Spring Portlet MVC is similar to integrating it with Spring Web MVC. Integration simply boils down to defining a `PortletFlowController` in the application context of the `DispatcherPortlet`:

```
<bean id="flowController"
  class="org.springframework.webflow.executor.mvc.PortletFlowController">
  <property name="flowExecutor" ref="flowExecutor"/>
</bean>

<flow:executor id="flowExecutor" registry-ref="flowRegistry">
  <flow:execution-attributes>
    <flow:alwaysRedirectOnPause value="false"/>
  </flow:execution-attributes>
</flow:executor>
```

The `PortletFlowController` wraps `PortletContext`, `PortletRequest`, and `PortletResponse` inside `PortletExternalContext`. Just like the `FlowController`, the `PortletFlowController` also uses a `FlowExecutorArgumentHandler` to extract `FlowExecutor` arguments. The `FlowExecutorArgumentHandler` and `FlowExecutor` used can be configured with the `argumentHandler` and `flowExecutor` properties respectively.

When using Spring Web Flow in a Portlet environment, you should be aware of a few technical constraints caused by peculiarities in the Portlet specification:

- The Portlet specification already identifies separate render and action requests. This makes use of the POST-REDIRECT-GET idiom and "always redirect on pause" impossible in a Portlet environment. Notice how the flow executor configuration in the preceding example disables "always redirect on pause".

- The `PortletFlowController` uses the `PortletSession` to pass information from the Portlet action request to the render request. This means that Spring Web Flow Portlet applications will always require a session, even when using the client continuation repository.

- The `PortletFlowController` launches new flow executions in the Portlet render request. This has two implications. First, refreshing the first page of a flow will always cause a new flow execution to be launched. Second, the first view rendered by the flow cannot be a redirect, because a Portlet render request cannot issue a redirect.

Views selected by Spring Web Flow are mapped to view implementations using the installed `ViewResolver`, just as in the case of the Spring Web MVC integration.

Developing views that participate in a web flow running in a Portlet environment is not much different from developing a normal Portlet page. Just follow the general guidelines described in the "Spring Web Flow View Development" section, and use the `<portlet:actionURL>` custom tag to build request URLs:

```
<a href="
  <portlet:actionURL>
    <portlet:param name="_flowExecutionKey"
      value="<%=request.getAttribute("flowExecutionKey") %>" />
    <portlet:param name="_eventId" value="next" />
    <portlet:param name="debitAccount"
      value="<%=((Account)pageContext.getAttribute("account")). \
        getNumber().toString() %>"/>
  </portlet:actionURL>">
  ${account.number}
</a>
```

# Struts

Spring Web Flow also integrates with the classic Apache Struts web MVC framework. In Struts, controller components are represented as `Action` classes.[1] Spring Web Flow integrates into Struts using a `FlowAction`, which is defined as any other Struts action in `struts-config.xml`:

```
<action-mappings>

  ...

  <action path="/flowAction" name="actionForm" scope="request"
    type="org.springframework.webflow.executor.struts.FlowAction"/>

  ...

</action-mappings>
```

If you're using the preceding configuration, all `/flowAction.do` requests will be handled by Spring Web Flow.

The `FlowAction` acts as a flow executor front-end. It wraps the incoming request and response in a `StrutsExternalContext`, extracts any relevant flow executor arguments, and invokes the flow executor. The `FlowAction` will look for beans named `flowExecutor` and `argumentHandler` in the root web application context to determine the `FlowExecutor` and `FlowExecutorArgumentHandler` to use. To set up a root web application context, you'll have to add Spring's `ContextLoaderListener` to the `web.xml` deployment descriptor:

```
<web-app ...>

  ...

  <context-param>
    <param-name>contextConfigLocation</param-name>
    <param-value>/WEB-INF/webflow-config.xml</param-value>
  </context-param>
```

---

1. Don't confuse a Struts `org.apache.struts.action.Action` with a Spring Web Flow `org.springframework.webflow.execution.Action`. The two concepts are unrelated.

```
<listener>
  <listener-class>
    org.springframework.web.context.ContextLoaderListener
  </listener-class>
</listener>

...

</web-app>
```

Since the referenced `webflow-config.xml` file is a normal Spring application context XML file, you can use Spring Web Flow's configuration schema to define the flow executor, argument handler, flow definition registry, and any other required beans. Keep in mind, however, that the bean name of the `FlowExecutor` bean needs to be `flowExecutor`, and `argumentHandler` needs to be the bean name for the `FlowExecutorArgumentHandler` bean.

Configuring the flow executor and argument handler as described previously has the disadvantage that all `FlowActions` in your application use the same flow executor and argument handler. As an alternative `FlowAction` configuration mechanism, you can also use Spring's `DelegatingActionProxy` (or `DelegatingRequestProcessor`). This will allow you to configure Struts actions as normal Spring beans in an application context, taking advantage of Spring's dependency injection techniques to configure your `FlowAction` implementation or implementations. Consult the Spring reference documentation for more details on its Struts support (Johnson et al 2003).

---

**Tip** You can use a single `FlowAction` to drive all flow executions in your Struts application. This will drastically cut down on the number of action definitions you have to add to the `struts-config.xml` file.

---

To map the views selected by Spring Web Flow to actual JSP pages, you need to add the necessary forwards to the `struts-config.xml` file. If you're using a single `FlowAction` to execute multiple flows, you'll typically want to use global forwards:

```
<global-forwards>
  <forward name="selectDebitAccount"
    path="/WEB-INF/jsp/selectDebitAccount.jsp"/>
  <forward name="enterPaymentInfo"
    path="/WEB-INF/jsp/enterPaymentInfo.jsp"/>

  ...

</global-forwards>
```

The general view development guidelines covered in the "Spring Web Flow View Development" section also apply when using Spring Web Flow in combination with Struts. Displaying data binding and validation messages deserves some special attention however.

## Data Binding and Validation

Struts has its own data binding and validation mechanism based on `ActionForm` objects. Those `ActionForm` objects are stored in either the `HttpServletRequest` or the `HttpSession`, in other words, outside of a Spring Web Flow flow execution. You can use classic Struts `ActionForm` objects in combination with Spring Web Flow, which leaves data binding and validation to Struts and lets the flow access the data in the `ActionForm` object in the request or session.

An alternative is to not use Struts `ActionForm` objects at all, and instead use Spring Web Flow's `FormAction`, as discussed in the "The Form Action" section of Chapter 5. The downside of this approach is that you will no longer be able to use the traditional Struts tag libraries to display form-backing object information and validation errors. Instead, you'll have to use Spring's binding and form tag libraries.

There is a third approach based on Spring's `SpringBindingActionForm`, for which the `FlowAction` has special support. Using `SpringBindingActionForm` allows you to leverage the `FormAction` and still use the traditional Struts tag libraries. All you need to do is use `SpringBindingActionForm` as the form bean type in `struts-config.xml` and reference that form bean from your `FlowAction` definition:

```
<form-bean name="actionForm"
  type="org.springframework.web.struts.SpringBindingActionForm"/>
```

The `SpringBindingActionForm` will automatically pick up on the form-backing object and `Errors` instance managed by Spring Web Flow's `FormAction`. You can then use that `FormAction` to do data binding and validation from inside your flow and display the results in the JSP page with the help of the traditional Struts tag libraries:

```
<html:form action="flowAction" method="post">

  ...

  <td colspan="2">
   Amount:
   <html:text property="amount" errorStyleClass="error"/>
   &euro;
  </td>

  ...
```

```
<input type="hidden" name="_flowExecutionKey"
  value="${flowExecutionKey} "/>
<html:button property="_eventId_next" value="Next"/>
<html:button property="_eventId_cancel" value="Cancel"/>
</html:form>
```

## JavaServer Faces

The integration of Spring Web Flow into JavaServer Faces (JSF) is elegant and powerful. Under the covers, it is quite a bit more complex than the integrations with other web MVC frameworks, but luckily, this does not impact you as an application developer. A primary goal of Spring Web Flow's integration with JSF is making it feel natural for JSF developers.

When integrated into JSF, Spring Web Flow fulfills two important roles:

- It handles navigation between JSF views, allowing you to use flow definitions to define the allowed navigational paths.

- It resolves variables referenced by JSF expressions. This will allow JSF components to access model information stored in one of Spring Web Flow's flow execution scopes.

Both responsibilities naturally complement JSF's component model, making the combination of JSF and Spring Web Flow an attractive offering. Plain JSF views can participate in a flow execution and can transparently access information managed by that flow execution. Furthermore, other popular JSF view technologies such as Facelets (`https://facelets.dev.java.net`), ICEfaces (`http://www.icefaces.org`), and Apache MyFaces Trinidad (`http://myfaces.apache.org/trinidad`) are not impacted by all of this.

### Configuration

Configuring JSF to use Spring Web Flow requires some simple definitions in JSF's `faces-config.xml` configuration file:

```
1  <faces-config>
2    <application>
3      <navigation-handler>
4        org.springframework.webflow.executor.jsf.FlowNavigationHandler
5      </navigation-handler>
6      <variable-resolver>
7        org.springframework.webflow.executor.jsf.DelegatingFlowVariableResolver
```

```
8         </variable-resolver>
9       </application>
10
11      <lifecycle>
12        <phase-listener>
13          org.springframework.webflow.executor.jsf.FlowPhaseListener
14        </phase-listener>
15      </lifecycle>
16    </faces-config>
```

Here are the key points to note about the preceding listing:

- *Line 3*: The FlowNavigationHandler will signal a JSF action outcome, such as a command button click, as an event in the active flow execution.

---

**Tip** If a request does not participate in an ongoing flow execution, the FlowNavigationHandler will simply delegate to the standard JSF NavigationHandler, which reads navigation rules from faces-config.xml. This allows you to use Spring Web Flow for some use cases in your application and standard JSF for other situations.

---

- *Line 5*: The DelegatingFlowVariableResolver will try to resolve normal JSF binding expressions, such as #{payment.amount}, to objects managed in one of Spring Web Flow's flow execution scopes. The flash, flow, and conversation scopes will be scanned, in that order, until a match is found. If no matching object can be located, the DelegatingFlowVariableResolver will delegate to the next variable resolver in JSF's variable resolver chain.

---

**Note** Notice that the DelegatingFlowVariableResolver does not resolve request scope variables. As a consequence, you cannot reference objects in request scope from JSF components using JSF's expression language. Binding components onto request-scoped objects is problematic in a JSF environment, because those objects are longer available when JSF restores the component view state on a subsequent postback request.

Recall the best practice of putting large objects in the request scope and reloading them every time using a view state render action. Since the request scope is not available using Spring Web Flow's JSF integration, you can no longer strictly follow this best practice. Instead, consider loading large objects using a view state entry action and storing them in the flash scope.

---

- *Line 12*: Spring Web Flow's `FlowPhaseListener` manages flow executions in a JSF environment. As a flow executor front-end, it launches, resumes, and refreshes flow executions as required. The `FlowPhaseListener` wraps the incoming JSF request (a `FacesContext`) in a `JsfExternalContext` and makes the flow execution available to other JSF artifacts that might need access to it, such as variable resolvers.

---

### ACCESSING THE FLOW EXECUTION FROM PLAIN JSF ARTIFACTS

You can access the flow execution from inside your own JSF artifacts, for instance an `ActionListener`, as follows:

```
FacesContext context = FacesContext.getCurrentInstance();
FlowExecution flowExecution =
  FlowExecutionHolderUtils.getRequiredCurrentFlowExecution(context);
```

This will obtain the flow execution from a thread locally managed by the `FlowPhaseListener`.

---

As you can see from the preceding configuration, Spring Web Flow's JSF integration does not directly use a `FlowExecutor`. To make configuration consistent with the other environments, the `FlowPhaseListener` and `FlowNavigationHandler` automatically pick up any relevant configuration from a `flowExecutor` bean defined in the root web application context. Consequently, you have to set up a root web application context, typically using Spring's `ContextLoaderListener` in the `web.xml` deployment descriptor of the web application:

```
<web-app ...>

  ...

  <context-param>
    <param-name>contextConfigLocation</param-name>
    <param-value>/WEB-INF/webflow-config.xml</param-value>
  </context-param>

  <listener>
    <listener-class>
      org.springframework.web.context.ContextLoaderListener
    </listener-class>
  </listener>
```

...

```
</web-app>
```

In the preceding example, the root web application context will simply contain Spring Web Flow configuration. Of course, it can also contain other supporting services used by the application. You can define the flow executor as usual, along with a flow definition registry, and possibly a conversation manager. Just make sure to use the `flowExecutor` name for the `FlowExecutor` bean:

```
<flow:executor id="flowExecutor" registry-ref="flowRegistry"/>

<flow:registry id="flowRegistry">
  <flow:location path="/WEB-INF/flows/*-flow.xml" />
</flow:registry>
```

---

**Caution** Spring Web Flow 1 does not allow you to have multiple flow executors, each with a different configuration, in a single JSF application. You might be able to work around this limitation, for instance, using multiple FacesServlets and Spring's delegating JSF proxies (Johnson et al 2003), but this workaround is not supported out of the box.

---

### System Cleanup

The JSF specification is not sufficiently strict to allow the `FlowPhaseListener` to clean up the Spring Web Flow artifacts related to a request in all possible situations. For instance, JSF will never call back into the `FlowPhaseListener` if fatal errors occur during request processing. To work around this problem and make sure everything is cleaned up properly for every request, Spring Web Flow includes a `FlowSystemCleanupFilter`, which you can configure in `web.xml`:

```
<web-app ...>

  ...

  <filter>
    <filter-name>cleanupFilter</filter-name>
    <filter-class>
      org.springframework.webflow.executor.jsf.FlowSystemCleanupFilter
    </filter-class>
  </filter>
```

```
<filter-mapping>
  <filter-name>cleanupFilter</filter-name>
  <url-pattern>*.faces</url-pattern>
</filter-mapping>

...

</web-app>
```

Typically, you'll want to map the `FlowSystemCleanupFilter` to the same URL pattern as the JSF `FacesServlet` (`*.faces` in the preceding example).

---

**JSF AND SPRING WEB FLOW BEFORE VERSION 1.0.2**

The `DelegatingFlowVariableResolver` was only introduced in Spring Web Flow version 1.0.2. Earlier versions used primitive `FlowVariableResolver` and `FlowPropertyResolver` implementations that could only resolve variables in flow scope. Although this code is still available, using the `DelegatingFlowVariableResolver` instead is recommended. Consult the Spring Web Flow API and reference documentation for more information on these classes.

---

## Launching flows

To allow standard JSF components to launch new flow executions, Spring Web Flow's JSF integration recognizes JSF action outcomes that adhere to a special format. An action outcome that has the `flowId:` prefix will launch the identified flow, for instance:

```
<h:commandLink value="Enter Payment" action="flowId:enterPayment-flow"/>
```

The preceding command link launches the `enterPayment-flow`. Alternatively, you can also use a simple URL targeted at the JSF `FacesServlet` that contains the `_flowId` request parameter and no `_flowExecutionKey` request parameter:

```
<a href="controller.faces?_flowId=enterPayment-flow">Enter Payment</a>
```

This is in line with the way flows are launched in the other environments Spring Web Flow integrates with.

## Developing Flows in a JSF Environment

Let's take a look at how to develop flows when using Spring Web Flow combined with JSF.

### Flow Definitions

JSF is a component-based web MVC framework. JSF components elegantly handle data binding and validation logic. With the help of the DelegatingFlowVariableResolver, JSF components can directly bind onto objects stored in one of the flow execution scopes. As a result, data binding and validation will no longer have to be integrated into the flow definition using the FormAction. This leads to flow definitions that are generally simpler and more focused on expressing navigational rules. Here is an extract that shows what a section of the enterPayment-flow would look like in a JSF environment:

```
<view-state id="showSelectDebitAccount" view="/selectDebitAccount.jsp">
  <entry-actions>
    <bean-action bean="accountRepository" method="getAccounts">
      <method-arguments>
        <argument expression="externalContext.sessionMap.user.clientId"/>
      </method-arguments>
      <method-result name="accounts" scope="flash"/>
    </bean-action>
  </entry-actions>
  <transition on="next" to="showEnterPaymentInfo"/>
</view-state>

<view-state id="showEnterPaymentInfo" view="/enterPaymentInfo.jsp">
  <transition on="next" to="showConfirmPayment"/>
  <transition on="selectBeneficiary" to="launchBeneficiariesFlow"/>
</view-state>
```

As you can see, there are no references to the FormAction. Also notice that the view names used in the view states above use the standard JSF view identifier format, using a leading forward slash and ending with a suffix. The suffix is .jsp in this case, but it could be something else; for instance, it's .xhtml when using Facelets. JSF will directly map these view names to a corresponding view implementation. Also notice how the accounts list resulting from the bean action is explicitly stored in the flash scope. This is necessary, since JSF views cannot reference request-scoped objects, as mentioned previously.

## View Development

JSF views participating in a web flow are plain JSF views, with no Spring Web Flow–
specific elements. This is true regardless of the view technology used, for example, JSP
or Facelets. Here is an extract from a JSF view using JSP technology:

```
<f:view>

  ...

  <h:form id="paymentInfoForm">

    ...

    <td colspan="2">
      Amount:
      <h:inputText id="amount" value="#{payment.amount} " required="true">
        <f:validateDoubleRange minimum="0.01"/>
      </h:inputText>
      &euro;
    </td>

    ...

    <h:commandButton type="submit" value="Next" action="next"/>
    <h:commandButton type="submit" value="Cancel" action="cancel"/>
  </h:form>

  ...

</f:view>
```

The flow execution key is automatically tracked in the JSF view root, so there is no need
to manually submit a _flowExecutionKey request parameter with every request. The
action outcomes specified by the command buttons in the preceding example will automatically signal the corresponding event in the flow execution. Also notice how the JSF
expression #{payment.amount} transparently accesses the payment object in the conversation scope.

**Facelets** Facelets (https://facelets.dev.java.net) is an alternative view definition technology for JSF. It was explicitly designed for use with JSF and solves many of the problems
related to using JSP to define JSF views. Since Facelets is very popular among JSF developers, quickly showing its usage in combination with Spring Web Flow seems useful.

Configuring a JSF application to use Facelets is easy. You simply need to add the required JAR files to the application and add a context parameter to the web.xml deployment descriptor to instruct JSF to use Facelets XHTML files as view definitions:

```
<context-param>
  <param-name>javax.faces.DEFAULT_SUFFIX</param-name>
  <param-value>.xhtml</param-value>
</context-param>
```

Next, you have to configure JSF to use the Facelets view handler by adding the following to your faces-config.xml:

```
<application>

  ...

  <view-handler>com.sun.facelets.FaceletViewHandler</view-handler>
</application>
```

This view handler complements the Spring Web Flow–specific configuration in faces-config.xml. The application is now set up to use Facelets. As far as Spring Web Flow is concerned, the only impact of using Facelets is the slightly different view IDs specified in the flow definition:

```
<view-state id="showEnterPaymentInfo" view="/enterPaymentInfo.xhtml">
  <transition on="next" to="showConfirmPayment"/>
  <transition on="selectBeneficiary" to="launchBeneficiariesFlow"/>
</view-state>
```

View names now end with the .xhtml suffix. As was the case with JSP view definitions, the Facelets view definitions themselves contain no Spring Web Flow–specific details.

---

**Note** JSF puts the view developer at a slightly higher level of abstraction. Instead of directly creating requests that submit a flow execution key and an event, you can use JSF actions to signal events while the flow execution key is automatically tracked. Internally, JSF constructs the actual requests. Since controlling the FlowExecutorArgumentHandler does not really make sense in this context, the JSF integration doesn't provide a direct way to configure the argument handler used.

---

### Deep Integration Between JSF and Spring Web Flow

The previous examples illustrate how Spring Web Flow's JSF integration allows you to use value bindings to bind JSF components to model objects managed inside a flow execution. For instance, the following JSF data table definition directly uses the `accounts` list of `Account` objects available in the flash scope:

```
<h:dataTable value="#{accounts}" var="account" border="1">

  ...

  <h:column>
    <h:commandLink action="next">
      <f:param name="debitAccount" value="#{account.number}"/>
      <h:outputText value="#{account.number}"/>
    </h:commandLink>
  </h:column>

  ...

</h:dataTable>
```

The JSF data table component will automatically convert the `List<Account>` to a JSF `ListDataModel`. In this case, the flow is unaware of JSF's rich component model. Consequently, the command link used to select one of the listed accounts needs to explicitly submit the relevant account number as a request parameter.

This style of JSF usage essentially uses JSF as a powerful tag library, similar to the way `Displaytag` is used when using Spring Web MVC. Some people prefer this style, and it is certainly a simple and elegant approach. The downside is that you can't leverage JSF's powerful component model. To be able to do that, you need to take a slightly different approach.

In classic JSF development, it is typical to have a backing bean manage all data and behavior required for a particular page. You can mimic this way of working using flow variables and evaluate actions. Recall the way evaluate actions can be used to directly invoke methods on objects stored inside the flow execution, typically flow variables; this was explained in the "Evaluate Actions" section of Chapter 5. Using a flow variable, you can set up a flow-backing bean in one of the flow execution scopes:

```
<var name="backingBean" scope="conversation"/>
```

This flow-backing bean will manage all data and behavior required by the flow, just like a traditional JSF-backing bean. The flow can invoke functionality provided by the backing bean using evaluate actions:

```
<view-state id="showSelectDebitAccount" view="/selectDebitAccount.jsp">
  <entry-actions>
    <evaluate-action
      expression="conversationScope.backingBean.loadAccounts()"/>
```

```
    </entry-actions>
    <transition on="next" to="showEnterPaymentInfo">
      <evaluate-action
        expression="conversationScope.backingBean.setDebitAccount()"/>
    </transition>
</view-state>
```

Notice how the first evaluate action in this listing does not directly expose the list of loaded accounts to the flow. It is the responsibility of the backing bean to do that:

```
1   public class EnterPaymentFlowBackingBean implements Serializable {
2
3     private transient AccountRepository accountRepository;
4     private Long clientId;
5     private Payment payment = new Payment();
6     private ListDataModel accounts;
7
8     public void setAccountRepository(AccountRepository accountRepository) {
9       this.accountRepository = accountRepository;
10    }
11
12    public void setClientId(Long clientId) {
13      this.clientId = clientId;
14    }
15
16    public Payment getPayment() {
17      return payment;
18    }
19
20    public ListDataModel getAccounts() {
21      return accounts;
22    }
23
24    public void setAccounts(ListDataModel accounts) {
25      this.account = accounts;
26    }
27
28    public void loadAccounts() {
29      accounts = new ListDataModel(accountRepository.getAccounts(clientId));
30    }
31
32    public void setDebitAccount() {
33      payment.setDebitAccount((Account)accounts.getRowData());
```

```
34    }
35
36    ...
37
38  }
```

There are several interesting things to highlight in the preceding code fragment:

- *Line 1*: Because the flow-backing bean is stored inside the flow execution, it needs to be serializable (especially when it would be stored in the flow scope).

- *Line 3*: The backing bean obviously needs access to the AccountRepository to be able to load the list of accounts. Since the backing bean is defined as a normal Spring bean, we can simply inject the AccountRepository:

```
<bean id="backingBean" scope="prototype"
  class="com.ervacon.springbank.web.EnterPaymentFlowBackingBean">
  <property name="accountRepository" ref="accountRepository"/>
</bean>
```

There is one problem however: the backing bean needs to be serializable! To avoid the accountRepository from being serialized along with the rest of the backing bean, it is marked as *transient*. This introduces another problem: when the backing bean is restored from its serialized state, the accountRepository member will be null. The solution to this problem is to *rewire* all objects in the flow execution when the flow execution is restored. Spring Web Flow provides a specialized JSF AutowiringPhaseListener to do this. You need to add this phase listener to faces-config.xml, along with the FlowPhaseListener:

```
<lifecycle>
  <phase-listener>
    org.springframework.webflow.executor.jsf.FlowPhaseListener
  </phase-listener>
  <phase-listener>
    org.springframework.webflow.executor.jsf.AutowiringPhaseListener
  </phase-listener>
</lifecycle>
```

The AutowiringPhaseListener will automatically rewire all objects found in any of the flow execution scopes *by name*. In the case of the enterPayment-flow backing bean, it will reinject the AccountRepository bean.

- *Line 4*: The clientId of the currently logged in user will be stored in the HTTP session, as you will see in Chapter 9. Using Spring 2's scoped bean feature, which was already discussed in the "Accessing Scoped Beans" section, we can make the client ID of the current user available to the backing action.

- *Line 6*: The backing bean directly holds on to a ListDataModel instance. The standard JSF ListDataModel is not serializable. To work around that problem, Spring Web Flow provides serializable versions of the JSF model classes in the org.springframework.webflow.executor.jsf.model package.

The JSF data table used to display the list of debit accounts now becomes quite a bit simpler:

```
<h:dataTable value="#{backingBean.accounts}" var="account" border="1">

  ...

  <h:column>
    <h:commandLink action="next">
     <h:outputText value="#{account.number}"/>
    </h:commandLink>
  </h:column>

  ...

</h:dataTable>
```

Note how it is no longer required to submit the account number of the selected account as a request parameter. The JSF data table will automatically track the selected account in the ListDataModel, making it available using getRowData(). The EnterPaymentFlowBackingBean listing shown earlier illustrated this.

### ACCESSING JSF COMPONENTS FROM INSIDE A FLOW

You can also use *component bindings* to make actual JSF component instances available to the backing bean, for instance:

```
<h:panelGroup binding="#{backingBean.warningPanel}">
  ...
</h:panelGroup>
```

This allows you to directly manipulate the components from inside your backing bean.

# Summary

The flow executor front-ends discussed in this chapter integrate Spring Web Flow into several popular web MVC frameworks.

The chapter started off explaining the general approach to integrating Spring Web Flow into a hosting framework and introduced the concept of a `FlowExecutorArgumentHandler` along the way. General guidelines related to Spring Web Flow view development were also covered, detailing the model data exposed to the view and how to build requests that launch a new flow execution, signal an event, or refresh a flow execution.

Integrating Spring Web Flow into request-based web MVC frameworks is straightforward. There is a `FlowController` for Spring Web MVC, a `PortletFlowController` for Spring Portlet MVC, and a `FlowAction` for Struts. All of these integrations simply delegate to a `FlowExecutor` implementation.

Integrating with JSF, a component-based web MVC framework, requires a slightly different approach. In a JSF environment, Spring Web Flow provides advanced navigation-handling capabilities and transparent resolution of variables that live in a flow execution. The end result is a development experience that fits very naturally with what JSF developers are used to. JSF views participating in a web flow contain no Spring Web Flow–specific elements. Even the flow execution key is tracked automatically.

You now have all the details of using Spring Web Flow in a runtime environment. You know how to define a flow, how to set up a flow executor to manage executions of that flow, and how to integrate that flow executor with your hosting framework of choice. The next chapter will explain how to use your flows in a test environment.

# CHAPTER 8

■ ■ ■

# Testing with Spring Web Flow

The previous chapter talked about driving flow executions from inside a deployed web application. There is another important execution environment to consider however: the test environment. No modern framework can ignore the need for unit testing. Spring Web Flow facilitates testing in several different ways:

- By abstracting away the details of the runtime environment behind an ExternalContext interface, Spring Web Flow makes it easy to test outside the container (Servlet engine or application server).

- Special support classes help you test Spring Web Flow–specific artifacts, such as Action implementations, in isolation.

- Spring Web Flow flow execution tests provide an innovative way of doing integration tests. They allow you to drive a flow execution from inside a JUnit test.

The test support provided by Spring Web Flow ranges from isolated unit tests to end-to-end integration tests. As a general guideline, you should have simple unit tests verifying the behavior of any custom web flow code you have developed. For instance, testing an Action implementation, a FlowExecutionExceptionHandler, a FlowExecutionListener, and so on.

Once the individual pieces of the puzzle have been tested, you can use Spring Web Flow's flow execution test support to test an entire flow definition and the executions thereof. Such a flow execution test will typically use mock or stub implementations of back-end services. Alternatively, you can use a flow execution test as a true integration test, interacting with real services.

---

■**Caution** Because of internal restructuring of the framework, the flow execution test support has changed considerably between Spring Web Flow 1 and Spring Web Flow 2. If you are planning to migrate to Spring Web Flow 2 in the near future, focus your efforts on testing individual flow artifacts, rather than flow execution tests. Know that migrating flow execution tests to Spring Web Flow 2 will take some effort.

---

Let's start by discussing isolated unit tests of custom flow artifacts.

# Unit Testing

Unit testing Spring Web Flow code is generally easy, since Spring Web Flow internally uses simple POJOs (plain old Java objects) that you can instantiate using the new operator. To further help you unit test your Spring Web Flow–specific code, mock implementations of key artifacts such as RequestContext are provided. These mock implementations reside in the org.springframework.webflow.test package and are explained in the following sections.

## MockRequestContext

Most Spring Web Flow code artifacts that live *inside* the flow execution, such as Action, TransitionCriteria, or ViewSelector implementations, interact with the flow execution using a RequestContext. MockRequestContext is a mock implementation of the RequestContext interface. It defines methods that allow you to freely manipulate the state of RequestContext to test your code.

## MockRequestControlContext

MockRequestControlContext is a mock implementation of the RequestControlContext interface that is designed for testing flow artifacts that need access to a RequestControlContext, for instance, FlowExecutionExceptionHandler.

## MockExternalContext

MockExternalContext is the mock implementation of the ExternalContext interface, and it's particularly useful to test code that queries the external environment for things such as the web application context path; a FlowExecutorArgumentHandler implementation is an example.

---

**Tip** If the code you are testing downcasts the external context to an environment-specific subclass, for example, ServletExternalContext in a Spring Web MVC application, consider using a normal ServletExternalContext wrapping mock implementations of ServletContext, HttpServletRequest, and HttpServletResponse. The Spring Framework ships with mock implementations of these servlet artifacts.

---

# MockParameterMap

MockParameterMap is the mutable mock implementation of the ParameterMap interface; it allows you to directly manipulate a map of request parameters. This class is used internally by MockExternalContext, but you can also directly use it in your unit tests.

# MockFlowExecutionContext

MockFlowExecutionContext is a mock implementation of the FlowExecutionContext interface. MockRequestCotext provides access to MockFlowExecutionContext, giving you control over the mocked flow execution context in which a test runs.

# MockFlowSession

MockFlowSession is a mock implementation of the FlowSession interface, used internally by the MockFlowExecutionContext. You typically access a MockFlowSession through MockRequestContext and its MockFlowExecutionContext to manipulate the status of the flow session for a particular unit test.

# MockFlowServiceLocator

To help you test flow builders, MockFlowServiceLocator provides a mock implementation of the FlowServiceLocator interface. MockFlowServiceLocator allows you to register subflow definitions and other artifacts needed by a flow using the registerSubflow(subflow) and registerBean(beanName, bean) methods, respectively.

This class is also used by the flow execution test support provided by Spring Web Flow, which will be discussed in the "Flow Execution Testing" section.

# Testing with Mock Objects

Using the mock objects listed in the preceding sections, you can test Spring Web Flow artifacts in a simple unit test, isolated from the environment in which they normally execute. To illustrate this, let's create a unit test for the PaymentAction developed in Chapter 4. Recall the PaymentAction as it was presented in Listing 4-12:

```
public class PaymentAction extends MultiAction {

  private PaymentProcessingEngine engine;
```

```
    public void setEngine(PaymentProcessingEngine engine) {
      this.engine = engine;
    }

    protected Event submitPayment(RequestContext context) throws Exception {
      try {
        Payment payment =
          (Payment)context.getConversationScope().get("payment");
        engine.submit(payment);
        return success();
      }
      catch (PaymentProcessingException ex) {
        return error(ex);
      }
    }
  }
}
```

---

**Note** The final version of the "enter payment" web flow of the Spring Bank sample application does not use PaymentAction. Instead, it uses a bean-invoking action to directly invoke the submit(payment) method of the PaymentProcessingEngine service.

---

A unit test for PaymentAction that verifies correct exception handling would look like this:

```
public class PaymentActionTests extends TestCase {

  public void testSubmitPaymentError() throws Exception {
    PaymentAction action = new PaymentAction();
    action.setEngine(new PaymentProcessingEngine() {
      public void submit(Payment payment) throws PaymentProcessingException {
        throw new PaymentProcessingException("test", "Testing");
      }
    } );

    MockRequestContext context = new MockRequestContext();
    context.getConversationScope().put("payment", new Payment());
    Event event = action.submitPayment(context);
```

```
    assertEquals("error", event.getId());
    assertTrue(event.getAttributes().contains(
      "exception", PaymentProcessingException.class));
  }
}
```

As you can see, PaymentActionTests is a plain JUnit test case. The testSubmitPaymentError() unit test directly instantiates the PaymentAction and configures it with a local mock implementation of the PaymentProcessingEngine service that always generates an exception. The submitPayment(context) method of the PaymentAction is then invoked with a MockRequestContext containing a payment object in conversation scope. Finally, correct processing is verified by checking the action result event.

It is equally simple to write a testSubmitPaymentSuccess() unit test that verifies PaymentAction processing in the sunny day scenario.

## Flow Execution Testing

The mock objects discussed in the previous section are great for testing Action implementations and other Spring Web Flow artifacts. Spring Web Flow also provides support to test its primary development product: flow definitions. Testing a flow definition essentially means testing an execution of that flow definition, verifying that the flow reacts as expected when events are signaled, when exceptions occur, and so on. The AbstractFlowExecutionTests class makes this possible. It is a base JUnit TestCase class that allows you to drive a flow execution from inside a unit test. Figure 8-1 shows the AbstractFlowExecutionTests class hierarchy.

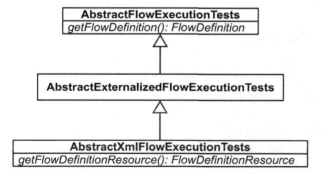

**Figure 8-1.** *AbstractFlowExecutionTests class diagram*

## Testing Java Flow Definitions

The base flow execution test support class is `AbstractFlowExecutionTests`. It is primarily useful when you want to test flow executions of flow definitions built using a Java flow builder. All you need to do is subclass `AbstractFlowExecutionTests` and define the `getFlowDefinition()` method, returning the flow definition you want to test:

```
public class EnterPaymentFlowExecutionTests extends
    AbstractFlowExecutionTests {

  protected FlowDefinition getFlowDefinition() {
    EnterPaymentFlowBuilder builder = new EnterPaymentFlowBuilder();
    return new FlowAssembler("enterPayment-flow", builder).assembleFlow();
  }

  ...

}
```

Notice how the `EnterPaymentFlowBuilder` is passed into a `FlowAssembler` to assemble the flow, as discussed in Chapter 4.

Typically, you will want to configure the flow builder with a `MockFlowServiceLocator` to have the flow use mocked services. The following code example uses the EasyMock (http://www.easymock.org) framework to construct mocks for the `AccountRepository` and `PaymentProcessingEngine` services used by the "enter payment" flow:

```
import static org.easymock.EasyMock.createMock;

public class EnterPaymentFlowExecutionTests extends
    AbstractFlowExecutionTests {

  private AccountRepository accountRepository =
    createMock(AccountRepository.class);
  private PaymentProcessingEngine paymentProcessingEngine =
    createMock(PaymentProcessingEngine.class);

  protected FlowDefinition getFlowDefinition() {
    EnterPaymentFlowBuilder builder = new EnterPaymentFlowBuilder();

    MockFlowServiceLocator serviceRegistry = new MockFlowServiceLocator();
    serviceRegistry.registerBean("accountRepository", accountRepository);
    serviceRegistry.registerBean("paymentProcessingEngine",
      paymentProcessingEngine);
```

```
    builder.setFlowServiceLocator(serviceRegistry);

    return new FlowAssembler("enterPayment-flow", builder).assembleFlow();
  }

  ...

}
```

## Testing XML Flow Definitions

Although you could also use `AbstractFlowExecutionTests` to test an XML flow definition and construct the flow using `XmlFlowBuilder`, it is easier to subclass `AbstractXmlFlowExecutionTests` in this case. All you need to do is define the `getFlowDefinitionResource()` method, returning a flow definition resource for the flow you want to test:

```
public class EnterPaymentFlowExecutionTests extends
  AbstractXmlFlowExecutionTests {

  protected FlowDefinitionResource getFlowDefinitionResource() {
    return createFlowDefinitionResource(
      "src/main/webapp/WEB-INF/flows/enterPayment-flow.xml");
  }

  ...
}
```

`AbstractXmlFlowExecutionTests` defines a number of `createFlowDefinitionResource(. . .)` convenience methods to create flow definition resources for XML flow definitions that *reside on the file system*. If you want to load an XML flow definition from the classpath, you can do that using Spring's `Resource` abstraction:

```
protected FlowDefinitionResource getFlowDefinitionResource() {
  return new FlowDefinitionResource("enterPayment-flow",
    new ClassPathResource("enterPayment-flow.xml"));
}
```

---

■**Note**  A `FlowDefinitionResource` object simply holds a flow ID and a Spring `Resource` containing the actual flow definition.

---

To allow you to register mock services used by the flow, AbstractXmlFlowExecutionTests defines two hook methods that you can implement. Using registerMockServices(serviceRegistry), you can register mock implementations of the services required by the flow. To override the services defined in the flow local application context (see the "Flow Local Bean Definitions" section of Chapter 4 for more details), you have to override registerLocalMockServices(flow, beanFactory). Here is an example equivalent to the one presented in the previous section:

```
import static org.easymock.EasyMock.createMock;

public class EnterPaymentFlowExecutionTests extends
  AbstractXmlFlowExecutionTests {

  private AccountRepository accountRepository =
    createMock(AccountRepository.class);
  private PaymentProcessingEngine paymentProcessingEngine =
    createMock(PaymentProcessingEngine.class);

  protected FlowDefinitionResource getFlowDefinitionResource() {
    return createFlowDefinitionResource(
      "src/main/webapp/WEB-INF/flows/enterPayment-flow.xml");
  }

  protected void registerMockServices(
      MockFlowServiceLocator serviceRegistry) {
    serviceRegistry.registerBean("accountRepository", accountRepository);
    serviceRegistry.registerBean("paymentProcessingEngine",
      paymentProcessingEngine);
  }

  ...

}
```

## Testing the "Enter Payment" Flow

Let's look at an actual flow execution test case for the "enter payment" flow. The previous section already set up the basic test class to test the enterPayment-flow.xml flow definition.

Using the registerMockServices(serviceRegistry) hook method, the test set up mock implementations of the AccountRepository and PaymentProcessingEngine services. The enterPayment-flow also uses a third service however: beneficiaries-flow. To test the enterPayment-flow isolated from the beneficiaries-flow, you will have to provide a mock flow definition for that flow. Instead of defining that mock flow in XML, or even using the Java flow builder, let's directly construct it using Spring Web Flow's basic flow definition artifacts:

```
private Account creditAccount = new Beneficiary("Credit", "Test-1");

protected void registerMockServices(
    MockFlowServiceLocator serviceRegistry) {
  serviceRegistry.registerBean("accountRepository",
    accountRepository);
  serviceRegistry.registerBean("paymentProcessingEngine",
    paymentProcessingEngine);

  // setup mock beneficiaries flow
  Flow beneficiariesFlow = new Flow("beneficiaries-flow");
  beneficiariesFlow.setOutputMapper(new AttributeMapper() {
    public void map(Object source, Object target, MappingContext ctx) {
      ((MutableAttributeMap)target).put("beneficiary", creditAccount);
    }
  } );
  new EndState(beneficiariesFlow, "endSelected");
  serviceRegistry.registerSubflow(beneficiariesFlow);
}
```

This code creates a simple beneficiaries-flow with a single endSelected state. The mock flow is configured with an output mapper that puts a beneficiary object in the sub-flow output map, simulating the selection of a beneficiary.

With the mock services set up, the enterPayment-flow is now isolated from its environment. There is one extra complexity to tackle however. In the next chapter, you will see that the enterPayment-flow expects a User object for the logged-in user to be available in the HTTP session. The test case will have to simulate this by creating an appropriate MockExternalContext object. To do that, you can override the createExternalContext(requestParameters) hook method:

```
protected ExternalContext createExternalContext(
    ParameterMap requestParameters) {
  MockExternalContext externalContext =
    new MockExternalContext(requestParameters);
  externalContext.getSessionMap().put("user",
    new User("test", "test", OL));
  return externalContext;
}
```

Writing actual test code that drives a flow execution of the enterPayment-flow is easy. You can use the many convenience methods provided by AbstractFlowExecutionTests to start the flow, signal events, refresh the flow, and verify the status of the flow or the view selections made by the flow. Here is a unit test that starts the flow:

```
private Account debitAccount = new Beneficiary("Debit", "Test-0");

public void testStartFlow() {
  expect(accountRepository.getAccounts(0L)).andReturn(
    Collections.<Account>singletonList(debitAccount));
  replay(accountRepository);

  ApplicationView view = applicationView(startFlow());
  assertCurrentStateEquals("showSelectDebitAccount");
  assertModelAttributeNotNull("payment", view);
  assertModelAttributeCollectionSize(1, "accounts", view);
}
```

The test first tells the EasyMock mock account repository to expect a call to getAccounts(clientId) and return a single account. It then starts the flow execution (using startFlow()) and checks that the flow is in the expected state and has returned the expected model data (the applicationView(viewSelection) method casts a ViewSelection to an ApplicationView; there are similar methods for the other view selection types).

The next step in the flow is the selection of a debit account, which can be tested in another unit test:

```
1   public void testSelectDebitAccount() {
2     testStartFlow();
3
4     reset(accountRepository);
5     expect(accountRepository.getAccount(
6       debitAccount.getNumber())).andReturn(debitAccount);
7     replay(accountRepository);
8
9     MockParameterMap params = new MockParameterMap();
10    params.put("debitAccount", "Test-0");
11    ApplicationView view =
12      applicationView(signalEvent("next", params));
13    assertCurrentStateEquals("showEnterPaymentInfo");
14    assertModelAttributeEquals(new AccountNumber("Test-0"),
15      "payment.debitAccount.number", view);
16  }
```

There are a few interesting things to notice in the preceding example:

- *Line 2*: The testSelectDebitAccount() test calls testStartFlow() to start the flow. It is typical for a flow execution test method to call the "previous" test method, bringing the flow execution to the appropriate point.

- *Line 12*: The test signals the next event, passing in request parameters identifying the selected debit account.

- *Line 14*: Notice how the assertModelAttributeEquals(. . .) method can use OGNL expressions to access model data, in this case, to verify that the payment form backing object has been updated with the selected debit account.

As a next step in the enterPayment-flow, let's look at selecting a beneficiary for the payment. The enterPayment-flow will launch the beneficiaries-flow to let the user select a beneficiary. For EnterPaymentFlowExecutionTests, the mock beneficiaries-flow has been created: it immediately ends in the endSelected state, returning a beneficiary object to the parent flow. As a result, the testSelectBeneficiary() test is simple. All it needs to do is verify that the payment form-backing object has been updated with the selected beneficiary:

```
public void testSelectBeneficiary() {
  testSelectDebitAccount();
  ApplicationView view =
    applicationView(signalEvent("selectBeneficiary"));
  assertCurrentStateEquals("showEnterPaymentInfo");
  assertModelAttributeEquals(new AccountNumber("Test-1"),
    "payment.creditAccount.number", view);
}
```

The last steps in the "enter payment" flow are entering all payment information (amount etcetera) and submitting the payment. Testing these steps is straightforward:

```
public void testEnterPaymentInfo() {
  testSelectBeneficiary();
  MockParameterMap params = new MockParameterMap();
  params.put("amount", "150");
  params.put("message", "Test transfer");
  ApplicationView view = applicationView(signalEvent("next", params));
  assertCurrentStateEquals("showConfirmPayment");
  assertModelAttributeEquals(new BigDecimal(150), "payment.amount", view);
  assertModelAttributeEquals("Test transfer", "payment.message", view);
}
```

```
public void testSubmit() throws Exception {
  testEnterPaymentInfo();

  paymentProcessingEngine.submit(
    (Payment)getFlowExecution().getConversationScope().get("payment"));
  replay(paymentProcessingEngine);

  ExternalRedirect redirect = externalRedirect(signalEvent("submit"));
  assertFlowExecutionEnded();
  assertEquals("/balances/show.html?confirmationMessage=paymentSubmitted",
    redirect.getUrl());
}
```

One interesting thing to notice here is that the testSubmit() test makes sure the flow execution ends when signaling the submit event, using assertFlowExecutionEnded().

## Using Flow Execution Listeners

Flow execution listeners were introduced in Chapter 6. They are often useful when writing flow execution tests, allowing you to verify things at particular points in the flow execution life cycle. For instance, the sessionEnded(context, session, output) method defined by the FlowExecutionListener interface makes it easy to check that a flow returns the output it is expected to return. You can also use this same method to verify that a flow ends in the correct end state.

To illustrate this, let's look at a unit test for the beneficiaries-flow. This flow has already been mentioned numerous times as a subflow of the enterPayment-flow. It allows the user to select a beneficiary for a payment, and that selected beneficiary is returned to the parent flow. Here is the complete flow definition for the beneficiaries-flow:

```
<flow>
  <start-state idref="showBeneficiaries"/>

  <view-state id="showBeneficiaries" view="beneficiaries">
    <render-actions>
      <bean-action bean="accountRepository" method="getAccounts">
        <method-arguments>
          <argument
            expression="externalContext.sessionMap.user.clientId"/>
        </method-arguments>
```

```
          <method-result name="accounts"/>
        </bean-action>
        <bean-action bean="accountRepository" method="getBeneficiaries">
          <method-arguments>
            <argument
              expression="externalContext.sessionMap.user.clientId"/>
          </method-arguments>
          <method-result name="beneficiaries"/>
        </bean-action>
      </render-actions>
      <transition on="select" to="loadBeneficiary"/>
      <transition on="cancel" to="endCancel"/>
    </view-state>

    <action-state id="loadBeneficiary">
      <bean-action bean="accountRepository" method="getAccount">
        <method-arguments>
          <argument expression="requestParameters.accountNumber"/>
        </method-arguments>
        <method-result name="beneficiary" scope="flow"/>
      </bean-action>
      <transition on="success" to="endSelected"/>
    </action-state>

    <end-state id="endSelected">
      <output-mapper>
        <output-attribute name="beneficiary"/>
      </output-mapper>
    </end-state>

    <end-state id="endCancel"/>
</flow>
```

A flow execution test that verifies that the beneficiaries-flow returns the selected beneficiary on completion could look like this:

```
1  public void testSelect() {
2    setFlowExecutionListener(new FlowExecutionListenerAdapter() {
```

```
3      public void sessionEnded(RequestContext context,
4          FlowSession session, AttributeMap output) {
5        assertEquals("endSelected", session.getState().getId());
6        assertTrue(output.contains("beneficiary"));
7      }
8    } );
9
10    testStartflow();
11
12    reset(accountRepository);
13    expect(accountRepository.getAccount("9")).andReturn(
14      new Beneficiary("Beneficiary", "9"));
15    replay(accountRepository);
16
17    MockParameterMap params = new MockParameterMap();
18    params.put("accountNumber", "9");
19    nullView(signalEvent("select", params));
20    assertFlowExecutionEnded();
21  }
```

The key details from the preceding code snippet are explained here:

- *Line 2*: Using setFlowExecutionListener(listener), the test attaches a listener
  to the flow execution. The attached listener verifies that the flow ends in the
  endSelected state and has correctly filled the output map.

- *Line 12*: This test is again using EasyMock to create mock objects. When the select
  event is signaled to select a beneficiary, the selected beneficiary will be loaded with
  a call to AccountRepository.getAccount(accountNumber).

- *Line 19*: Signaling the select event will cause the beneficiaries-flow to end. At that
  point, the attached listener will be invoked and will check expectations.

# Integration Testing

The flow execution tests discussed in the previous section used mock services and even
mock subflow definitions to provide the means to test a flow definition in isolation. Flow
execution tests can also be used for integration tests, giving you an innovative and lightweight end-to-end integration test system.

When using a flow execution test as an integration test, you load, initialize, and register actual services with the FlowServiceLocator. The following example is taken from an integration test testing the "enter payment" use case of the Spring Bank application:

```
1   public class EnterPaymentFlowUseCaseTests extends
2       AbstractXmlFlowExecutionTests {
3
4     private BeanFactory beanFactory;
5     private UserService userService;
6     private AccountRepository accountRepository;
7
8     protected void setUp() throws Exception {
9       // boot real service layer because this is an integration test
10      beanFactory = new ClassPathXmlApplicationContext("service-layer.xml");
11      userService = (UserService)beanFactory.getBean("userService");
12      accountRepository =
13        (AccountRepository)beanFactory.getBean("accountRepository");
14    }
15
16    protected FlowDefinitionResource getFlowDefinitionResource() {
17      return createFlowDefinitionResource(
18        "src/main/webapp/WEB-INF/flows/enterPayment-flow.xml");
19    }
20
21    protected FlowServiceLocator createFlowServiceLocator() {
22      // setup a flow definition registry for the subflows
23      FlowDefinitionRegistry subflowRegistry =
24        new FlowDefinitionRegistryImpl();
25
26      FlowServiceLocator flowServiceLocator =
27        new DefaultFlowServiceLocator(subflowRegistry, beanFactory);
28
29      // load beneficiaries subflow and register it
30      XmlFlowRegistrar registrar = new XmlFlowRegistrar(flowServiceLocator);
31      registrar.addResource(createFlowDefinitionResource(
32        "src/main/webapp/WEB-INF/flows/beneficiaries-flow.xml"));
33      registrar.registerFlowDefinitions(subflowRegistry);
34
35      return flowServiceLocator;
36    }
```

```
37
38    ...
39
40  }
```

Here are the salient points in the preceding snippet:

- *Line 8*: Test setup involves loading the actual service layer. The Spring Bank sample application does not use a database, but a real application would typically also set up a data source connecting to a test database at this point.

- *Line 16*: The flow definition resource is loaded as in a normal flow execution test.

- *Line 21*: Instead of relying on registerMockServices(serviceRegistry), an integration test overrides createFlowServiceLocator() to set up an actual FlowServiceLocator. This flow service locator wraps the application context defining the application services and a flow definition registry containing the actual beneficiaries-flow.

The preceding setup code makes the enterPayment-flow run in a realistic environment, interacting with real application services and the real beneficiaries-flow. Interacting with real services, of course, impacts the test code. For instance, the unit tests selecting a beneficiary now look like this, actually driving the use case through the beneficiaries-flow:

```
public void testLaunchBeneficiariesFlow() {
  testSelectDebitAccount();

  ApplicationView view = applicationView(signalEvent("selectBeneficiary"));
  assertActiveFlowEquals("beneficiaries-flow");
  assertCurrentStateEquals("showBeneficiaries");
  assertModelAttributeCollectionSize(2, "accounts", view);
  assertModelAttributeCollectionSize(2, "beneficiaries", view);
}

public void testSelectBeneficiary() {
  testLaunchBeneficiariesFlow();

  MockParameterMap params = new MockParameterMap();
  params.put("accountNumber", "SpringBank-1");
  ApplicationView view = applicationView(signalEvent("select", params));
  assertActiveFlowEquals("enterPayment-flow");
  assertCurrentStateEquals("showEnterPaymentInfo");
```

```
assertModelAttributeEquals(new AccountNumber("SpringBank-1"),
  "payment.creditAccount.number", view);
}
```

Notice how the tests use the `assertActiveFlowEquals(flowId)` method to check the flow that is currently running.

Testing whether the flow correctly submits the payment also looks different in an integration test. The test can now interact with the service layer to check the payment was correctly submitted:

```
public void testSubmit() {
  testEnterPaymentInfo();

  ExternalRedirect redirect = externalRedirect(signalEvent("submit"));
  assertFlowExecutionEnded();
  assertEquals("/balances/show.html?confirmationMessage=paymentSubmitted",
    redirect.getUrl());

  assertEquals(9850.0D, accountRepository.getAccount(
    new AccountNumber("SpringBank-0")).getBalance().doubleValue());
  assertEquals(2150.0D, accountRepository.getAccount(
    new AccountNumber("SpringBank-1")).getBalance().doubleValue());
}
```

# Summary

Like any modern framework, Spring Web Flow actively promotes unit testing. Being a lightweight, POJO-based framework is an absolute plus in this regard. Spring Web Flow's abstraction of the runtime environment also helps you test outside of the container.

Unit testing Spring Web Flow code artifacts is facilitated by a number of mock implementations shipped with Spring Web Flow, and `MockExternalContext` is certainly the most important example.

In addition to simple mock classes, Spring Web Flow also provides advanced flow execution test support, allowing you to drive flow executions from inside a JUnit test. Flow execution tests were designed to test executions of flow definitions. However, they also provide an innovative and elegant technique for integration testing.

This chapter concludes the discussion of Spring Web Flow's feature set. Every available feature has now been covered. The next few chapters provide some more examples of using Spring Web Flow and illustrate how to extend the framework.

# CHAPTER 9

# The Sample Application

This chapter will discuss the Spring Bank sample application in detail. Earlier chapters of this book used examples from this sample application to illustrate various Spring Web Flow features. The following sections will cover the entire application, from its domain model all the way up to the presentation tier.

Studying the Spring Bank sample application should give you a feeling for what a realistic application that uses Spring Web Flow looks like. Although it is only a sample application, Spring Bank tries to present a realistic implementation:

- It builds on the Spring Framework as architectural glue, while Spring Web MVC is used as a base web MVC framework.

- It uses a rich and expressive domain model to manage accounts and process payments.

- Real user authentication and authorization are implemented using Spring Security (formerly Acegi Security System for Spring).

- Proper exception handling is provided: the application doesn't just spit stack traces at the user—something that would be unacceptable in a real electronic banking application.

- All messages displayed by the application have been internationalized, making multilingual use possible.

- The application has a polished look and feel. It uses SiteMesh (http://www.opensymphony.com/sitemesh) as a web page layout engine, and Displaytag (http://displaytag.sourceforge.net) for table display, allowing for data export and sorting.

Let's get started by looking at the functional requirements implemented in the Spring Bank sample application.

# Functional Requirements

Spring Bank is a simplified electronic banking application. Because it is only a sample application, Spring Bank will not provide every possible functionality for a real online banking application. Instead, it contains key use cases demonstrating important Spring Web Flow features. The use cases implemented in the Spring Bank application follow:

*User login and logout*: The application will authenticate a user during login, identifying the Spring Bank client associated with the user. Once logged in, users can log out, ending their sessions with the application.

*Account balances overview*: Logged in users can request an overview of the balances of all their accounts. They can then drill down into a particular account to see all entries for the selected account.

*Enter payment*: A logged in user can enter a new payment. Entering a payment is a multistep process in which all payment information is gathered and submitted to the payment processing system.

Chapters 4 and 5 used the "enter payment" use case as an example. Refer to those chapters, particularly to Figure 4-1, for more details on the "enter payment" process.

---

**Tip**  The Spring Bank sample application also gives you an excellent starting point to exercise your new Spring Web Flow expertise. For instance, you could try to implement additional use cases such as managing beneficiaries, opening and closing accounts, and so on.

---

Let's start by taking a quick look at where you can download the Spring Bank source code and how the application can be built.

# Downloading and Building

The source code of the Spring Bank application is stored in the Ervacon Subversion repository and is available at https://svn.ervacon.com/public/spring/samples/trunk/springbank. To check out the entire source tree, type the Subversion **svn co** command:

```
erwin@alex:~$ svn co https://svn.ervacon.com/public/spring/samples \
  /trunk/springbank springbank
A    springbank/project.properties
A    springbank/ivy.xml
```

```
A    springbank/src
A    springbank/src/test

...

A    springbank/src/main/webapp/css/style.css
A    springbank/build.xml
 U    springbank
Checked out revision 103.
```

Alternatively, you can use a graphical Subversion client for your platform, for instance, TortoiseSVN (http://tortoisesvn.tigris.org).

Spring Bank uses the Spring Jumpstart build system discussed in the "Spring Jumpstart" section of Chapter 2. The ivy.xml dependency descriptor lists the dependencies of the project:

```
<ivy-module version="1.1">
  <info organization="com.ervacon" module="springbank"/>

  <configurations>
    <conf name="global" visibility="private"/>
    <conf name="buildtime" visibility="private"/>
    <conf name="test" visibility="private"/>

    <conf name="default" extends="global"/>
  </configurations>

  <dependencies defaultconf="global->default">
    <!-- buildtime dependencies -->
    <dependency org="javax.servlet" name="servlet-api" rev="2.4"
      conf="buildtime->default" />

    <!-- global dependencies -->
    <dependency org="log4j" name="log4j" rev="1.2.14"/>
    <dependency org="taglibs" name="standard" rev="1.1.2"/>
    <dependency org="jstl" name="jstl" rev="1.1.2"/>
    <dependency org="opensymphony" name="sitemesh" rev="2.3"/>
    <dependency org="displaytag" name="displaytag" rev="1.1"/>
    <dependency org="commons-beanutils" name="commons-beanutils" rev="1.7.0"/>
    <dependency org="commons-lang" name="commons-lang" rev="2.4"/>
    <dependency org="commons-collections" name="commons-collections" rev="3.2.1"/>
```

```
    <dependency org="com.lowagie" name="itext" rev="1.4.8"/>
    <dependency org="org.springframework" name="spring-webflow" rev="1.0.6"/>
    <dependency org="org.springframework.security" name="spring-security-core" \
                rev="2.0.3"/>
    <dependency org="org.springframework" name="spring-aop" rev="2.5.3"/>

    <!-- test-time only dependencies -->
    <dependency org="junit" name="junit" rev="3.8.2"
      conf="test->default"/>
    <dependency org="org.easymock" name="easymock" rev="2.2"
      conf="test->default" />
  </dependencies>
</ivy-module>
```

As you can see, the application uses Spring Web Flow in its default configuration that is integrated with Spring Web MVC. Further dependencies are Log4j, the standard JSTL implementation, SiteMesh, Displaytag, iText (for PDF exports), and Spring Security. JUnit and EasyMock are used for unit testing.

Before you can build the project, you first have to edit the project.properties file to specify the location of the common build system on your computer:

common.build.dir=**/java/spring-webflow-1.0.6/common-build**

You can now build a deployable WAR file by simply typing the **ant dist** command from inside the springbank/ project directory:

```
erwin@alex:~/springbank$ ant dist
Buildfile: build.xml

force.env.load:


...


BUILD SUCCESSFUL
Total time: 5 seconds
```

The generated WAR file can be found in the target/artifacts/war/ directory and can be deployed to any Servlet 2.4–compatible Servlet engine (for instance Tomcat 5 or Jetty 6) running on Java 5 or later. As a sample application, Spring Bank does not use a real database, so you don't need to set up a database or configure a data source.

# The Domain Model

Most of the Java code in the Spring Bank application is part of the domain model implementation, which resides in the com.ervacon.springbank.domain package. As its core domain responsibility, the Spring Bank application needs to track bank accounts for clients of the bank, and correctly process payments submitted by those clients (see Figure 9-1).

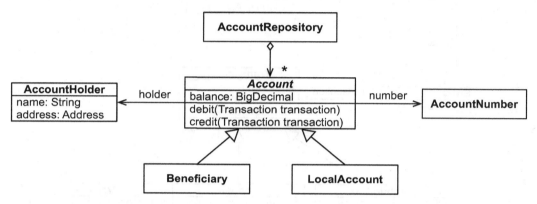

**Figure 9-1.** *Account class diagram*

The central class is the abstract Account class, modeling a bank account. Every Account is identified by an AccountNumber (which serves as a natural key) and has an AccountHolder (the owner of the account). Accounts track their balance and can be debited and credited in the context of a transaction.[1] An AccountRepository manages all accounts processed by the system. Not all of those accounts are local to Spring Bank. For instance, a user can transfer money from his local Spring Bank account (a LocalAccount) to an account from another bank. Such external accounts are generically captured as Beneficiary accounts. In a real application, an external Beneficiary would act as a facade for communication with another bank.

We don't know much about external beneficiaries (Beneficiary objects), only the account number is required. Optionally, we also have name and address information. The situation is somewhat different for local accounts, accounts associated with Spring Bank clients. Figure 9-2 shows the LocalAccount class diagram. The holder of a LocalAccount is a Client of Spring Bank. Those clients are managed by a ClientRepository. Each Client tracks his or her account numbers.

---

1. A transaction here is a monetary transaction, not a database transaction.

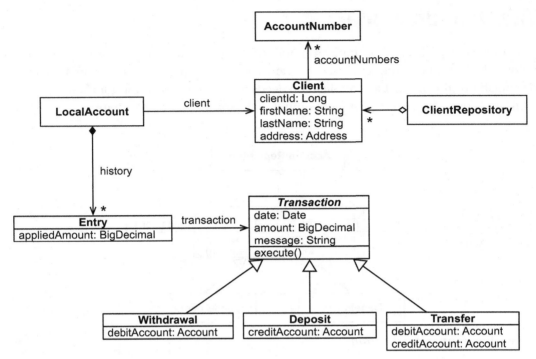

**Figure 9-2.** *LocalAccount class diagram*

The Spring Bank application is responsible for tracking all transactions involving local accounts. To this end, a LocalAccount maintains an entry history. Each Entry tracks the amount that was applied to the account (for example, –10.0 when the account is debited, 10.0 when it is credited) and the Transaction that caused the entry to be created. A Transaction object models a monetary transaction, moving an amount from or to an account on a particular date. Three types of transactions are supported:

- Withdrawal: Withdrawing cash from a debit account

- Deposit: Depositing cash on a credit account

- Transfer: Transferring money from a debit account to a credit account

As simple command objects, Transaction objects can be instantiated and executed:

```
Account creditAccount = accountRepository.getAccount(
  new AccountNumber("UBS-2291"));
new Deposit(500.0d, "Savings", creditAccount).execute();
```

Transaction objects are low-level, internal constructs of the domain model. The PaymentProcessingEngine service provides a high-level facade that calling code (such as the presentation tier) can use to submit a Payment. This is illustrated in Figure 9-3.

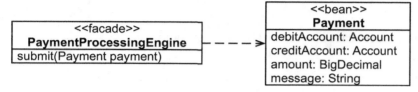

**Figure 9-3.** *Payment class diagram*

The PaymentProcessingEngine applies a payment policy to check whether or not the payment is allowed and translates the Payment into a Transfer transaction:

```
public void submit(Payment payment) throws PaymentProcessingException {
  Account debitAccount = accountRepository.getAccount(
    payment.getDebitAccount().getNumber());
  Account creditAccount = accountRepository.getAccount(
    payment.getCreditAccount().getNumber());
  enforcePaymentPolicy(debitAccount, creditAccount, payment.getAmount());
  new Transfer(payment.getAmount(), payment.getMessage(),
    debitAccount, creditAccount).execute();
}
```

Unlike Transfer objects, Payment objects are simple beans—parameter objects that are part of the PaymentProcessingEngine facade.

This domain model is capable of serving all the needs expressed earlier in the use cases of the Spring Bank application. For the "account balances overview" use case, the system looks up the accounts associated with a logged in Client (user) using the AccountRepository. A user can then drill down into the Entry history of an account. The "enter payment" use case involves creating a Payment object and submitting it to the PaymentProcessingEngine.

# Application Setup

In essence, the Spring Bank application is a Java EE web application. Since it uses Spring as architectural glue, the root web application context is set up using Spring's ContextLoaderListener in web.xml:

```
<context-param>
  <param-name>contextConfigLocation</param-name>
  <param-value>
```

```
    classpath:service-layer.xml
    /WEB-INF/security.xml
  </param-value>
</context-param>
<listener>
  <listener-class>
    org.springframework.web.context.ContextLoaderListener
  </listener-class>
</listener>
```

The root web application context contains the core service layer and security-related beans (which will be discussed in a minute). The service-layer.xml application context definition is loaded from the classpath and sets up the core services needed by the application:

```
<?xml version="1.0" encoding="UTF-8"?>
<beans xmlns="http://www.springframework.org/schema/beans"
  xmlns:xsi="http://www.w3.org/2001/XMLSchema-instance"
  xmlns:security="http://www.springframework.org/schema/security"
  xsi:schemaLocation="
    http://www.springframework.org/schema/beans
    http://www.springframework.org/schema/beans/spring-beans-2.5.xsd
    http://www.springframework.org/schema/security
    http://www.springframework.org/schema/security/spring-security-2.0.xsd">

  <bean id="clientRepository"
    class="com.ervacon.springbank.domain.InMemoryClientRepository"/>

  <bean id="accountRepository"
    class="com.ervacon.springbank.domain.InMemoryAccountRepository">
    <constructor-arg ref="clientRepository"/>
  </bean>

  <bean id="paymentProcessingEngine"
    class="com.ervacon.springbank.domain.PaymentProcessingEngineImpl">
    <constructor-arg ref="accountRepository"/>
  </bean>

  <bean id="userService"
    class="com.ervacon.springbank.user.UserServiceImpl">
    <constructor-arg ref="clientRepository"/>

    <security:custom-authentication-provider/>
```

```
  </bean>

  <!-- load sample data -->
  <bean class="com.ervacon.springbank.sampledata.SampleDataLoader"
    lazy-init="false" init-method="initSampleData">
    <constructor-arg ref="accountRepository"/>
    <constructor-arg ref="clientRepository"/>
    <constructor-arg ref="userService"/>
  </bean>
</beans>
```

Since Spring Bank is just a sample application, it uses in-memory implementations of AccountRepository, ClientRepository, and UserService (which will be introduced in the "Implementing the 'User Login and Logout' Use Case" section). Also notice the SampleDataLoader bean, which initializes some test data on application startup.

Defining core services in the root application context of the application is a Spring best practice. It isolates service layer beans from beans in other application tiers and makes the core services available to the rest of the application.

# The Presentation Tier

The Spring Bank presentation tier uses the Spring Web MVC framework, integrated with Spring Web Flow. In addition to these core components, a number of other well known frameworks are used for particular features of the application, namely SiteMesh, Displaytag, and Spring Security.[2]

## Spring Web MVC Setup

Spring Web MVC uses a DispatcherServlet as its front controller. This servlet is defined in the web.xml deployment descriptor:

```
<servlet>
  <servlet-name>dispatcher</servlet-name>
  <servlet-class>
    org.springframework.web.servlet.DispatcherServlet
  </servlet-class>
  <load-on-startup>1</load-on-startup>
</servlet>
<servlet-mapping>
```

---

2. This section does not cover all the details of using these frameworks. Refer to the relevant documentation and web sites for more information.

```
  <servlet-name>dispatcher</servlet-name>
  <url-pattern>*.html</url-pattern>
</servlet-mapping>
```

All `*.html` requests will be handled by the `DispatcherServlet`, which will by default load its configuration from a Spring application context: `/WEB-INF/dispatcher-servlet.xml`. A core piece of configuration is the definition of the view resolver:

```
<bean id="viewResolver"
  class="org.springframework.web.servlet.view.InternalResourceViewResolver">
  <property name="prefix" value="/WEB-INF/jsp/"/>
  <property name="suffix" value=".jsp"/>
  <property name="viewClass"
    value="org.springframework.web.servlet.view.JstlView"/>
</bean>
```

All JSP pages of the application are located in the `/WEB-INF/jsp/` directory. Since the application uses the JSTL, Spring's `JstlView` view class is used.

Another important piece of Spring Web MVC configuration is the handler mapping:

```
<bean id="handlerMapping"
  class="org.springframework.web.servlet.handler.SimpleUrlHandlerMapping">
  <property name="mappings">
    <props>
      <prop key="/session/*.html">sessionController</prop>
      <prop key="/balances/*.html">balancesController</prop>
      <prop key="/flows.html">flowController</prop>
    </props>
  </property>
</bean>
```

Using Spring's `SimpleUrlHandlerMapping`, the `DispatcherServlet` will dispatch requests to a `sessionController`, a `balancesController`, or a Spring Web Flow `flowController`. Let's take a look at each of those controllers.

## Implementing the "User Login and Logout" Use Case

Correctly implementing the "user login and logout" use case requires authentication of application users. The Spring Bank domain model includes a `Client` object, representing a Spring Bank client. Instead of directly basing authentication on a `Client` object, the application defines a `User` object, linking authentication credentials to a `Client`. Figure 9-4 illustrates this class setup.

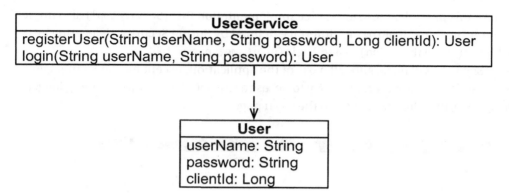

**Figure 9-4.** *User class diagram*

A `UserServices` takes care of actual authentication during login.

Using the authentication credentials stored in `User` objects, Spring Bank authenticates users with the help of the Spring Security framework. Spring Security also enforces URL-based security. To be able to do this, a Spring Security servlet filter intercepts all requests into the application and processes them using beans defined in the `security.xml` application context file:

```
<filter>
  <filter-name>springSecurityFilterChain</filter-name>
  <filter-class>
    org.springframework.web.filter.DelegatingFilterProxy
  </filter-class>
</filter>
<filter-mapping>
  <filter-name>springSecurityFilterChain</filter-name>
  <url-pattern>/*</url-pattern>
</filter-mapping>
```

The `service-layer.xml` application context marked the `userService` bean as a custom authentication provider:

```
<bean id="userService"
  class="com.ervacon.springbank.user.UserServiceImpl">
  <constructor-arg ref="clientRepository"/>

  <security:custom-authentication-provider/>
</bean>
```

To make this possible, the UserService implementation (UserServiceImpl) also imple-ments the AuthenticationProvider interface defined by Spring Security, delegating an authenticate(authentication) call to login(userName, password).

Spring Security will make sure all parts of the application, except for the login page, require an authenticated user. If you try to access a restricted area without being logged in, Spring Security will redirect you to the login page:

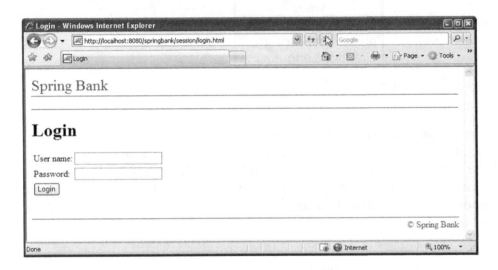

---

**Tip** Try to log in using user name erwinv and password foobar. The erwinv user is part of the sample data.

---

Presenting the login page is the responsibility of the SessionController (notice the URL in the preceding image), which is a simple Spring Web MVC MultiActionController. When the login page is submitted, Spring Security will authenticate the user using the UserService and, on successful authentication, forward the request to the /session/prepare.html URL, which again maps to the SessionController:

```
public ModelAndView prepare(HttpServletRequest request,
    HttpServletResponse response) throws Exception {
  User user = (User)SecurityContextHolder.getContext().getAuthentication() \
                   .getDetails();
  request.getSession(true).setAttribute("user", user);
  return new ModelAndView(new RedirectView("/balances/show.html", true));
}
```

As you can see, `prepare(request, response)` prepares the application for use, storing the authenticated `User` object in the HTTP session. It then redirects to the account balances overview page.

The last responsibility of the `SessionController` is handling logout. In response to a `/session/logout.html` request, the `SessionController` will simply invalidate the session and display the login page. Invalidating the session will also clean up the authenticated `User` object.

### Implementing the "Account Balances Overview" Use Case

Handling the "account balances overview" use case is the responsibility of another simple Spring Web MVC `MultiActionController`: `BalancesController`.

In response to a `/balances/show.html` request, the `BalancesController` will load all accounts of the logged in user from the `AccountRepository`:

```
public ModelAndView show(HttpServletRequest request,
    HttpServletResponse response) throws Exception {
  User user = (User)request.getSession(false).getAttribute("user");
  List<Account> accounts =
    accountRepository.getAccounts(user.getClientId());
  return new ModelAndView("balances", "accounts", accounts);
}
```

The list of balances is then rendered using Displaytag, allowing the user to sort the information by clicking a column header:

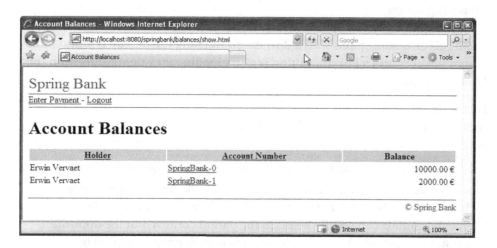

Clicking an account in this list will trigger a request to `/balances/entries.html` with an `accountNumber` request parameter. In response to such a request, the `BalancesController` will load the identified account and display its entry history. Displaytag's data export facilities are used to allow the user to export the history entries to various formats (XML, PDF, and so on):

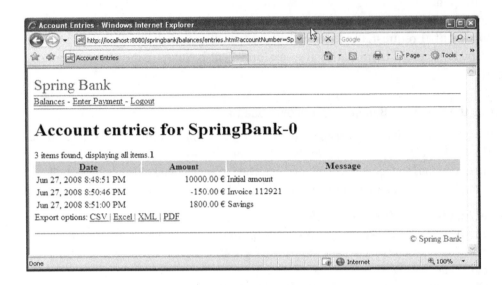

## Implementing the "Enter Payment" Use Case

Since the "enter payment" use case is a multistep process, it's best implemented using Spring Web Flow. Implementing this use case with Spring Web Flow is covered in depth in earlier chapters of this book. Instead of repeating that material here, let me just point out a few interesting things.

All /flows.html requests will be dispatched to a standard Spring Web Flow FlowController.

The FlowController is configured with a flow executor using the default continuation flow execution repository and a flow definition registry loading flow definitions from the /WEB-INF/flows/ directory:

```
<flow:registry id="flowRegistry">
  <flow:location path="/WEB-INF/flows/**/*-flow.xml"/>
</flow:registry>
```

The enterPayment-flow has a flow local application context: enterPayment-context.xml. This application context will be a child context of the DispatcherServlet application context, which will, in turn, be a child of the root web application context, as shown in Figure 9-5. A child context can see the beans in the parent context, but the opposite isn't true. As a result, the enterPayment-flow has access to all services provided by the application.

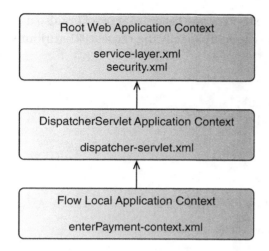

**Figure 9-5.** *Application context hierarchy*

Flow execution tests for the enterPayment-flow and beneficiaries-flow are included in the src/test/java directory. Type the **ant tests** command to run all unit tests for the project:

```
erwin@alex:~/springbank$ ant tests
Buildfile: build.xml

...

tests-local:
    [junit] Running com.er...springbank.web.BeneficiariesFlowExecutionTests
    [junit] Tests run: 3, Failures: 0, Errors: 0, Time elapsed: 1.347 sec
    [junit] Running com.er...springbank.web.EnterPaymentFlowExecutionTests
    [junit] Tests run: 7, Failures: 0, Errors: 0, Time elapsed: 1.842 sec
    [junit] Running com.er...springbank.web.EnterPaymentFlowUseCaseTests
    [junit] Tests run: 8, Failures: 0, Errors: 0, Time elapsed: 2.39 sec

tests:

BUILD SUCCESSFUL
Total time: 11 seconds
```

The JSP pages participating in the enterPayment-flow and beneficiaries-flow also use Displaytag. To make that work, you just have to explicitly specify the requestURI attribute of the <display:table> tag:

```
<display:table name="accounts" id="account"
  requestURI="/flows.html" style="width: 100%;">
  <display:column titleKey="holder" sortable="true"
    property="holder.name"/>

  ...
```

This will cause Displaytag to generate requests looking like this:

```
/flows.html?d-1327631-s=1&_flowExecutionKey=_c808..._k6C1...
```

These requests contain a _flowExecutionKey request parameter but no _eventId. Consequently, they trigger a flow execution refresh, simply rerendering the current page with a different sort order.

When the enterPayment-flow ends in the end end state (after having successfully submitted the payment), it sends a request parameter along to the BalancesController:

```
<end-state id="end" view="externalRedirect: \
  /balances/show.html?confirmationMessage=paymentSubmitted"/>
```

The balances.jsp page, displayed by the BalancesController, will detect the request parameter and display a confirmation message to the user:

```
<c:if test="${ param.confirmationMessage != null} ">
  <div class="confirmation">
    <fmt:message key="${ param.confirmationMessage} "/>
  </div>
</c:if>
```

And that's how a Spring Web MVC controller and a web flow can interoperate.

---

■**Tip**  Although the Spring Bank application doesn't illustrate sending input to a flow, recall that you can do so by including appropriate request parameters in the flow launch request: /flows.html?_flowId=foo-flow&a=x&b=y.

The preceding request launches foo-flow, passing in an input attribute a with value x and an input attribute b with value y.

---

# Internationalization

To make Spring Bank usable in an international setting, all text messages have been internationalized and are obtained from resource bundles. Those resource bundles are loaded using Spring's ReloadableResourceBundleMessageSource, which is configured in dispatcher-servlet.xml:

```
<bean id="messageSource"
  class="org.springframework.context.support. \
    ReloadableResourceBundleMessageSource">
  <property name="fallbackToSystemLocale" value="false"/>
  <property name="basename" value="/WEB-INF/messages"/>
  <property name="useCodeAsDefaultMessage" value="true"/>
  <property name="cacheSeconds" value="5"/>
</bean>
```

The actual resource bundle property files are located in the /WEB-INF/ directory. Since the application uses Spring's JstlView, message resources can simply be accessed from a JSP page using JSTL's <fmt:message> tag:

```
<h1><fmt:message key="enterPaymentInfo"/></h1>
```

Translation of error messages is equally simple, because the application makes sure to always include an error code that can be used to look up appropriate messages. For instance, the PaymentProcessingException generated by the PaymentProcessingEngine includes an error code:

```
if (debitAccount.getBalance().compareTo(amount) < 0) {
  throw new PaymentProcessingException(
    "error.insufficientBalance",
    "The balance of the debit account is insufficient");
}
```

Furthermore, Spring's DataBinder will automatically assign error codes to all data binding and validation errors using a DefaultMessageCodesResolver (see the JavaDoc of that class for more details). Including appropriate message resources for those error codes will make sure they are translated before being presented to the user. For instance, the following message will be used when there is a type mismatch on the amount field of the Payment form-backing object:

```
typeMismatch.amount=Enter a decimal number
```

> **■Tip** The interesting thing to keep in mind here is that Spring Web Flow does not influence internationalization. You can internationalize pages participating in a web flow using normal Spring Web MVC techniques.

## Exception Handling

To avoid showing ugly stack traces to the user when things go wrong, the Spring Bank application uses Spring Web MVC's HandlerExceptionResolver mechanism. The dispatcher-servlet.xml application context contains a bean definition for a SimpleMappingExceptionResolver:

```
<bean id="exceptionResolver"
  class="org.springframework.web.servlet.handler. \
    SimpleMappingExceptionResolver">
  <property name="exceptionMappings">
    <value>
      NoSuchFlowExecutionException=flowError
      java.lang.Exception=error
    </value>
  </property>
</bean>
```

When a NoSuchFlowExecutionException occurs, the flowError.jsp page will be shown. All other exceptions will be shown using the error.jsp page. Spring Web Flow will generate a NoSuchFlowExecutionException when a request comes in including an invalid _flowExecutionKey. This could happen, for instance, if the user uses the back button after having completed the enterPayment-flow:

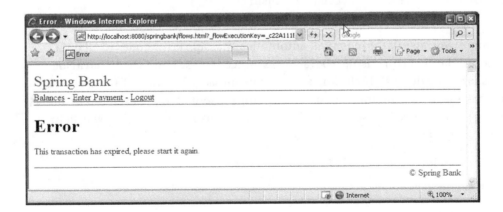

## Page Layout

A final interesting aspect of the Spring Bank application is its use of the SiteMesh page layout framework. SiteMesh uses a servlet filter to *decorate* every request:

```
<filter>
  <filter-name>sitemesh</filter-name>
  <filter-class>
    com.opensymphony.module.sitemesh.filter.PageFilter
  </filter-class>
</filter>
<filter-mapping>
  <filter-name>sitemesh</filter-name>
  <url-pattern>*.html</url-pattern>
  <dispatcher>REQUEST</dispatcher>
  <dispatcher>FORWARD</dispatcher>
</filter-mapping>
```

The decoration process extracts pieces of HTML from the generated pages and places them into an overall page layout defined by a decorator JSP (/WEB-INF/decorators/ main.jsp in the case of the Spring Bank application). This elegantly centralizes all layout and styling responsibilities of the application in a single place.

# Summary

This chapter presented an overview of the Spring Bank sample application. Spring Bank is a Spring Web MVC–based web application with a rich domain model, using Spring Jumpstart as its build system. It implements three key use cases: user login and logout, account balances overview, and enter payment.

Using Spring Security, Spring Bank implements form-based authentication and URL-based security. Leveraging Spring Security's flexibility, an application-specific UserService was used as the primary authentication provider.

The implementation of the "account balances overview" use case relies on simple Spring MVC controller technology, while the more complex "enter payment" use case is implemented using Spring Web Flow. The design and implementation of the enterPayment-flow and beneficiaries-flow were extensively covered in earlier chapters of this book.

To serve as a realistic implementation example, the Spring Bank application also leverages several other frameworks. Displaytag is used to display tables of information, while SiteMesh takes care of page layout. Furthermore, the application is fully internationalized and has realistic exception handling.

An important theme to take away from this sample application is the fact that Spring Web Flow plays nicely with all the other frameworks used in the application. Pages participating in web flows can use Displaytag, be secured using Spring Security, or be decorated using SiteMesh, just as any other page in the application. As a controller component in a web MVC framework, Spring Web Flow does not influence the use of these frameworks.

# CHAPTER 10

■ ■ ■

# Real-World Use Cases

**E**arlier chapters of this book covered Spring Web Flow's feature set in considerable detail. In this chapter, you will see that feature set in action as I show you a number of real-world use cases. One way of looking at this chapter is as a list of answers to frequently asked questions.

Most of the following sections show you how you can apply and leverage Spring Web Flow functionality to solve particular problems. In addition to this, I will also describe how to load and stress test an application using Spring Web Flow.

---

**Tip** If you can't find the answer to your question in this chapter, or in the rest of this book, you can always search Spring Web Flow's active user forums for an answer. If your search comes up empty, post your question to the forum, which is available at `http://forum.springframework.org`. Chances are that other people have struggled with the same problem and are willing to help you.

---

## Accessing the Host Environment

Spring Web Flow abstracts a developer from the details of the host framework and runtime environment, while still providing access to that host environment through the `ExternalContext` interface. This was already discussed in the "Flow Executions" section of Chapter 4, "Spring Web Flow Basics," as well as in Chapter 7, "Driving Flow Executions."

In some situations, however, you might want direct access to objects of the host environment that are not accessible through the `ExternalContext` interface. An example could be a Spring Web Flow `Action` that wants to write PDF data loaded from a database directly to the `HttpServletResponse`Åtypically in conjunction with a view state with a *null view*, that is, with no view name specified. How can this be accomplished?

The answer is simple: any Spring Web Flow artifact (Action, FlowExecutionListener, etc.) that has access to the external context can downcast the ExternalContext to an environment-specific subclass:

```
public class ShowPdfAction extends MultiAction {

  private PdfService pdfService;

  public void setPdfService(PdfService pdfService) {
    this.pdfService = pdfService;
  }

  protected Event showPdf(RequestContext context) throws Exception {
    ServletExternalContext externalContext =
      (ServletExternalContext)context.getExternalContext();
    HttpServletResponse response = externalContext.getResponse();
    response.setContentType("application/pdf");
    response.getOutputStream().write(pdfService.loadPdf());
    return success();
  }
}
```

The preceding example downcasts ExternalContext to ServletExternalContext and uses the HttpServletResponse available from that object to send a PDF to the client.

Each environment into which Spring Web Flow integrates has its own ExternalContext subclass, giving you access to the constructs specific to that environment. Chapter 7 mentioned the available ExternalContext subclasses, while Chapter 8, "Testing with Spring Web Flow," introduced the MockExternalContext for use in test environments. Table 10-1 presents an overview of all ExternalContext variants.

**Table 10-1.** *ExternalContext Variants*

| Environment | External Context | Remarks |
| --- | --- | --- |
| Spring Web MVC | ServletExternalContext | Also usable in a straight servlet environment; provides access to ServletContext, HttpServletRequest, and HttpServletResponse |
| Spring Portlet MVC | PortletExternalContext | Provides access to PortletContext, PortletRequest, and PortletResponse, as well as to the Portlet user information attributes |
| Struts | StrutsExternalContext | Subclasses ServletExternalContext and allows you to access the Struts ActionMapping and ActionForm |

**Table 10-1.** *ExternalContext Variants*

| Environment | External Context | Remarks |
| --- | --- | --- |
| JavaServer Faces | JsfExternalContext | Provides access to the JSF FacesContext and the ID and outcome of the last JSF action |
| Unit test | MockExternalContext | Mutable external context implementation that is only intended for testing purposes |

Downcasting ExternalContext is simple and functional, but doing so has one important downside: it ties your flow into one particular environment. For instance, testing a flow containing the previous ShowPdfAction requires additional effort. By default, the AbstractFlowExecutionTests will use a MockExternalContext, which would cause ShowPdfAction to throw ClassCastException because MockExternalContext and ServletExternalContext are not type compatible. As a workaround, you can explicitly use a real ServletExternalContext from inside your test code, wrapping a Spring MockServletContext, MockHttpServletRequest, and MockHttpServletResponse:

```
public class SampleFlowExecutionTests extends AbstractFlowExecutionTests {


  public void testStartFlow() {
    startFlow(new LocalAttributeMap(),
      new ServletExternalContext(new MockServletContext(),
        new MockHttpServletRequest(), new MockHttpServletResponse()));
  }

  ...

}
```

---

■**Tip** It is a good idea to try to keep your flows *environment independent*. If you really need access to the host environment, consider moving that code into a FlowExecutionListener. Listeners are not an integral part of a flow and can be plugged into executions of a flow depending on the runtime environment.

---

# Flow Definition Parameterization

It is not uncommon for an application to contain several similar web flows. For instance, part of an application might provide CRUD-style management of a number of entity types: persons, organizations, and so on. Every entity type has a corresponding web flow to edit the entity: an editPerson-flow for people and an editOrganization-flow for organizations. If the only differences between each of those flows are the type of entity they edit and the web pages used for editing, you end up with a number of essentially equivalent flow definitions. This clearly violates the DRY (*don't repeat yourself*) principle.

The Java flow builder offers an elegant solution to the problem. Chapters 4 and 5 already highlighted the flexibility of the Java flow builder. We can use that flexibility to define a single `EditEntityFlowBuilder` that can be parameterized with the entity type:

```
public class EditEntityFlowBuilder extends AbstractFlowBuilder {

  private String viewPath;
  private FormAction formAction;

  public EditEntityFlowBuilder(Class entityType) {
    // configure form action
    formAction = new FormAction();
    formAction.setFormObjectName("entity");
    formAction.setFormObjectClass(entityType);

    // calculate view path prefix
    viewPath = ClassUtils.getShortNameAsProperty(entityType) + "/";
  }

  public void buildStates() throws FlowBuilderException {

    ...

    addViewState("showEditEntity", viewPath + "editEntity",
        invoke("setupForm", formAction),
        transition(on(submit()), to("saveEntity"),
          ifReturnedSuccess(invoke("bindAndValidate", formAction))));

    ...

  }
}
```

When the `EditEntityFlowBuilder` is constructed, it initializes a `FormAction` using the specified entity type as form object class. The builder also calculates a view path based on the entity type (i.e., the views for editing `Person` entities reside in the `person/` directory). The `formAction` and `viewPath` are then used when adding states to the flow.

The parameterizable EditEntityFlowBuilder can now be reused for every entity type. Reuse in this context means registering multiple flows built by the same flow builder in the flow definition registry, each with a different flow ID:

```
public class ApplicationFlowRegistry extends
    AbstractFlowBuilderFlowRegistryFactoryBean {

  protected void doPopulate(FlowDefinitionRegistry registry) {
    registerFlowDefinition(registry, "editPerson-flow",
      new EditEntityFlowBuilder(Person.class));
    registerFlowDefinition(registry, "editOrganization-flow",
      new EditEntityFlowBuilder(Organization.class));
  }
}
```

Deploying this registry in your application is as simple as adding a corresponding bean definition to your application context:

```
<bean id="flowRegistry" class="sample.ApplicationFlowRegistry"/>
```

### PAREMETERIZING XML FLOW DEFINITIONS

Parameterizing an XML flow definition is also possible but quite a bit more cumbersome. In this case, you will have to rely on flow attributes to parameterize your flow. Recall that all flow definition constructs can have associated metadata attributes. A good example is the validatorMethod attribute recognized by FormAction. You can specify these attributes inside the flow definition, but the XmlFlowRegistryFactoryBean also allows you to specify attributes when registering a flow definition in the flow definition registry:

```
<bean id="flowRegistry"
  class="org.springframework.webflow.engine.builder.xml. \
    XmlFlowRegistryFactoryBean">
  <property name="flowDefinitions">
    <value>
      editPerson-flow=classpath:editPerson-flow.xml
      editOrganization-flow=classpath:editOrganization-flow.xml
    </value>
  </property>
  <property name="flowAttributes">
    <map>
      <entry key="editPerson-flow">
        <map>
          <entry key="entityType" value="foo.bar.Person"/>
        </map>
      </entry>
```

```
        <entry key="editOrganization-flow">
          <map>
            <entry key="entityType" value="foo.bar.Organization"/>
          </map>
        </entry>
      </map>
    </property>
</bean>
```

The preceding example registers editPerson-flow and editOrganization-flow with the flow registry but assigns a different entityType attribute value in each case. The attributes will be associated with the created Flow objects.

Simply defining the attributes is not enough. In this example, you would also have to subclass FormAction to take the attribute values into account, for instance:

```
public class EntityFormAction extends FormAction {

  protected Object createFormObject(RequestContext context)
      throws Exception {
    String entityType = (String)
      context.getActiveFlow().getAttributes().get("entityType");
    return Class.forName(entityType).newInstance();
  }

  ...

}
```

Using OGNL expressions would allow you to take the entity type into account in the view attribute of view and end states.

# Leveraging Listeners

Flow execution listeners are one of the most interesting Spring Web Flow features. As was explained in the "Flow Execution Listeners" section of Chapter 6, "Flow Execution Management," a FlowExecutionListener is an implementation of the Observer pattern: it can observe the life cycle of a flow execution.

You have already seen how useful flow execution listeners are when writing flow execution tests. Let's look at a few more examples illustrating their flexibility.

## Securing a Flow

The aspect-like nature of a flow execution listener makes it an ideal candidate to add security checks to a flow. As an example, consider a flow that contains a state that can only be entered by users that have a particular role. The stateEntering(context, state) method provides an ideal place to hook in this check:

```
public class SecurityListener extends FlowExecutionListenerAdapter {

  ...

  public void stateEntering(RequestContext context, StateDefinition state)
      throws EnterStateVetoException {
    if (!allowed(state)) {
      throw new EnterStateVetoException(context, state,
        "You are not allowed to enter this state");
    }
  }

  private boolean allowed(StateDefinition state) {

    ...

  }
}
```

Spring Web Flow even provides an EnterStateVetoException that you can use for this purpose, although this is not technically required.

Such a security listener can, of course, rely on the authorization services provided by a security framework such as Spring Security or the Servlet API (HttpServletRequest. isUserInRole(role)). Besides enforcing security when entering a state, you can also do security checks when a flow session starts using sessionStarting(context, definition, input) or when an event is signaled using eventSignaled(context, event).

## A Global Back Transition

A question that frequently pops up on the Spring Web Flow forums is whether Spring Web Flow automatically supports a back transition to move the flow back to the previous page. Spring Web Flow 1 does not provide this out of the box, because there is no single agreed-upon definition for "back." Does "back" mean going back to the previous view state? What if there are subflows or if a view state is entered several times in a row (e.g., in a loop in the flow definition)?

If you can specify exactly what it means to go back in your application, it should be easy to write a flow execution listener that will make a global back transition possible. For instance, let's assume going back simply means returning to the previous view state in the current flow session (so this doesn't take into account subflows). The following

BackListener code shown makes it possible to add a global "back" transition to the flow, like so:

```
<global-transitions>
  <transition on="back" to="${flashScope.previousViewStateId} "/>
</global-transitions>
```

This transition moves the flow to the previousViewStateId, which is tracked by the BackListener:

```
1   public class BackListener extends FlowExecutionListenerAdapter {
2
3     private Stack<String> getViewStateIds(RequestContext context) {
4       return (Stack<String>)context.getFlowScope().get("viewStateIds");
5     }
6
7     public void sessionCreated(RequestContext context,
8         FlowSession session) {
9       session.getScope().put("viewStateIds", new Stack<String>());
10    }
11
12    public void eventSignaled(RequestContext context, Event event) {
13      if ("back".equals(event.getId())) {
14        if (!getViewStateIds(context).isEmpty()) {
15          context.getFlashScope().put(
16            "previousViewStateId", getViewStateIds(context).pop());
17        }
18      }
19    }
20
21    public void stateEntered(RequestContext context,
22        StateDefinition previousState, StateDefinition state) {
23      if (previousState instanceof ViewState) {
24        if (previousState.getId().equals(state.getId())) {
25          return;
26        }
27
28        if ("back".equals(context.getLastEvent().getId())) {
29          return;
30        }
31
```

```
32              getViewStateIds(context).push(previousState.getId());
33          }
34      }
35  }
```

These are the key details to note in the previous code snippet:

- *Line 7*: Every time a new flow session is spawned, the listener adds a viewStateIds stack to flow scope. This stack is used to track the view state history.

- *Line 12*: When the back event is signaled, the listener puts the previousViewStateId in the flash scope, popping it from the viewStateIds stack. The previousViewStateId in the flash scope is available for use by the transition or by a view (e.g., to decide whether or not to render a Back button).

- *Line 21*: Whenever a transition takes the flow from a view state to another state, the listener records that previous view state by pushing it onto the viewStateIds stack. Some additional checks are necessary however, because we do not want to record a transition that doesn't move the flow into another state or executes the back transition.

## Breadcrumbs

The BackListener class presented in the previous section tracks the ID of the previous view state. A listener can also track more general navigational history information to, for instance, to build up a trail of breadcrumbs. The purpose of a breadcrumb trail is to give users a way to keep track of their location within the application. Here is an example taken from the JSPWiki (http://www.jspwiki.org/) application, which uses breadcrumbs to track a user's trail through the available pages:

You could add a breadcrumb to the trail for every view state the flow enters, but this is generally too fine grained. A better approach is to have a breadcrumb for every flow spawned by the user, resulting in a trail when the user moves into a subflow. Using a breadcrumb at the level of a flow also enforces the notion that a flow is a self-contained module. The following code example implements this in a `BreadcrumbListener`:

```
public class BreadcrumbListener extends FlowExecutionListenerAdapter {

  public void sessionStarting(RequestContext context,
      FlowDefinition definition, MutableAttributeMap input) {
    LinkedList<String> trail =
      (LinkedList<String>)context.getConversationScope().get("trail");
    if (trail == null) {
      trail = new LinkedList<String>();
      context.getConversationScope().put("trail", trail);
    }
    trail.add(definition.getId());
  }

  public void sessionEnding(RequestContext context,
      FlowSession session, MutableAttributeMap output) {
    LinkedList<String> trail =
      (LinkedList<String>)context.getConversationScope().get("trail");
    if (trail != null) {
      trail.removeLast();
    }
  }
}
```

The listener adds a breadcrumb to the trail every time a new flow session starts. When that flow session ends again, the breadcrumb is removed. Notice that `trail` is stored in the conversation scope. This is necessary because the trail needs to be global for the entire flow execution (conversation) and not linked to a particular flow session.

# Load and Stress Testing

Let's shift gears a bit and move from discussing Spring Web Flow features to the topic of load and stress testing an application. Load testing an application provides valuable insights into the application's performance characteristics. Stressing an application beyond the expected load can highlight potentially problematic areas.

Load and stress testing are important parts of the testing process any application should go through. Web applications using Spring Web Flow are no exception. There are many tools available to perform load or stress tests on web applications, in both the commercial and open source spaces. The only peculiarity these tools need to deal with when testing a Spring Web Flow application is tracking the *flow execution key*.

---

**Note** As I mentioned in Chapter 7, you don't need to manually submit the flow execution key when you integrate Spring Web Flow with JSF.

---

Recall that every request that participates in an ongoing flow execution needs to include a _flowExecutionKey request parameter, identifying the execution in which it is participating. Refer to the "Flow Executors" section of Chapter 6 for more details.

---

**Tip** When load or stress testing an application using Spring Web Flow, disabling "always redirect on pause" at the level of the flow executor is often interesting. This will avoid the extra request introduced by the POST-REDIRECT-GET idiom and will generally make your load and stress tests simpler. The impact of POST-REDIRECT-GET on the server load should be minimal. You can, of course, also leave "always redirect on pause" enabled and configure the test to handle the extra GET request.

---

To illustrate load testing a Spring Web Flow application, I will explain how to test the Spring Bank sample application using Apache JMeter (http://jakarta.apache.org/jmeter). JMeter is a Java desktop application designed to load and stress test web applications.

**Note**  The JMeter project file for Spring Bank, called `Spring Bank.jmx`, is included in the Spring Bank project available from `https://svn.ervacon.com/public/spring/samples/trunk/springbank`. The test configuration assumes the application is configured with "always redirect on pause" *disabled*.

When testing an application using Spring Web Flow with JMeter, two pieces of test configuration are of particular importance. First of all, you need to add an HTTP Cookie Manager to the test. This is necessary to have JMeter manage the cookies used to track HTTP sessions. By default, Spring Web Flow's `SessionBindingConversationManager` uses the HTTP session to store conversational state.

Second, you can use JMeter's Regular Expression Extractor to extract the `_flowExecutionKey` from the response pages and put it in a variable. The following screenshot shows the relevant JMeter configuration:

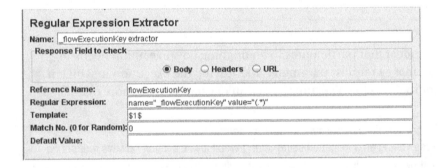

JMeter will post process every request using the Regular Expression Extractor. A subsequent request can use the `${flowExecutionKey}` variable to send the flow execution key extracted from the response of the previous request back to the server:

Extracting a flow execution key from a response is only useful when dealing with pages generated by Spring Web Flow. You can scope the Regular Expression Extractor by nesting it under a simple controller. This nesting is illustrated in the following screenshot, along with the rest of the test tree:

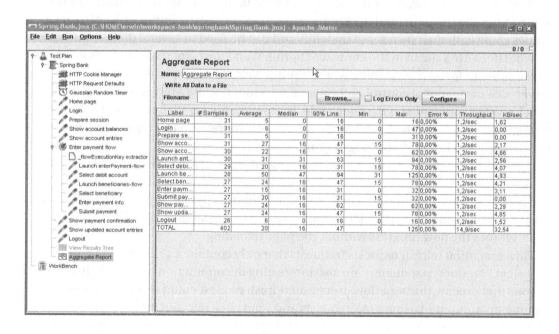

The test scenario simulates a user that logs into the application, checks account entries, submits a payment, and then checks the account entries again to verify the balance was updated. Finally, the user logs out.

---

■**Note**   The Spring Web Flow framework itself was put through rigorous performance testing and optimization. Performance concerns should not stop you from using Spring Web Flow. Keeping a close eye on memory utilization under load is a more interesting characteristic, especially if you are putting large objects into one of the flow execution scopes.

---

# Spring Web Flow and AJAX

AJAX has lately been a popular technique to make web applications more interactive. With AJAX, parts of a page might be updated individually, and relevant data might be loaded from the server behind the scenes without reloading the entire page. AJAX techniques come with their own set of tradeoffs and can be used in several different ways.

What does AJAX mean in the context of Spring Web Flow? Not that much. As a controller component for web MVC frameworks, Spring Web Flow is mainly concerned with server-side navigational control and state management, while AJAX is tightly coupled with view development and the client side. In essence, Spring Web Flow and AJAX are orthogonal: they do not really influence each other. There are a few interesting ways to put Spring Web Flow and AJAX together however.

One way of driving a flow execution is through the use of AJAX. Using an AJAX framework such as Prototype (http://www.prototypejs.org), you can submit requests to a flow and receive results back from the flow, rendering them as part of larger web page. From the point of view of Spring Web Flow, this results in a normal flow execution, while the end user sees the flow progress without the page reloading.

Flow execution refresh requests (requests that only contain a _flowExecutionKey but no _eventId request parameter) are also interesting in conjunction with AJAX. Render actions that execute during a flow execution refresh request could recognize request parameters submitted using AJAX requests and send back relevant information from one of the flow execution scopes. This allows a Spring Web Flow flow execution to also serve as the execution context of JavaScript code running in the client browser.

Spring Web Flow 2 comes with specialized support for AJAX techniques, allowing you to trigger partial rendering of a view from an AJAX request.

# Summary

This chapter presented answers to a number of frequently asked questions. It showed you how to leverage Spring Web Flow's feature set to implement several real world use-cases. You learned how to interact with the native host environment in which Spring Web Flow is running, an elegant way to parameterize Java flow definitions, and how to use flow execution listeners to solve several interesting problems.

Since stress and load testing are important activities, this chapter illustrated this kind of testing using Apache JMeter and the Spring Bank sample application. The chapter concluded by looking at AJAX and Spring Web Flow and at how these two technologies can work together.

In the next chapter, we continue the trend of this chapter and will look at how to extend Spring Web Flow to meet exotic requirements.

# CHAPTER 11

■ ■ ■

# Extending Spring Web Flow

**W**hile studying Spring Web Flow's flow definition language and flow execution management system, you already learned about many of the possible extension points the framework offers. This chapter will present a broad overview of how you can extend Spring Web Flow, plugging custom implementations of particular artifacts into the system.

I will also show you two examples of Spring Web Flow extensions: a custom `ConversationManager` that stores conversational state in a database using JDBC and a custom flow executor front-end, integrating Spring Web Flow into the raw Servlet API. Before getting to that, let's start by looking at some common extension points.

## Common Extension Points

Spring Web Flow's basic feature set should cover the majority of use cases. In some situations, however, you need specialized custom functionality. Most of the time, you can get the exact behavior you want by plugging in a custom implementation of a Spring Web Flow artifact, through one of its many extension points.

This section focuses on plugging custom artifacts into Spring Web Flow flow definitions. Examples of extending Spring Web Flow's flow execution management are provided in the sections called "A Database-Backed Conversation Manager" and "A Flow Servlet."

---

**Tip** Recall that the Java flow builder provides quite a bit more flexibility when it comes to using custom flow definition artifacts. Java flow definitions use standard Java syntax and can use the full flexibility of the Java language to instantiate and configure custom artifacts. If you want to use several customizations to the flow definition language, the Java flow builder might be a good idea.

---

## Using Bean References

Both the XML and Java flow definition syntax provide ways to reference custom artifact implementations deployed as beans in a Spring application context. The application context defining those custom artifact beans is typically the flow local application context or one of its parent contexts.

Custom Action implementations (Spring Web Flow's most important extension point) can easily be referenced as beans in an application context:

```
<action bean="paymentAction" method="submitPayment"/>
```

```
invoke("submitPayment", action("paymentAction"))
```

You have seen many examples of this. Plugging in your own FlowExecutionExceptionHandler to handle exceptions that occur in a flow execution of your flow can be done in a similar way:

```
<exception-handler bean="myExceptionHandler"/>
```

```
getFlowServiceLocator().getExceptionHandler("myExceptionHandler")
```

The same is true if you want to use a custom FlowAttributeMapper to have fine-grained control over subflow state input and output mapping:

```
<attribute-mapper bean="customMapper"/>
```

```
attributeMapper("customMapper")
```

Refer to Chapters 4 and 5 for more details.

Bean references for some flow definition artifacts, notably TransitionCriteria, TargetStateResolver, and ViewSelector, use a slightly different technique. A custom implementation of these strategies can be referenced using the bean: prefix in a flow definition. This technique was introduced in Chapter 5.

TransitionCriteria objects are responsible for matching transitions as eligible for execution. An XML flow definition can do something like this:

```
<transition on="bean:myCriteria" to="nextState"/>
```

while a Java flow builder has a similar possibility:

```
transition(on("bean:myCriteria"), to("nextState"))
```

These two transition definitions refer to a `myCriteria` bean defined in a Spring application context:

```
<bean id="myCriteria" class="my.CustomTransitionCriteria"/>
```

The `bean:` prefix can also be used to plug in a custom `TargetStateResolver` responsible for calculating the target state of a transition at runtime. Here are two examples:

```
<transition on="cancel" to="bean:cancelStateIdCalculator"/>

transition(on("cancel"), to("bean:cancelStateIdCalculator"))
```

The same technique can also be used for custom `ViewSelector` implementations that are responsible for selecting a view and preparing the model data that will be exposed to the view. A custom `ViewSelector` is particularly useful if you want to control the model that will be exposed to the view, for instance:

```
<end-state id="endCancel" view="bean:cancelViewSelector"/>

addEndState("endCancel", "bean:cancelViewSelector")
```

---

**Tip** When using the Java flow builder, it is typically more elegant and convenient to directly instantiate the custom `TransitionCriteria`, `TargetStateResolver`, or `ViewSelector` object, instead of using the `bean:` prefix: `transition(on(new CustomTransitionCriteria()), to("nextState"))`. This avoids the need for an extra bean definition.

---

## Extending the Flow Definition Constructs

The previous section discussed plugging in custom implementations of certain strategy objects referenced by a flow definition. Spring Web Flow also allows you to customize the core flow definition artifacts: flows, states, and transitions. Customizing these artifacts requires you to subclass the corresponding types defined by the Execution Engine layer. You can then override one of the behavioral methods or set up a default configuration for your custom artifact type.

Each core flow definition artifact class defines behavioral methods capturing the responsibilities of that class.

### Flow

The Flow class defines four behavioral methods that you can override:

- start(context, input) is called when a new flow session for the flow is started. The default implementation sets up all flow variables, does input mapping using configured input mappers, executes all flow start actions, and enters the start state.

- Every time an event occurs in a flow session of a Flow, its onEvent(context) method is called. By default, the Flow will simply propagate the event to the current state of the flow session. This method is also responsible for making global transitions work: if signaling the event in the current state of the flow session results in a NoMatchingTransitionException, the flow will look for a matching global transition.

- Whenever a flow session of a Flow ends, its end(context, output) method is invoked. The default implementation executes all flow end actions and does output mapping using the configured flow output mappers.

- The last behavioral hook method of the Flow class is handleException(exception, context), which will be called every time an exception occurs in a flow session of a Flow. The default implementation simply delegates exception handling to any registered FlowExecutionExceptionHandler instances.

### State

The abstract State class defines two behavioral methods:

- enter(context) is called when the flow enters the state. The enter(context) method defined by the State class is actually final. It executes the state entry actions and then delegates to the abstract doEnter(context) method that subclasses must override.

- If an exception occurs in the state, handleException(exception, context) is invoked. The default implementation of this method will delegate exception handling to any FlowExecutionExceptionHandlers registered with the state.

## TransitionableState

`TransitionableState` is the superclass of all states that are *transitionable*, in other words, states that have transitions. `TransitionableState` adds three additional behavioral methods to those inherited from the `State` superclass:

- `onEvent(context)` is invoked whenever an event is signaled in the state. The default implementation simply looks for a matching transition and executes that.

- When a transition was matched as eligible for execution but rolled back because the transition execution criteria failed, the source state will be reentered with a call to `reenter(context)`. The default implementation just calls `enter(context)`, as defined by the `State` class. If you want different enter and reenter behavior, override this method.

- If a fired transition does not roll back and instead enters its target state, it will first invoke `exit(context)` to leave the source state. By default, exiting a transitionable state simply executes the state exit actions.

## Transition

The `Transition` class defines a single behavioral method: `execute(sourceState, context)`. This method will be called whenever the transition is matched as eligible for execution and executed. The default implementation will use the transition execution criteria to check if the transition can complete execution. If so, it will exit the source state and enter the target state; if not, it will reenter the source state.

All of these hook methods are summarized in Figure 11-1.

---

■**Tip** Instead of directly subclassing `State` or `TransitionableState`, it is better to extend one of Spring Web Flow's default state types: `ViewState`, `ActionState`, `EndState`, `DecisionState`, or `SubflowState`.

---

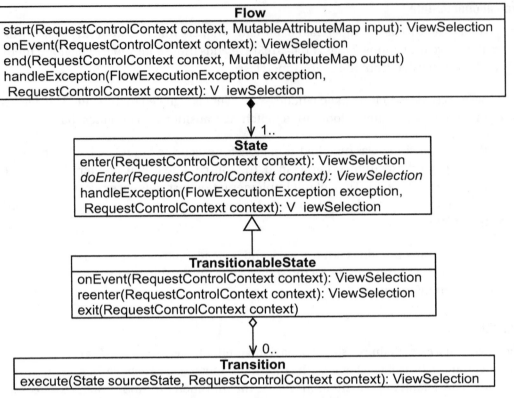

**Figure 11-1.** *Behavioral hook methods of the core flow definition artifacts*

Once you have your custom flow definition artifacts implemented, you still need to plug them into your flow definition. This is simple in the case of the Java flow builder, because you can directly instantiate your custom artifact type and add it to your flow, for instance:

```
FormState state =
  new FormState(getFlow(), "showEnterPaymentInfo", action("formAction"));
```

The preceding example uses a hypothetical FormState, a view state configured with a FormAction for handling an input form, as discussed in Chapter 5.

---

■**Tip**  Recall that instantiating a state automatically adds it to the flow passed into the constructor.

---

Things are a little bit more involved when using the XML flow builder. The flow builder delegates creation of core flow definition artifacts to a FlowArtifactFactory. As a result, you have to configure a flow builder with a custom `FlowArtifactFactory` to plug in the custom artifact types.

As an example, let's look at how you can plug the `FormState` mentioned previously into an XML flow definition. Once the `FormState` itself is implemented, you have to set up a custom flow artifact factory:

```
1  public class CustomFlowArtifactFactory
2      extends FlowArtifactFactory {
3
4    public State createViewState(String id, Flow flow,
5        Action[] entryActions, ViewSelector viewSelector,
6        Action[] renderActions, Transition[] transitions,
7        FlowExecutionExceptionHandler[] exceptionHandlers,
8        Action[] exitActions, AttributeMap attributes)
9        throws FlowArtifactLookupException {
10     if (id.startsWith("form_")) {
11       FormAction formAction = new FormAction();
12
13       String className = attributes.getString("formObjectClass");
14       try {
15         formAction.setFormObjectClass(Class.forName(className));
16       }
17       catch (ClassNotFoundException e) {
18         throw new FlowArtifactLookupException(id, FormState.class,
19             "Cannot load form object class: " + className);
20       }
21
22       FormState formState = new FormState(flow, id, formAction);
23       if (viewSelector != null) {
24         formState.setViewSelector(viewSelector);
25       }
26
27       // configure other properties
28       ...
29
30       return formState;
31     }
32     else {
33       return super.createViewState(id, flow, entryActions,
34           viewSelector, renderActions, transitions,
35           exceptionHandlers, exitActions, attributes);
36     }
```

```
37    }
38
39    ...
40  }
```

There are a few interesting things to notice here:

- *Line 4*: Since the FormState is assumed to be a specialized view state, the createViewState(...) method is overridden.

- *Line 10*: Based on a state ID naming convention, the factory decides whether to build a FormState or a normal ViewState.

- *Line 13*: The factory queries the state attributes to find the necessary FormAction configuration.

With the CustomFlowArtifactFactory ready to go, you just need to configure the XmlFlowRegistryFactoryBean to use it. You cannot use the <flow:registry> element in this case. Here is an example definition:

```
<bean id="flowRegistry"
  class="org.springframework.webflow.engine.builder.xml. \
    XmlFlowRegistryFactoryBean">
  <property name="flowLocations" value="classpath:enterPayment-flow.xml"/>
  <property name="flowArtifactFactory">
    <bean class="my.CustomFlowArtifactFactory"/>
  </property>
</bean>
```

Finally, an XML view state definition that would cause a FormState to be created would look like this:

```
<view-state id="form_showEnterPaymentInfo" view="enterPaymentInfo">
  <attribute name="formObjectClass"
    value="com.ervacon.springbank.domain.Payment"/>

  <transition on="bindAndValidate_next" to="showConfirmPayment"/>
  <transition on="bind_selectBeneficiary" to="launchBeneficiariesFlow"/>
</view-state>
```

This example essentially uses convention over configuration: by detecting prefixes in the state ID and transition IDs, the artifact factory knows how to configure the corresponding objects.

**Note**  Next to creating `Flow` and `Transition` objects, Spring Web Flow's `FlowArtifactFactory` only supports the five state types provided out of the box: `ViewState`, `ActionState`, `EndState`, `DecisionState`, and `SubflowState`. In other words: if you're using the XML flow builder you are limited to subclassing the existing state types and cannot introduce a brand new state type. This makes sense because the XML flow definition syntax is completely focused at those five core state types.

## Custom Flow Builders

If you are using custom extensions of particular flow definition constructs, for instance, a custom state type, adding direct support for this at the flow builder level can be useful. Doing that allows you to enhance the flow definition language with syntax for your custom constructs, for instance, `<form-state>` XML elements.

**Note**  For Java flow builders, customizing the flow builder to add support for your own extensions is less relevant, since Java is used as the flow definition language. In this case, adding helper methods to a builder superclass is the equivalent of introducing new flow definition syntax.

A very nice example of a custom flow definition language implemented by a specialized flow builder is the Groovy-based flow definition syntax offered by Grails (http://www.grails.org). Here is a simple example:

```
class BookController {

  def shoppingCartFlow = {
    getBooks {
      action {
        [ bookList:Book.list() ]
      }
      on("success").to "showCatalogue"
      on(Exception).to "handleError"
    }
    showCatalogue {
      on("chooseBook") {
        if(!params.id) return error()
```

```
        def items = flow.cartItems
        if(!items) items = [] as HashSet
        items << Book.get(params.id)
        flow.cartItems = items
      } .to "showCart"
    }
    showCart {
      on("checkout").to "enterPersonalDetails"
      on("continueShopping").to "showCatalogue"
    }

    ...

  }
}
```

There are other reasons why you might want to use a custom flow builder. One fairly typical example is building flows from definitions residing in a database. Your application might, for instance, allow particular users to define flows by editing relevant definitions via the web interface and storing those in the database. Other users will launch flow executions for those flows, causing Spring Web Flow to load the definitions from the database and build the corresponding Flow.

# A Database-Backed Conversation Manager

Spring Web Flow has a well-defined ConversationManager service tasked with storing conversational state. A ConversationManager manages Conversation objects, which are little more than simple attribute collections (similar to an HttpSession defined by the Servlet API for instance). While a ConversationManager is responsible for actually persisting the conversational state in between individual requests, a FlowExecutionRepository decides when and how to store conversation state using the ConversationManager (this was discussed in much more detail in the "Conversation Management" section of Chapter 6).

---

**Tip** If you want to change the way a ConversationManager is used, consider implementing a custom FlowExecutionRepository, which is considerably more complex but also provides more flexibility. An example could be a continuations-based repository that does not rely on Java object serialization to produce flow execution snapshots.

---

Recall the ConversationManager and Conversation interfaces. Both interfaces are simple and fairly straightforward to implement:

```
package org.springframework.webflow.conversation;

public interface ConversationManager {

  public Conversation beginConversation(ConversationParameters params)
    throws ConversationException;
  public Conversation getConversation(ConversationId id)
    throws ConversationException;
  public ConversationId parseConversationId(String encodedId)
    throws ConversationException;
}

public interface Conversation {

  public ConversationId getId();
  public void lock();
  public Object getAttribute(Object name);
  public void putAttribute(Object name, Object value);
  public void removeAttribute(Object name);
  public void end();
  public void unlock();
}
```

The trickiest part to implementing your own ConversationManager is the getConversation(id) method. This method is expected to return a handle allowing the caller to manipulate the identified conversation, *in the current execution thread.* For instance, the following code is legal:

```
ConversationManager manager = ...;
ConversationId id = ...;
Conversation conv = manager.getConversation(id);
conv.lock();
try {
  Conversation localReference = manager.getConversation(id);
  // no need to lock since conversation 'id' is already locked
  localReference.putAttribute("foo", "bar");
  Object foo = conv.getAttribute("foo");
}
```

```
finally {
  conv.unlock();
}
```

---

**Note**  Whether the handle returned by the `getConversation(id)` method is the actual `Conversation` or a specialized handle object is up to the `ConversationManager` implementation.

When deciding on an implementation strategy, keep in mind that Spring Web Flow will ensure that a single conversation is *never* concurrently accessed from multiple different execution threads.

---

As an example of implementing a `ConversationManager`, I will discuss a `DaoConversationManager`, which persists conversational state in a database using a `ConversationDao`. The "Downloading and Building the Conversation Manager" sidebar explains where you can download the source code for this conversation manager.

### DOWNLOADING AND BUILDING THE CONVERSTATION MANAGER

The source code for the `DaoConversationManager` discussed in this section, as well as the `FlowServlet` covered in the next section, are available in the Ervacon Subversion repository located at `https://svn.ervacon.com/public/spring/samples/trunk/swfextensions`. You can check out the code using your favorite Subversion client. The `swfextensions` project uses the Spring Jumpstart build system (discussed in the "Spring Jumpstart" section of Chapter 2). To build a JAR file, simply type the **ant dist** command in the project directory.

Figure 11-2 shows the structure of the conversation manager.

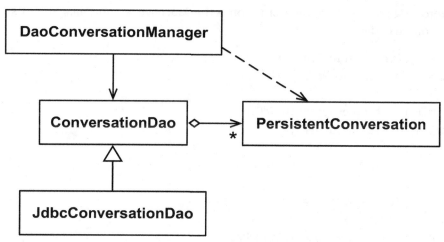

**Figure 11-2.** *DaoConversationManager class diagram*

A single ConversationDao implementation is provided: JdbcConversationDao. This is a simple Spring JdbcDaoSupport-based data access object (DAO) that stores PersistentConversation objects in a simple CONVERSATION database table (HSQLDB syntax is shown):

```
create table CONVERSATION(
  ID char(48) primary key,
  ATTRIBUTES varbinary not null
);
```

---

■**Tip**  Since the data access object used by the DaoConversationManager is pluggable, you could implement your own ConversationDao, for instance, using the Java Persistence API (JPA) or Hibernate (http://www.hibernate.org).

---

The most interesting part of the implementation is the DaoConversationManager. Let's take a look at its source code:

```
1   public class DaoConversationManager
2       implements ConversationManager {
3
4   private UidGenerator conversationIdGenerator =
5     new RandomGuidUidGenerator();
6
7   private ConversationDao conversationDao;
8
9   public void setConversationDao(
10        ConversationDao conversationDao){
11    this.conversationDao = conversationDao;
12    }
13
14  public Conversation beginConversation(
15        ConversationParameters params)
16        throws ConversationException {
17    ConversationId convId = new SimpleConversationId(
18        conversationIdGenerator.generateUid());
19    conversationDao.createConversation(
20        new PersistentConversation(convId, conversationDao));
21    return getConversation(convId);
22    }
23
24  public Conversation getConversation(ConversationId id)
25        throws ConversationException {
26    if (PersistentConversationHolder.holdsConversation(id)) {
27      // we already loaded the conversation for the calling thread
28      return PersistentConversationHolder.getConversation(id);
29    }
30    else {
31      // load the conversation
32      PersistentConversation conversation =
33        conversationDao.readConversation(id);
34      if (conversation == null) {
35        throw new NoSuchConversationException(id);
36      }
37      // cache it for the calling thread
38      PersistentConversationHolder.putConversation(conversation);
39      return conversation;
```

```
40        }
41    }
42
43    public ConversationId parseConversationId(String encodedId)
44          throws ConversationException {
45        return new SimpleConversationId(
46          conversationIdGenerator.parseUid(encodedId));
47    }
48  }
```

Several lines in the preceding code snippet bear further explanation:

- *Line 14*: Beginning a new conversation will create an entry for the conversation in the database. Instead of directly returning the created entry, getConversation(id) is called.

- *Line 24*: Obtaining a conversation by ID is a bit more involved. As explained previously, getConversation(id) might be called multiple times, and the returned handle must allow the caller to manipulate the identified conversation in the current execution thread. To make that possible, the DaoConversationManager uses a PersistentConversationHolder that manages PersistentConversation objects in a Java ThreadLocal.

  If the identified conversation is present in the PersistentConversationHolder, that object is returned. Otherwise, the conversation is loaded from the database and placed in the PersistentConversationHolder.

- *Line 43*: Parsing a string-encoded conversation ID simply re-creates the corresponding ConversationId object. Note that the SimpleConversationId class is part of Spring Web Flow's SessionBindingConversationManager implementation.

There is an error looming in the code of the DaoConversationManager shown previously: it stores PersistentConversation objects in a ThreadLocal but never removes them again. The code that removes the object from the PersistentConversationHolder is found inside the PersistentConversation class:

```
1  public class PersistentConversation
2    implements Conversation, Serializable {
3
4    ...
5
6    public PersistentConversation(
7        ConversationId id, ConversationDao dao) {
8      this.id = id;
```

```
 9        this.attributes = new HashMap<Object, Object>();
10        this.dao = dao;
11    }
12
13    public void lock() {
14        lock.lock();
15        lockCount++;
16    }
17
18    public void unlock() {
19        lockCount--;
20        lock.unlock();
21        if (lockCount == 0) {
22          if (!ended) {
23            dao.updateConversation(this);
24          }
25          PersistentConversationHolder.removeConversation(id);
26        }
27    }
28
29    public void end() {
30        dao.deleteConversation(id);
31        ended = true;
32    }
33
34    ...
35
36  }
```

The salient details from the preceding code follow:

- *Line 13*: A conversation needs to be locked before it is manipulated (that is, has its getAttribute(name), putAttribute(name, value), removeAttribute(name), or end() method called). Spring Web Flow will make sure this contract is respected.

  The PersistentConversation implementation uses this strict lock-unlock contract to clean up the PersistentConversationHolder. If the outermost lock is unlocked, the conversation data is updated in the database, and the PersistentConversation object is removed from ThreadLocal.

- *Line 29*: If a conversation ends, it removes itself from the database using the ConversationDao. To make this possible, the PersistentConversation receives a reference to the DAO that loaded it during construction.

As you can see, DaoConversationManager and PersistentConversation are closely coupled. These classes work together to implement a single component: a DAO-based conversation manager with a pluggable ConversationDao.

Configuring the flow executor to use a custom conversation manager was already discussed in the "Custom Conversation Managers" section of Chapter 6. Here is an example configuration using the DaoConversationManager together with the JdbcConversationDao:

```
<flow:executor id="flowExecutor" registry-ref="flowRegistry">
  <flow:repository type="continuation"
    conversation-manager-ref="conversationManager"/>
</flow:executor>

<bean id="conversationManager" class="
  com.ervacon.swfextensions.conversation.dao.DaoConversationManager">
  <property name="conversationDao">
    <bean class="com.ervacon.swfextensions.conversation.dao. \
      JdbcConversationDao">
      <property name="dataSource" ref="dataSource"/>
    </bean>
  </property>
</bean>

<bean id="transactionManager" class="
  org.springframework.jdbc.datasource.DataSourceTransactionManager">
  <property name="dataSource" ref="dataSource"/>
</bean>

<bean id="dataSource"
  class="org.springframework.jdbc.datasource.DriverManagerDataSource">
  <property name="driverClassName" value="org.hsqldb.jdbcDriver"/>
  <property name="url"
    value="jdbc:hsqldb:hsql://localhost/conversations"/>
  <property name="username" value="sa"/>
  <property name="password" value=""/>
</bean>

<tx:annotation-driven/>
```

Notice that this example still uses the continuation flow execution repository. The only difference with the default conversation manager is that the continuation snapshots will now be stored in the database. Also notice the <tx:annotation-driven/> tag instructing

Spring to do annotation-driven transaction management. The ConversationDao interface uses the @Transactional annotation to indicate its methods have transactional semantics:

```
@Transactional
public interface ConversationDao {

  public void createConversation(PersistentConversation conv);
  public PersistentConversation readConversation(ConversationId id);
  public void updateConversation(PersistentConversation conv);
  public void deleteConversation(ConversationId id);
}
```

# A Flow Servlet

As a second example extension, this section will show you how to directly integrate Spring Web Flow into the Servlet API, without a web MVC framework in between. In essence, the Servlet API defines a request-based web MVC framework: the Servlet engine acts as a front controller, dispatching requests to servlets, which act as controllers. JSP pages serve as view implementations, and request attributes can be used to hold model data. This simple and functional model avoids any framework-specific dependencies.

A FlowServlet class will act as a flow executor front-end. Since the Servlet API is request based, integration will follow the general process outlined in the "Flow Executor Integration" section of Chapter 7 and will be implemented by the FlowRequestHandler helper class. FlowServlet is a simple HttpServlet overriding the service(request, response) method:

```
public class FlowServlet extends HttpServlet {

  ...

  protected void service(HttpServletRequest request,
      HttpServletResponse response)
      throws ServletException, IOException {
    log("servicing flow request");
    FlowRequestHandler handler =
      new FlowRequestHandler(flowExecutor, argumentHandler);
```

```
    ServletExternalContext context =
      new ServletExternalContext(
        getServletContext(), request, response);
    handleResponse(handler.handleFlowRequest(context), context);
  }

  ...

}
```

As you can see, a request will simply be wrapped in a ServletExternalContext (which is part of Spring Web Flow itself and is also used by the Spring Web MVC integration) and is then handled using a FlowRequestHandler instance. The ResponseInstruction instance returned by FlowRequestHandler is turned into a servlet response by the handleResponse(ri, context) method:

```
1   private void handleResponse(final ResponseInstruction ri,
2       final ServletExternalContext context) {
3     log("handling flow response: " + ri);
4
5     new ResponseInstructionHandler() {
6
7       protected void handleApplicationView(ApplicationView view)
8           throws Exception {
9         @SuppressWarnings("unchecked")
10        Map<String, Object> model =
11          new HashMap<String, Object>(view.getModel());
12        argumentHandler.exposeFlowExecutionContext(
13            ri.getFlowExecutionKey(), ri.getFlowExecutionContext(),
14            model);
15        for (String key : model.keySet()) {
16          context.getRequest().setAttribute(key, model.get(key));
17        }
18        context.getRequest().getRequestDispatcher(
19          "/WEB-INF/jsp/" + view.getViewName() + ".jsp").
20          forward(context.getRequest(), context.getResponse());
21      }
22
```

```
23      protected void handleFlowDefinitionRedirect(
24          FlowDefinitionRedirect redirect) throws Exception {
25        String flowUrl =
26          argumentHandler.createFlowDefinitionUrl(
27            redirect, context);
28        context.getResponse().sendRedirect(flowUrl);
29      }
30
31      protected void handleFlowExecutionRedirect(
32          FlowExecutionRedirect redirect) throws Exception {
33        String flowExecutionUrl =
34          argumentHandler.createFlowExecutionUrl(
35            ri.getFlowExecutionKey(), ri.getFlowExecutionContext(),
36            context);
37        context.getResponse().sendRedirect(flowExecutionUrl);
38      }
39
40      protected void handleExternalRedirect(
41          ExternalRedirect redirect) throws Exception {
42        String externalUrl = argumentHandler.createExternalUrl(
43          redirect, ri.getFlowExecutionKey(), context);
44        context.getResponse().sendRedirect(externalUrl);
45      }
46
47      protected void handleNull() throws Exception {
48        // nothing to do
49      }
50
51    }.handleQuietly(ri);
52  }
```

A different type of response is issued depending on the type of view selection contained in the ResponseInstruction. The internal ResponseInstructionHandler helper class forces you to deal with each view selection type defined by Spring Web Flow.

Particularly important lines in the preceding listing are explained here:

- *Line 7*: In the case of an ApplicationView, a model map is prepared using the FlowExecutorArgumentHandler. The model data is then copied into the request attributes, exposing it to the view (JSP page). Rendering is done by simply forwarding the request to the selected JSP page.

- *Line 23*: Handling any of the redirect view selections is as simple as constructing a URL using the argument handler and then redirecting to that URL with the help of the HttpServletResponse.sendRedirect(url) method.

- *Line 47*: Finally, handling a null view selection is trivial: the FlowServlet just doesn't generate any response in this case.

---

**Tip**  Looking at the source code of the FlowController, or any of the other flow executor front-ends, will show very similar code. Study this existing source code if you are planning to integrate Spring Web Flow into a particular web MVC framework.

---

There is one question left to answer: where do the flowExecutor and argumentHandler variables used in the FlowServlet code come from? The FlowServlet initializes these member variables in its init() method:

```
public void init() throws ServletException {
  log("initializing flow servlet");
  try {
    // setup flow registry
    FlowDefinitionRegistry flowRegistry = ...;

    // setup flow executor
    flowExecutor = ...;

    // setup flow executor argument handler
    argumentHandler =
      new RequestParameterFlowExecutorArgumentHandler();
  }
```

```
  catch (Exception e) {
    throw new ServletException(
      "FlowServlet initialization failed", e);
  }
}
```

Instead of directly instantiating a flow definition registry, a flow executor, and an argument handler—like in this sample code—the FlowServlet class could also have looked up relevant beans in a Spring root web application context (loaded by ContextLoaderListener). In that case, standard Spring Web Flow configuration could have been used to define the flow definition registry and flow executor.

To deploy FlowServlet in a web application, simply add a corresponding servlet definition to the web.xml deployment descriptor:

```
<servlet>
  <servlet-name>flow-servlet</servlet-name>
  <servlet-class>
    com.ervacon.swfextensions.servlet.FlowServlet
  </servlet-class>
  <load-on-startup>1</load-on-startup>
</servlet>
<servlet-mapping>
  <servlet-name>flow-servlet</servlet-name>
  <url-pattern>/flows.html</url-pattern>
</servlet-mapping>
```

The preceding mapping will cause all /flows.html requests to be routed to FlowServlet, which will delegate handling to Spring Web Flow. The FlowServlet class will recognize the _flowId, _eventId, and _flowExecutionKey request parameters, just like the other flow executor front-ends discussed in Chapter 7.

# Building Spring Web Flow

If your need for customization goes beyond what is possible using the provided extension points, you can also customize Spring Web Flow itself and use your own modified version. Customization is a straightforward process since you have all of Spring Web Flow's source code available to you (its open source!), and building Spring Web Flow JAR files is easy.

> ### IS SPRING WEB FLOW CUSTOMIZATION A GOOD IDEA?
>
> Before diving into the Spring Web Flow source code to modify it and build your own custom version, you need to consider a few things. Although customizing the source code provides the ultimate form of flexibility, it also comes at a fairly high cost.
>
> First, understand that using a customized Spring Web Flow will make it much harder to get support on the Spring Web Flow forums and will likely void any commercial support you might have.
>
> Second, you'll have to manage and maintain the changes you make to the source code yourself. Consider what would happen if you wanted to upgrade to a new version of Spring Web Flow. You would have to reapply the modifications, possibly changing them along the way because Spring Web Flow's internals might have changed. All of this, of course, implies an additional maintenance cost.
>
> Finally, the onus is on you as far as documentation and testing goes. New people coming into the team who are familiar with Spring Web Flow need to be brought up to speed regarding the customizations made. This is true for all kinds of customizations, but particularly with those made by modifying Spring Web Flow's source code.
>
> My advice would be to steer clear of using a custom Spring Web Flow build, unless you have pressing requirements that cannot be met in any other way.

This book has given you a detailed picture of Spring Web Flow's architecture and structure. Looking at the source code and understanding how it works shouldn't be too hard. The full source code is included inside the Spring Web Flow distribution archive in the `projects/` directory. Two projects are of particular importance:

- The source code for *Spring Web Flow* itself is contained in `projects/spring-webflow/`. If you want to modify Spring Web Flow's source code, change the Java source files you find in this directory. Building this source code will give you a new `spring-webflow.jar` file.

- The source code for the *Spring Data Binding* framework, an internal helper library used by Spring Web Flow, is found in `projects/spring-binding/`. Building this project results in a new `spring-binding.jar` file.

To help you develop, you can import the `spring-webflow` and `spring-binding` projects into the Eclipse IDE. Both projects contain Eclipse project descriptors.

Spring Web Flow and the Spring Data Binding framework use the Spring Jumpstart build system, discussed in the "Spring Jumpstart" section of Chapter 2. As a result, building is easy. Just move into either the `projects/spring-webflow/` or `projects/spring-binding/`

directory, and type the **ant dist** command. Before doing that, however, you should modify the `project.properties` file contained in each of those projects and indicate a custom version number:

```
project.base.version=CUSTOM 1.0.6
project.version=${project.base.version}
ivy.status=release
```

Remove the `project.version` and `ivy.status` entries if you are building not a final release but just an intermediate snapshot.

Once the build has finished, your customized JAR files are published in the Ivy integration repository found in the `projects/integration-repo/` directory:

```
erwin@alex:~/spring-webflow-1.0.6/projects/spring-webflow$ ant dist
Buildfile: build.xml

...

   [echo] project spring-webflow released with version CUSTOM 1.0.6

...

BUILD SUCCESSFUL
Total time: 18 seconds
```

You can also find the generated JAR file, along with a ZIP file containing the accompanying sources, in the `target/artifact/lib/` directory inside the project directory (`projects/spring-webflow` in this case).

# Summary

This chapter discussed extending Spring Web Flow to meet special requirements that go beyond the out-of-the-box feature set.

Flow definitions allow you to reference custom flow definition artifacts deployed as beans in a Spring application context. These extension points should cover most cases. The Java flow builder is an ideal choice if you need to use several such extensions. If you need more flexibility, you can customize Spring Web Flow's core flow definition constructs or even implement your own flow builder.

The second part of this chapter showed two examples of customizing Spring Web Flow's flow execution management system: a database-backed conversation manager and a FlowServlet integrating Spring Web Flow into the raw Servlet API. Both examples serve as excellent starting points for developing your own extensions.

The chapter concluded with a quick introduction to modifying and building the Spring Web Flow distribution. Although building your own distribution provides the ultimate form of customization, it should only be done in special circumstances.

In the next and final chapter of this book, we conclude our investigation of Spring Web Flow.

# Epilogue

I hope this book has given you a clear and detailed picture of Spring Web Flow and has gotten you excited about using it. The best way to learn about a new framework is by understanding the problems it tries to solve. Following that ideology, I started the book explaining the challenges Spring Web Flow is facing in realizing its core goals:

- Controlling user navigation in web applications

- Managing state associated with *conversations*, multistep interactions users can have with a web application

- Allowing elegant modularization and reuse, making it possible to build complex applications from self-contained, coarse-grained modules with a well defined input-output contract

As a stateless environment geared toward free browsing, the World Wide Web makes implementing these goals a difficult task. Spring Web Flow deals with many of the issues involved, such as the double submit problem, and automatically applies web development best practices such as the POST-REDIRECT-GET idiom and the Synchronizer Token pattern.

Spring Web Flow is a focused tool, a controller component for web MVC frameworks targeted at use cases requiring controlled navigation. It integrates into most frameworks, such as Spring Web MVC and JavaServer Faces, providing a very low adoption overhead. While promoting a POJO-based programming model, Spring Web Flow itself is a lightweight framework well suited for agile environments requiring a rapid feedback cycle and excellent test support.

UML state diagrams naturally translate into web flows expressed in Spring Web Flow's flow definition language, which makes the flow definition language easy to understand and pick up and bridges the gap between analysis, design, and implementation. As far as runtime flow execution management is concerned, Spring Web Flow does all the heavy lifting for you. All you need to take care of is simple configuration.

Besides covering Spring Web Flow's flow definition language and flow execution management system in-depth, I also tried to give you an overview of Spring Web Flow's architecture, allowing you to understand many of the Spring Web Flow concepts and classes in a broader context.

In line with the Spring Framework itself, Spring Web Flow has a flexible and extensible design. Plugging custom implementations into the many extension points allows the framework to fit into most environments and fulfill exotic requirements.

# Spring Web Flow 2

In June of 2008, the first production-quality release of Spring Web Flow 2 was made available to the general public. Spring Web Flow 2 truly represents the next generation of the framework, building on the rock-solid feature set provided by Spring Web Flow 1 (and described in this book). Although the development process and user experience are largely unchanged, Spring Web Flow 2 introduces important architectural changes inside the framework. The most important of these changes is the fact that Spring Web Flow 2 no longer acts as a pure controller component for a web MVC framework. In addition to its controller responsibilities, Spring Web Flow 2 also takes care of view rendering. This change implies that Spring Web Flow 2 no longer plugs into a hosting framework like Spring Web Flow 1 does. Instead, it is an extension to the Spring Web MVC and Spring Portlet MVC frameworks.

Why this drastic change, you might ask? Since Spring Web Flow 2 is now in control of the view rendering process, it can elegantly provide functionality that would have been very hard or impossible to implement correctly on top of Spring Web Flow 1, notably

*Flow-managed persistence*: Spring Web Flow 2 provides the ability to link a Hibernate `Session` or JPA `PersistenceContext` with a flow execution, implementing a pattern that could be called Open Session in Flow. This way, Spring Web Flow 2 can allocate a persistence context when a flow starts, and commit all changes to persistent entities when the flow ends (commits). You also no longer have to worry about lazy-loading problems, because Spring Web Flow 2 will keep the persistence context available when rendering the view (something that would not have been possible in Spring Web Flow 1).

*Deep JSF integration*: Although Spring Web Flow 1 has impressive JSF integration capabilities, some issues still need ironing out. Spring Web Flow and JSF are both stateful models, with their own state management. Spring Web Flow stores flow executions in a flow execution repository, while JSF uses a `StateManager` to persist the view state of a component tree. In Spring Web Flow 1, flow execution and view state persistence are independent of each other, which can lead to all kinds of subtle problems. With Spring Web Flow 2, Spring Web Flow itself executes the JSF life cycle and renders the JSF component tree. This makes it easy to store JSF component state inside the flow execution, bringing flow execution and view state persistence in sync.

As I mentioned previously, Spring Web Flow 2 builds on top of the Spring Web MVC and Spring Portlet MVC frameworks. Therefore, it no longer integrates into third-party hosting frameworks like Struts and JSF. JSF is still supported, however, since Spring Web Flow 2 has the ability to render JSF views, essentially acting as a JSF implementation (called Spring Faces).

Next to the architectural rework, several other new themes emerged in the Spring Web Flow 2 release.

Simplification was an important goal. Rapid web development frameworks such as Ruby on Rails (http://www.rubyonrails.org) and Grails (http://www.grails.org) highlighted the value of convention over configuration and the DRY (don't repeat yourself) principle. Spring Web Flow 2 adheres to these principles more closely, bringing you an even more intuitive development experience.

The flow definition language is key in Spring Web Flow 2. It was simplified considerably, while becoming more powerful and consistent. To get a feeling for what has changed, look at the following Spring Web Flow 2 definition for the enterPayment-flow definition of the Spring Bank sample application, as discussed in Chapter 9:

```
<flow>
  <view-state id="selectDebitAccount" model="conversionScope.payment">
    <on-render>
      <evaluate
        expression="accountRepository.getAccounts( \
            externalContext.sessionMap.user.clientId)"
        result="requestScope.accounts"/>
    </on-render>
    <transition on="next" to="enterPaymentInfo"/>
  </view-state>

  <view-state id="enterPaymentInfo" model="conversionScope.payment">
    <transition on="next" to="confirmPayment"/>
    <transition on="selectBeneficiary" to="beneficiariesFlow"/>
  </view-state>

  <subflow-state id="beneficiariesFlow" subflow="beneficiaries-flow">
    <transition on="endSelected" to="showEnterPaymentInfo">
      <evaluate expression=" \
        conversationScope.payment.setCreditAccount( \
        currentEvent.beneficiary)"/>
    </transition>
    <transition on="endCancel" to="showEnterPaymentInfo"/>
  </subflow-state>
```

```
<view-state id="confirmPayment">
  <transition on="submit" to="submitPayment"/>
</view-state>

<action-state id="submitPayment">
  <evaluate expression="paymentProcessingEngine.submit( \
      conversationScope.payment)"/>
  <transition on="success" to="end"/>
  <transition on-exception=" \
      com.ervacon.springbank.domain.PaymentProcessingException"
    to="confirmPayment"/>
</action-state>

<end-state id="end" view="externalRedirect:/balances/show.html? \
  confirmationMessage=paymentSubmitted"/>

<end-state id="endCancel"
  view="externalRedirect:balances/show.html"/>

<global-transitions>
  <transition on="cancel" to="endCancel"/>
</global-transitions>

<bean-import resource="enterPayment-context.xml"/>
</flow>
```

An important motivation for changing Spring Web Flow 2's architecture was seamless integration with systems such as JSF and JPA. Spring Web Flow 2 also offers built-in support for securing flows with Spring Security.

Modern web techniques such as AJAX and partial view rendering are explicitly supported in Spring Web Flow 2. The framework comes bundled with a JavaScript module and a simple JSF component library to enable AJAX and client-side validation functionality in a progressive manner. All of this helps you develop rich web applications.

And finally, as you would expect from any new version of a framework, Spring Web Flow 2 also adds several new features. Notable examples are support for runtime monitoring and management using Java Management Extensions (JMX), direct support for the unified expression language defined by Java Enterprise Edition 5 as an alternative to Object Graph Navigation Language, XML flow definition inheritance, and integration of Spring Web Flow's flow execution scopes with Spring 2's scoped bean feature.

# Choosing Between Spring Web Flow 1 and 2

Spring Web Flow 2 is an exciting framework. Are there reasons why you would still want to use Spring Web Flow 1? Indeed there are. It should be clear by now that Spring Web Flow 1 and Spring Web Flow 2 are essentially different products. Because Spring Web Flow 2 is not backward compatible with Spring Web Flow 1, you can't just upgrade the JAR files; rather, you have to migrate to the new version using the provided migration tools. When choosing between the two frameworks, consider the following things:

- Keep in mind that Spring Web Flow 2 builds on top of the Spring Web MVC and Spring Portlet MVC frameworks. There might be constraints (political, technical, etc.) in your organization that prevent your from using Spring Web MVC; for instance, use of a particular JSF implementation or Struts may be mandated. If this is the case, Spring Web Flow 1 is your only option.

- If you are not constrained by the first item, you should generally prefer Spring Web Flow 2 for new applications. If you want to integrate Spring Web Flow into an existing application, for instance, a Struts-based application, Spring Web Flow 1 is a better fit.

- Spring Web Flow 2 requires Java 1.4 or later and Spring 2.5.4 or later, while Spring Web Flow 1 will run on top of Java 1.3 using Spring 1.2.7 or later.

- At the time of this writing, Spring Web Flow 2 does not have a Java flow definition syntax.

- Spring Web Flow 1 offers four different flow execution repositories, as discussed in Chapter 6. In contrast, Spring Web Flow 2 currently offers only the continuation-based flow execution repository.

---

**Caution** Because of the important architectural changes in Spring Web Flow 2, Spring Web Flow 1 and Spring Web Flow 2 cannot be used concurrently in the same application.

---

# Concluding Thoughts

Hoping you have enjoyed this book, I will conclude by asking you to send all feedback and remarks to swfbook@ervacon.com and encouraging you to become an active member of the Spring Web Flow community. Have fun!

# References

Alur, Deepak, John Crupi, and Dan Malks. 2003. *Core J2EE patterns: Best practices and design strategies*. 2nd ed. Santa Clara: Sun Microsystems Press.

Apache Software Foundation. 2004. Apache license version 2.0. http://www.apache.org/licenses/LICENSE-2.0.html.

Belapurkar, Abhijit. 2004. *Use continuations to develop complex Web applications: A programming paradigm to simplify MVC for the Web. developerWorks.* http://www-128.ibm.com/developerworks/java/library/j-contin.html.

Evans, Eric. 2004. *Domain-driven design: Tackling complexity in the heart of software.* Boston: Pearson Education, Inc.

Fielding, Roy. 2000. Architectural styles and the design of network-based software architectures. PhD diss., University of California, Irvine.

Fowler, Martin. 2000. *UML distilled: A brief guide to the standard object modeling language.* Boston Addison-Wesley.

———. 2003. *Patterns of enterprise application architecture.* Boston: Addison-Wesley.

———. 2004. Mocks aren't stubs. http://www.martinfowler.com/articles/mocksArentStubs.html.

———. 2005. Fluent interface. http://www.martinfowler.com/bliki/FluentInterface.html.

Gamma, Erich, Richard Helm, Ralph Johnson, and John Vlissides. 1995. *Design patterns: Elements of reusable object-oriented software.* Boston: Addison-Wesley.

The Internet Society. 1999. Hypertext transfer protocol—HTTP/1.1. *World Wide Web Consortium.* http://www.w3.org/Protocols/rfc2616/rfc2616.html.

Java Community Process. 2003. JSR 168 portlet specification. http://jcp.org/aboutJava/communityprocess/final/jsr168/.

Johnson, Rod, Juergen Hoeller, Colin Sampaleanu, Alef Arendsen, Rob Harrop, Thomas Risberg, Darren Davison, et al. 2003. Spring documentation. *The Spring Framework.* http://www.springframework.org/documentation.

Jouravlev, Michael. 2004. Redirect after post. *TheServerSide.com.* http://www.theserverside.com/tt/articles/article.tss?l=RedirectAfterPost.

Wikipedia. *Finite state machine.* http://en.wikipedia.org/wiki/Finite_state_machine.

World Wide Web Consortium. XML schema. *World Wide Web Consortium.* http://www.w3.org/XML/Schema.

# Index

# You Need the Companion eBook

**Your purchase of this book entitles you to buy the companion PDF-version eBook for only $10. Take the weightless companion with you anywhere.**

W e believe this Apress title will prove so indispensable that you'll want to carry it with you everywhere, which is why we are offering the companion eBook (in PDF format) for $10 to customers who purchase this book now. Convenient and fully searchable, the PDF version of any content-rich, page-heavy Apress book makes a valuable addition to your programming library. You can easily find and copy code—or perform examples by quickly toggling between instructions and the application. Even simultaneously tackling a donut, diet soda, and complex code becomes simplified with hands-free eBooks!

Once you purchase your book, getting the $10 companion eBook is simple:

1. Visit www.apress.com/promo/tendollars/.

2. Complete a basic registration form to receive a randomly generated question about this title.

3. Answer the question correctly in 60 seconds, and you will receive a promotional code to redeem for the $10.00 eBook.

THE EXPERT'S VOICE™

2855 TELEGRAPH AVENUE | SUITE 600 | BERKELEY, CA 94705

**Offer valid through 04/2009.**